T0349985

Praise for *The New Extraordinary Leader*

"Much has been written on leadership; mostly these writings have been expressed through personal philosophies and beliefs. As a result, we have grown cynical on books about leadership. However, once again, Zenger and Folkman have broken through the chatter and generated new compelling insights on the topic. Based on a convincing body of evidence, *The New Extraordinary Leader* provides data-driven practices. I especially love the insight; powerful combinations produce nearly exponential results. It turns out that there is no universal truth for leading, but a few practices combined in the appropriate context can be breakthrough. Whether you are a leader, an aspiring leader, or a leadership coach, you must read this book."

> —MICHAEL J. ARENA,
> Former Chief Talent Officer, General Motors
> Author of *Adaptive Space*

"I fell in love with *The New Extraordinary Leader* on page one. From the moment I started reading I really got jazzed, and my enthusiasm only increased the more I read. You see, I'm just mad about books that attack cherished but unsupportable assumptions about anything, especially leadership. That's exactly what Jack Zenger and Joe Folkman do, and they do it persuasively, precisely, and professionally. *The New Extraordinary Leader* is no hackneyed rehashing of tired nostrums. Through their exceptional research, the authors demonstrate and prove that leadership *does* make a difference and that *you* can learn to lead. There are some profound insights in this book, and whether you've studied leadership for over 20 years, as I have, or you are brand new to the subject, Zenger and Folkman give you much more than your money's worth. And while their research gives the book distinctive credibility, their examples and practical applications give it life. This is a book that scholars and practitioners will be referring to for years to come. If your goal is to be a better leader than you are today, then you must read this book."

> —JAMES M. KOUZES
> Chairman Emeritus, Tom Peters Company
> Coauthor of *The Leadership Challenge*
> and *Encouraging the Heart*

"Read this book! Its approach to understanding leadership development is unique: It uses data, not opinion! Some of the insights are intuitive, but many are counterintuitive. Extraordinarily readable, this book represents some of the best thinking on leadership I've seen in a long while."

—E. David Spong
President, Military Aerospace Support
The Boeing Company

"This is a must-read for coaches, leaders, and those who develop them. *The New Extraordinary Leader* goes beyond anecdotes or 'war stories'; it builds upon comprehensive research. It is destined to be a classic in our field."

—Marshall Goldsmith
Named by *Forbes* as one of five top executive coaches and one of the *Wall Street Journal's* "Top 10" executive educators

"The authors' promise on the bottom of page three to do their best 'to unravel the mystery of leadership through careful analysis and observation' of a huge database 'by emulating Sherlock Holmes,' grabbed my attention. Always an avid mystery reader, I found myself compulsively turning pages, devouring the entire book, like any good mystery, in one sitting. I especially appreciated the wisdom found in Insights 1 to 20, the nonobvious competency companions, and the distinctions between mattress and tent leadership models. By the last chapter (when all at last had been revealed), I had deduced a far better way to help my organization become a company of leaders than I've been able to figure out in the past 20 years!"

—Sallie T. Hightower, EdD
Conoco University
Conoco, Inc.

"This book was a key tool to advance the cultural transformation of Santander Spain, helping our managers to significantly improve the effectiveness of their leadership. The model hooks managers and enables teams to transcend past performance."

—Elena Perez Berjón
Leadership Development Manager
Banco Santander Spain

"Finally someone has moved beyond theory and complicated models to tell us what great leaders really bring to the party. Zenger and Folkman have effectively summarized data on 20,000 leaders that help us understand what really makes leaders tick. Any serious student of leadership will both enjoy this book's journey and walk away with useful new insights that will help them and others."

—Ralph Christensen
Senior Vice President, Human Resources
Hallmark Cards, Inc.

"This book has changed the way I think! If you want to move from good to great as a leader, don't focus on a weakness; instead, take a strength and build on it. Jack Zenger and Joe Folkman have written an important book, full of insight and based on sound research. It will shape the way we help our clients develop executives."

—Douglas D. Anderson
Founder and Managing Partner
Center for Executive Development–Boston

"Ordinarily, I'd say the last thing we need is another book on leadership. But *The New Extraordinary Leader* by Jack Zenger and Joe Folkman is refreshingly different. Rather than serve up yesterday's anecdotes, they've performed the heavy lifting of empirical data collection and analysis. The foreword promises clarity, simplicity, and utility in addressing the real-world challenges of developing leaders, and this book delivers that and more. This is a must-read."

—Jon Younger, PhD
Senior Vice President, Leadership Development
National City Corporation

"I need to congratulate and thank Jack and Joe one more time after reading the manuscript of *The New Extraordinary Leader*. . . . in this edition they share with us new research findings and proven methods that any organization can apply to be successful in their overall leadership development initiatives. A must-read for all practitioners and professionals in the leadership and talent field."

—Pablo Riera
President, P&A Group

THE NEW

EXTRAORDINARY

LEADER

TURNING GOOD
MANAGERS
INTO GREAT LEADERS

JOHN H. ZENGER
JOSEPH R. FOLKMAN

New York Chicago San Francisco Athens London Madrid
Mexico City Milan New Delhi Singapore Sydney Toronto

2 3 4 5 6 7 8 9   LCR   29 28 27 26 25 24

ISBN: 978-1-260-45560-1
MHID: 1-260-45560-2

e-ISBN: 978-1-260-45561-8
e-MHID: 1-260-45561-0

Library of Congress Cataloging-in-Publication Data

Names: Zenger, John H., author. | Folkman, Joe, author.
Title: The new extraordinary leader / John H. Zenger, Joseph R. Folkman.
Description: Third edition. | New York : McGraw-Hill, [2020] | Includes
    bibliographical references and index.
Identifiers: LCCN 2019028359 (print) | LCCN 2019028358 (ebook) | ISBN
    9781260455601 (hardcover) | ISBN 9781260455618 (ebook) | ISBN
    9781260455618?q(ebook) | ISBN 9781260455601?q(hardcover)
Subjects: LCSH: Leadership.
Classification: LCC HD57.7 .Z46 2020 (ebook) | LCC HD57.7 (print) | DDC
    658.4/092--dc23
LC record available at https://lccn.loc.gov/2019028359

McGraw-Hill Education books are available at special quantity discounts to use as premiums and sales promotions or for use in corporate training programs. To contact a representative, please visit the Contact Us pages at www.mhprofessional.com.

We dedicate this book to our internal colleagues, along with our international strategic partners. They are a remarkable group who at once serve as a well-spring of excellent ideas, along with serving as a flywheel of stability. Always in good nature, they tolerate and encourage the authors chasing after their latest new idea. Of even greater importance, they collectively share the vision of making a positive impact in the world by helping to create better leaders. Because of that they make coming to work both rewarding and fun.

Jack and Joe

CONTENTS

Acknowledgments   vii

Introduction   xi

PART I

HOW INDIVIDUALS DEVELOP THEIR LEADERSHIP CAPABILITY

1 Demystifying Leadership   3

2 Great Leaders Make a Great Difference   31

3 The Competency Quest   53

4 How The Extraordinary Leader Behaves   71

5 Great Leaders Possess Multiple Strengths   91

6 Leaders Must Fit Their Organization   109

7 Fatal Flaws Must Be Fixed   127

8 Alternative Paths for Leadership Development   149

9 How Individuals Develop Themselves   177

PART II

THE ORGANIZATION'S ROLE IN FILLING THE LEADERSHIP PIPELINE

10 Tailor Leadership Development to the Organization   201

11 Define the Scale and Scope   213

12 Ensure Executive Support   223

13 Use Powerful Learning Methods   233

14 Embed Leadership Development into the Culture   241

15 Sustain and Follow-Through   251

PART III

TOPICS OF SPECIAL INTEREST

16 Women in Leadership   265

17 Measure Improvement   277

18 Develop Leadership Teams   285

Appendix: Research Methodology   295

Notes   309

Index   315

ACKNOWLEDGMENTS

This book began several years ago as I was walking down the hall looking over some statistical output and bumped into Jack Zenger. Jack's question was, "Are you doing anything that's interesting?" My response was, "Funny you should ask, look at these data." What began as a fascination with some statistical analysis grew into a compelling body of evidence that modified substantially the conventional wisdom people have about what makes great leaders and how they develop.

To anyone who reads a number of books on leadership, it becomes apparent that more than 90 percent of what you read has been said before. The packaging is different, the examples amusing, but fundamentally there is little that is new. I had no interest in writing that kind of book. Our approach was to do rigorous research and then formulate a theory to explain the results. In presentations on our findings to clients, we have been very pleased with the "Ah-ha's" that are apparent as we present the insights from our research. I am hopeful that readers of this book will have a similar experience.

One of the most interesting findings from our research is something called "powerful combinations." A powerful combination occurs when leaders combine two unique skills, which results in a substantial increase in overall effectiveness. In thinking about the process of getting this book written, I am very confident that neither Jack nor I could have accomplished this research and written this book alone. The combination of Jack's experience, knowledge, and conceptual skills with my research, measurement, and change management background created a very powerful combination.

Working through the laborious and demanding process of writing this book with Jack has been an absolute delight. I am grateful for his patience, gentle persuasion, and persistence.

Many people contributed substantially by doing research and editing on the book. Thanks to both our colleagues, staff members, and clients for their contributions and suggestions.

As is always the case with projects such as this, it was impossible to produce record revenues, carry a full client load, write a book, and manage my responsibilities as a husband and father. It was my wife and family who gave up the most and voluntarily carried an increased load. I appreciate their willingness to do so very much. I recognize in them much that is extraordinary.

Finally, I would like to dedicate this book to my clients. I am extremely grateful to brilliant clients in a broad range of industries. Universally, they are dedicated to improving organizations and the individuals who work in them. They are continually looking for ways to make people more successful. The data, which is the foundation on which this book is built, came from them.

JOE FOLKMAN

As a relatively young boy, I worked at the hospital for which my father was the administrator. From him I learned much about leadership and the challenges of being the senior executive. His relentless pursuit of improvement and willingness to abandon systems that were working for the promise of something better were great examples to me.

My academic interests in leadership began at UCLA as a research assistant in the Human Relations Research Group. I appreciate the tutelage of Robert Tannenbaum and the late Irv Weschler. Then at USC came an association with Bill Woolf, who exposed me to a sociologic and anthropologic view of leadership. Many others influenced my thinking, including Mel Sorcher, the creator of behavioral modeling training in industry.

I had many colleagues at Zenger-Miller who influenced me, beginning with Dale Miller, Steve Mann, Ed Musselwhite, Bob Sherwin, and dozens of others. Their association enriched my thinking about leadership and simultaneously helped build an extraordinary company. To them all I express appreciation. I wish to thank my current colleagues, who not only make the organization run smoothly but also are the genesis of countless good ideas. I could not ask for a more dedicated group with whom to work.

I would never have imagined that I'd be writing a book with a statistically inclined organizational psychologist. Joe Folkman's academic interests have been quite opposite from mine, but the experience has been extremely positive. Differences were quickly and painlessly resolved. The book is something that neither of us could have done alone.

Finally, I extend my deepest appreciation to my combined family. From our children, their spouses, and many grandchildren have come great lessons in leadership, along with opportunities to apply some of what I have learned. To my wife, Holly, I express special thanks. Besides being a good critic of whatever I write, her organization of our life together creates the time and environment in which it is possible to write a book.

JACK ZENGER

INTRODUCTION

What's different in this third edition of this book? First, we sought to bring up-to-date all of the data and our conclusions from the data. More than 15 years have elapsed since the first edition. The world changes in that time period. Second, we discovered new insights about leadership that expand our understanding. Rather than the 20 insights that were in the original, we now present 35. Finally, the original book was primarily focused on individuals as leaders and how they could best develop themselves. In this edition we added six chapters that describe how organizations can most effectively contribute to the development of their leaders.

Yet, much has remained the same. We originally had three objectives for this book. First was simplicity. We insisted that the book provide a clear, understandable message. Nothing is more irritating than to read a book on a topic of great personal interest and then close the book and not be able to summarize the book's point of view or basic thesis.

Our second objective was that the contents be actionable. We do not expect that every idea in the book will be something you can implement immediately, but success for us will be your ability to take much of our findings and be able to do something with them next Monday morning.

Our third objective was that the book be empirical. We insisted that it be based on hard data, facts, and statistical analyses. Huge sets of data were the touchstone to which we constantly returned. While the original book was based on analyzing 200,000 multi-rate feedback instruments

(360-degree feedback), pertaining to roughly 20,000 leaders; this edition contains data from more than a million instruments that analyze 120,000 leaders worldwide.

Frankly, we tire of books by executives and business writers that primarily express personal philosophies and beliefs, especially when they are so inconsistent. The discipline of leadership and those committed to developing leaders inside organizations surely deserve better. Our standard was to have every conclusion grounded in objective data. The combination of hard data and statistical analyses were to be the point of the spear. It then became our task to make sense of the data and to put logical explanations around our findings.

We welcome feedback from readers. The topic deserves a great deal of dialogue from all of us who are concerned with the future of our vital institutions—universities, schools, hospitals, government agencies, and businesses. These all need leaders to flourish. Our hope is that the information that follows will in some small way aid in the development of those much-needed leaders.

PART I

HOW INDIVIDUALS DEVELOP THEIR LEADERSHIP CAPABILITY

The first nine chapters of this book update research that was conducted 17 years ago, examining the nature of leadership, leadership competencies, the value of strengths, when to focus on leadership failings or weaknesses, and our discovery of an alternative pathway that leaders may use to build their strengths.

The original research involved our analysis of 200,000 multi-rater feedback instruments that pertained to 20,000 leaders. They were mostly from North America, with a smattering of data from Europe, the Pacific Rim, and South America. Now, 17 years later, we've done a significant update, analyzing more than a million feedback instruments assessing the behavior of 90,000 leaders worldwide. And our data encompass the global business community, with substantial representation from Europe, the Pacific Rim, South America, the Middle East, and Africa.

During the course of 17 years, we generated new insights about leadership, which are now included in these first chapters.

The overall theme of Part I is an analysis of leadership and how individuals can better develop their effectiveness as leaders.

1

DEMYSTIFYING LEADERSHIP

*Leadership is one of the most observed and
least understood phenomena on Earth.*
—J. M. BURNS

*The aura with which we tend to surround the
words leader and leadership makes it hard to think
clearly. Good sense calls for demystification.*
—JOHN GARDNER

The Mystery Remains

While we were seated at a dinner table recently, it became known that we were writing a book. A dinner guest immediately inquired, "What is the book about?"

"It is about leadership," one of us replied.

Without hesitation the guest inquired, "Do you really think people can be developed into leaders? Aren't they born that way?" (We'd like to have a dollar for every time that question has been asked of us over the past decades.) The question seems as hardy as cockroaches or crocodiles. People in general have that query at the tops of their minds and so do a lot of CEOs and public organization leaders.

And the question is really in two parts. If the question is answered using the popular party line that says, "Of course you can develop leadership in people," the immediate follow-up question is, "How do you do that?" It is to those two basic questions that we address in this book. In this new edition, six chapters have been added that address how organizations go about filling their leadership pipeline, in addition to what individuals can do to elevate their own leadership effectiveness.

Does the world need anything more written on the subject of leadership? On the one hand, it could be argued that the answer is a loud "No!" Consider the fact that more than 3.5 billion articles have been published about leadership in the past century. Whereas some are based on research, most reflect the personal opinions of the authors regarding leadership, derived from their own experiences or their observations of leaders. Many are written by successful business executives and reflect their own beliefs about what made them successful.

Included in the larger body of articles are approximately 419 million research studies that have been conducted on leadership and published in scholarly journals. Then add 499 million books that have been written about leadership over the past 100 years. (In recent years, that is more than four each day. Many of these were written by practicing leaders; others were written by academicians and consultants who sought to explain this important role that some people perform. Given that immense body of literature, it would seem futile to add yet one more book.

The Reasons for One More Book

Despite that extensive literature, leadership remains shrouded in mystery. Rather than making the subject clearer, one recognized leadership expert, Warren Bennis, summed it up by saying "We have more *information* now than we can use, and less knowledge and understanding than we need. Indeed, we seem to collect information because we have the ability to do so, but we are so busy collecting it that we haven't devised a means of using it. The true measure of any society is not what it knows but what it does with what it knows."[1] He summed up his concern by remarking, "the more that is written about leadership, the less we seem to know."

Regarding the enormous number of research studies that have been conducted, another respected scholar observed, "The results of many of these studies are contradictory or lack any clear conclusion."[2]

How Mysteries Are Solved?

There is an astonishing description of one approach to solving a mystery in Sir Arthur Conan Doyle's classic Sherlock Holmes tale.

The Sign of Four

Dr. Watson remarks to Sherlock Holmes, "I have a gold watch in my possession. Would you have the kindness to let me have an opinion upon the character or habits of the late owner?" Watson was testing Holmes and attempting to tone down his arrogant manner. Holmes then complained that because the watch had recently been cleaned, he was robbed of the most useful data. But after carefully examining the watch, Holmes then proceeded to tell Watson a series of hypotheses about the owner. These included:

- The watch belonged to his older brother, who inherited it from his father.
- He was a man of untidy habits.
- He had gone through a period of poverty, with intervals of prosperity.
- He had taken to heavy drinking before he died.

Watson sprang from his chair and accused Holmes of having made inquiries into the history of his unhappy brother and then pretending to deduce it from his observations of the gold pocket watch. He concluded by saying, "It is unkind and, to speak plainly, has a touch of charlatanism in it."

Holmes proceeded to explain how he had come to each of his conclusions by simply observing important data and seeing their implications. The initials on the watch's back, "H.W.," suggested a family member, and gold watches usually were passed from father to the elder son.

The watch was 50 years old. The initials appeared to be as old as the watch, and so it was most likely the father's watch, passed to Dr. Watson's brother. The owner's untidy habits were revealed by the dents and scratches that came from carrying this expensive watch in the same pocket with other hard objects such as coins or keys. Inside the case of the watch were scratched in pinpoint the numbers of a pawnbroker's ticket, suggesting that the owner had gone through a period of dire poverty. The fact that he regained possession of the watch would imply that he also had periods of prosperity. The owner's drinking problem was revealed by thousands of scratches around the keyhole where the winding key had slipped and scratched the case. Holmes noted, "That is characteristic of a drunkard's watch, not a sober man's."

Solving the Mystery of Leadership

Our hope is to take an enormous amount of data collected about and from leaders and, through careful analysis and observation, begin to unravel the mystery of leadership. We will do our best to emulate Sherlock Holmes. It would seem that if careful attention is given to the clues that lie inside huge databases, the continuing mystery of leadership might be penetrated.

Our objective is to provide readers with an empirical analysis of leadership, a simple and practical conceptual model of what leadership is, and a practical guide to helping leaders develop "greatness." Our approach and understanding comes from our analysis of hundreds of thousands of leadership assessments from the direct reports of leaders, their peers, their bosses, and themselves. We let our findings guide our development of a practical theory.

Because together the authors have roughly three-quarters of a century of experience in leadership development, we were surprised that the research changed some long-held beliefs about the nature of leadership and how best to develop it.

The Complexity of Defining and Describing Leadership, or Why the Mystery Exists

Everyone recognizes the challenge of trying to solve any problem that contains multiple unknowns. That is precisely the problem in trying to solve the leadership dilemma. There are a significant number of unknowns, and many of them are constantly changing.

Fifteen of those variables are described below.

1. Leadership occurs in extremely diverse environments. Some leadership produces prescribed results in a relatively defined and established organization. Such leadership may speed a product to market or escalate the revenue from a sales force, but it is not conceiving new directions or strategies for the organization. Other leadership is exhibited in a start-up organization in which there is no structure or form, and the leader must create it from scratch.

2. Different skills are required at different stages in a person's career. The research on career stages shows that people's careers

go through very predictable stages. Early on, people start as apprentices, learning some new discipline. They then move to become more independent in their work. From there, some people move into managerial positions in which they over-see the work of others or move from a narrow focus on their own work to a broader focus that involves coaching others to develop skill and expertise. Finally, a handful of people become pathfinders and visionaries who lead broad-scale organizational change and are the "statesmen" of their organization. Career stages are easily confused with organizational levels, but they are not identical. People who are promoted into managerial positions often continue to function as professional, individual contributors. They revert to the work they find most comfort-able and never take on the role of coach, mentor, or director of others. They continue doing technical work at which they are highly proficient. However, the stage of a person's career is another variable of the leadership equation.[3]

3. Leadership is driven by major events. Former New York mayor Rudolph Giuliani was catapulted into the national limelight because of his handling of the terrorist attacks on the World Trade Center. Prior to that, his career had been waning. His career next took a completely new turn when Donald Trump appointed him as his attorney-spokesperson, a role in which he garnered extremely mixed reviews. Winston Churchill had sought several leadership positions, but it was not until the events of Dunkirk that his talents were recognized. Through World War II he was a premier leader, and then when the war was over, his countrymen voted him out of office. When a friend suggested that this was a blessing in disguise, Churchill growled back, "If it is, the disguise is perfect."

4. The activities of leadership are not all the same. For exam-ple, not all leaders are required to "lead change." Some leaders spend a great deal of time on people development activities, whereas others are riveted to the operational or production ele-ments of their roles.

5. We confuse success and effectiveness as the general benchmark of leadership. If success is measured by dollars and titles, that is clearly not the same thing as effectiveness, or truly produc-ing the results that the organization needs. We believe this is

probably best measured by the feedback from subordinates who experience that leadership. Much of the research on leadership makes no distinction between success and effectiveness.

6. We lack agreed-upon measures, so it has been frustratingly difficult to get agreement on who is a good leader and who is not. We lack robust measures of leadership effectiveness and especially have no comprehensive measures that track the leader's impact on customers, employees, organizations, and shareholders.

7. We have not taken into account the evolving nature of leadership. That is, we have analyzed leadership around the characteristics that are required for success or effectiveness today but have not given much attention to the competencies that will be required in the future. Thus, much of the leadership analysis and development has been "looking in the rearview mirror" and not looking out over the horizon.

8. There has been no way to define the different constituencies of the leader. Thus, if a leader is in charge of "baby boomers" born from 1945 to 1955, this would call for some different values, motives, and skills than if the leader was responsible for a group of "Gen-Xers" born from 1975 to 1985. That complexity is now compounded with "Generation Y," those born from 1986 to 2000, and the soon to come "Generation Z," born in 2001 and beyond.

9. Still another variable is whether the leader is operating alone versus acting as part of a leadership team. Clearly there are organizations in which one person plays an extremely dominant part, exercising control and influence over the big issues, along with the day-to-day tactics. Other organizations have a leadership team that acts in concert. In some cases, a formal "office of the president" has people who act quite interchangeably in the organization.

10. A further dimension is the impact of technology. Effectiveness in some organizations would demand a high level of comfort with the latest computer and information technology, whereas others would tolerate a leader who could neither send nor receive email. New technologies exist to conduct virtual meetings, and in some organizations a comfort and familiarity with such technology would be a "must." A Dell Computer

employee reported, "My boss spent the entire weekend retyping a 25-page proposal that only needed corrections. She claims the file I gave her was corrupted and she could not edit it. The PDF file I gave her was 'read only,' but all she had to do was copy it into a word-processing program and make the corrections."

11. A new dimension of leadership is one of geography. Some leaders interact with a virtual team, whereas others have on-site staffs. This can be even further complicated by the fact that groups are often scattered across widely different time zones, thus making the leadership task even more complex. For example, holding meetings at one point in time can be cumbersome.

12. Another variable is the wide variety of leadership styles used within different organizations to motivate and inspire the front line. Some of the best research in this regard comes from Jon Katzenbach and is described in his book *Peak Performance*.[4] In that book, he describes firms that were extremely effective and successful but that used very different approaches to getting high performance from the people within. He described five of these:

- *Mission, values, and pride.* In this approach, the organization immerses everyone in the traditions, the spirit, the core values, and the mission of the organization. This in turn generates great pride, and people produce at high levels because of that pride in the organization. The U.S. Marine Corps is a good example of this.

- *Recognition and celebration.* Many organizations he studied practiced extensive recognition for their people and went to great lengths to celebrate successes. Southwest Airlines is a classic example of this approach.

- *Process metrics.* Many organizations post detailed charts showing productivity and quality metrics for every department. People are trained to understand these metrics, and the organization's success is measured and rewarded by performance against these metrics.

- *Individual achievement.* Other organizations excel by allowing individuals to accomplish extraordinary things. Organizational effectiveness is the addition of all these excelling individuals. Professional service firms function this way, and McKinsey & Company is a good example.

- *Entrepreneurial spirit.* Still another approach to motivating people to high performance is to let them enjoy a huge financial stake in the potential success of the firm. Many high-tech start-ups have relied on this appeal to someone's entrepreneurial spirit, and this has enabled such organizations to excel.

This is a good example of the complexity of leadership. All five of the above approaches work well. One is not right and the others wrong. What could end up being "wrong" is for a recognition and celebration leader to attempt to function that way in a process metrics organization. Chances are the organization would reject such a leader as the human body rejects any foreign substance implanted in it.

13. Who decides those who are good leaders? We have been unclear regarding who is in the best position to evaluate leadership effectiveness. Organizations have often relied on performance appraisals from the level above to evaluate the effectiveness of a leader. We have studies from several organizations showing absolutely no correlation between performance appraisals and their 360-degree feedback instruments. Yet the research for past decades has shown that subordinates were in the best position to appraise any leader's effectiveness. Research in the military proved that having the enlisted men select sergeants was more effective than having higher-ranking officers make those selections.

14. Several "companions" of leadership effectiveness have clouded the issue. For example, all of the following have been shown to have some correlation to leadership effectiveness:

- Intelligence, as measured by IQ scores
- Physical characteristics, such as height
- Emotional or personality characteristics, such as assertiveness and outgoingness
- Biochemical characteristics, such as testosterone levels in men

Because some correlation exists between these elements and leadership effectiveness, there has been a logical temptation to assume there to be a cause-and-effect relationship. At the same time, there was high interest in such conclusions from those responsible for leadership selection; the above elements did not help further the work of those concerned with development.

15. Language has an impact. Is the lack of adequate language partly responsible for the mystery that surrounds leadership? The Inuit (or as some call them, Eskimos) have some 23 words to describe snow. They can describe its hardness, texture, moisture content, color, age, and crystalline structure with their richer vocabulary. We, on the other hand, have roughly three words at best, as we talk about powder, slush, and corn snow. It is possible that if our vocabulary were more precise and robust, we could better succeed in describing what leadership is and how to more effectively develop it. Given our current condition, leadership is still nearly impossible to define or describe in detail or specificity. However, as Professor Karl Weick has suggested, any idea can be "simple, general or accurate, but never all three."[5] We will strive to be general and accurate, but not specific. That appears to be the best way to improve our understanding of this most important topic.

Research-Based Book

Our hope is to present a way for people to think about leadership in a highly practical and yet simple way. We will not review the past literature on leadership. Others have done that. Nor will we dwell on the theoretical. Nor will we attempt to describe all the tasks or activities of leaders. Others have done that also. Instead, we want to present a way for you personally to think about your own leadership abilities and how you might go about increasing those, if you choose. And for those who have subordinates, we provide suggestions about what they and their organizations can do to develop leadership in the people who report to them. For those with responsibility or interest in how organizations can best develop their leaders, Part II of this book is for you.

We believe this is best done by examining a huge body of data collected about leaders from their peers, their subordinates, their bosses, and themselves. Rather than describe our personal beliefs and prejudices about leadership, we will turn to more objective data. We think it enables us to discover some profound insights into the real nature of leadership. Where mysteries still remain, we call that to your attention and share our beliefs.

To answer intelligently the question "Are leaders born or made?" and the sequel "If they are made, then how do you do that?" we begin by providing the reader with a model of leadership that becomes our operational definition of a leader. That model then provides a workable vehicle with which to describe a practical way to make good managers into great leaders.

This book examines the leader as seen through the eyes of those being led (subordinates) and influenced (peers), of those who manage the leaders (the bosses), and of the leaders themselves. This process has become known as 360-degree feedback because of its comprehensive view of a leader's behavior, looked at from above, the side, and below. Indeed, we later describe our database of some 1,500,000 responses, using 360-degree questionnaires. We focus on the questions: What do these three groups (subordinates, peers, and bosses) notice? What do they see in "great leaders" that sets them apart from the average ones?

Of those three perspectives, we conclude that the best way to understand leadership is to examine the impact leaders have on the people they lead. It is the subordinates' view we value the most because we believe they collectively have the most complete and accurate data.

Peers see slices of a leader's behavior, but there is good evidence to conclude that their perceptions are less accurate than those of the people who report to the leader.

We strongly believe that this comprehensive pool of data is far more powerful and accurate than information that would come from interviews of leaders themselves. As Michael Polanyi noted in his book *Personal Knowledge*, "Most highly skilled performers in any activity, whether it be music, sports, or violin making, cannot accurately tell you what makes them so effective. Their behavior is often highly intuitive. You must actually observe them to accurately determine the true cause of their success."[6]

This database of approximately 1,500,000 questionnaires completed by subordinates, peers, and bosses about leaders collectively describes more than 121,000 leaders. They come from widely diverse industries.

These leaders are from North America, along with many from Europe, the Pacific Rim, Middle East, Africa, and South America.

To make our database and analysis more robust, we examined more than 44 different leadership assessment instruments. Rather than depending on the same set of assessment items for all 121,000 leaders, we examined a variety of different assessments, each built on different assumptions. This provided us with a database rich in diversity and helped give us a much clearer sense of what makes effective leadership and what doesn't. All together, we included in our analysis more than 2,000 unique assessment items.

Research Methodology

We began our analysis by identifying the top 10 percent of managers as seen through the eyes of their subordinates, peers, and bosses and compared them with the bottom 10 percent. The top 10 percent, with the highest aggregate scores, became a high-performing group, and the 10 percent with the lowest aggregate scores were placed in the bottom group. Next, we asked the question "What were the competencies or attributes that separated these groups?"

We were surprised by the results that came from analyzing all of these data. It opened our thinking to some highly promising new ways to look at leadership and provided new directions in the ways we go about developing leaders.

Moving Complexity Toward Simplicity

If you and 10 colleagues were asked to describe a computer, there would be some general consistency among the answers, but the answers would most likely focus on what a computer does, not what is going on inside it. Indeed, for most people, what goes on inside a laptop or desktop computer is a complete mystery. Most have never looked inside one. What's more, you don't need to. The output from the computer is all you care about; that can be spreadsheets, computer graphics, design simulations, email, or simple word processing.

Many people know that there is a hard drive inside and roughly know its capacity. They also know there is a microprocessor, and they have some idea about its speed. They know there is some memory capacity and approximately what the RAM of their computer is. In short, they know some general things about it and what it produces.

That is the level of understanding that practicing leaders need to have about leadership. They do not need to know the details, but it is helpful to have some general understanding of the components that come together to make a great leader.

The Leadership Tent—a Conceptual Framework

We propose approaching leadership in the same way. We will not add one more description of the inner character traits or thought processes of great leaders. The conceptual model we propose is rather simple and involves five elements, which we will compare with the poles in a tent.

Our empirical factor analysis of huge amounts of data collected on leadership competencies reveals that all vital and differentiating leadership competencies can be grouped into five clusters. For the sake of ease in remembering and analysis, we have created a diagram in the form of a tent floor (Figure 1.1) that shows the relationship of these building blocks to each other.

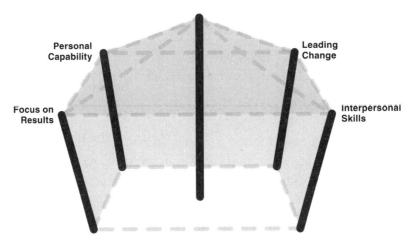

Figure 1.1. The Leadership Tent

Character

Our model in Figure 1.1 starts with a center pole representing the "character" of an individual. There is a huge body of writing on this subject. Indeed, some writers and researchers have argued that leadership is totally about character or integrity. We do not share that view, but we do agree that personal character is the core of all leadership effectiveness. We strongly concur that the ethical standards, integrity, and authenticity of the leader are extremely important.

With a strong personal character, the leader is never afraid to be open and transparent. In fact, the more people can see inside, the more highly regarded the leader will be. Without that personal character, on the other hand, leaders are forever in danger of being discovered. They are like a Hollywood set that from one side looks attractive, but after walking around it, the illusion is dispelled and the hollowness is obvious.

Personal Capability

On one side of the tent floor is the pole of personal capability. This describes the intellectual, emotional, and skill makeup of the individual. It includes analytical and problem-solving capabilities, along with the technical competence the person possesses. It requires an ability to create a clear vision and sense of purpose for the organization. Great leaders need a strong collection of these personal capabilities. Leadership cannot be delegated to others. The leader must be emotionally resilient, innovative, and knowledgeable enough to anticipate and solve problems.

Focus on Results

The third tent pole of leadership represents the behaviors that can broadly be described as "focusing on results." It describes the ability to have an impact on the organization. It means being capable of getting things accomplished. We fully subscribe to the main thesis in the book *Results-Based Leadership*,[7] which argues that leaders may be wonderful human beings, but if they don't produce sustained, balanced results, they simply are not good leaders. We will later examine the interplay of these three elements as a powerful predictor of leadership effectiveness.

Interpersonal Skills

The fourth tent pole of leadership puts into one cluster all of the interpersonal or people skills. There is an enormous body of evidence that says leadership is expressed through the communication process and is the impact that one person (the leader) has on a group of other people. It is the direct expression of the character of the individual and is often the window by which people understand the personal character of the leader. (Note, however, that leadership does not equal any one competency. It is expressed in a result. Yes, the competency is the tool or the manners in which that result is obtained. As such, it is worthy of understanding, but a competency is never an outcome, and leadership is ultimately about outcomes.) We have arbitrarily separated the leader's impact on people from the leader's ability to obtain good results in other arenas, such as financial outcomes, productivity improvement, enhanced customer relations, or greater organizational capability.

Leading Organizational Change

Fifth, as noted earlier, another expression of leadership comes in the ability to produce change within an organization. The highest expression of leadership involves change. Caretaker managers can keep things going on a steady path, but leaders are demanded if the organization is to pursue a new path or rise to a significantly higher level of performance.

A key point here is that for many leadership roles, the first four tent poles may be all that are required. It is not until a person gets into leading broad, strategic change that the final tent pole is required.

An Overview of Important Ideas in this Book

The first edition of this book presented 20 insights. With 15 additional years of research and implementation of these ideas, that number has nearly doubled. We know that many people who buy a book with the best of intentions of thoroughly reading it, but distractions come along, and only the first few chapters are read. Therefore, we now present the 33 insights that we think you would benefit from knowing.

The following chapters present further analysis of these ideas.

Insight 1. Great Leaders Make a Huge Difference

We have known for some time that huge differences exist between top performers and average performers in any job category. One meta-analysis (a synthesis of some 80 well-conducted studies on productivity) showed that for high-level jobs (and leaders certainly fit that category), the productivity difference between the top person out of 100 and the great majority is huge. For example, the top person performing high-complexity jobs is 127 percent more productive than the mean average person and infinitely more productive than the 100th person in that curve. The researchers said "infinitely" because the number was so large that it would be lacking precision to say anything other than "infinite."

Our research with a large mortgage company showed that the leaders in the top decile of ratings (90th to 99th), as rated by their managers, subordinates, and peers, produced twice as much net revenue to the organization (their term for profitability) as that of managers in the 11th through 89th percentiles. So, the difference between really great leaders and the others is extraordinary. We have found strong statistically significant relationships between leadership effectiveness and a variety of desirable business outcomes such as profitability, turnover, employee commitment, customer satisfaction, and intention of employees to leave. In almost every study where we have undertaken to understand the impact of various dimensions of organizational effectiveness, leadership effectiveness has consistently had substantial impact. This is discussed in Chapter 2.

Insight 2. One Organization Can Have Many Great Leaders

Being a great leader can be defined by selecting the top 5 or 10 percent from any distribution, but this is artificial. It was done for the sake of ease and objectivity in our research. However, greatness should ultimately be defined against a standard rather than merely comparing people against each other. There is no reason why half the leaders in an organization could not be great if they were developed properly. Better still, why not all? Great leadership is not a competitive activity in which one person's success detracts from another's success.

Somehow, we must change the mentality that holds that any organization can have only a few really good leaders. Chapter 2 covers this topic.

Insight 3. We Have Been Aiming Too Low

We contend that one of the major failings in leadership development programs has been the tendency to aim low. Michelangelo said, "The greatest danger for most of us is not that our aim is too high and we miss it, but that it is too low and we reach it."

We have often set the target as "getting a little bit better." We have not set our sights on getting people to become outstanding leaders. The more great leaders an organization develops, the more it will become an outstanding organization. There is no reason to accept mediocrity in leadership any more than in software programming, customer service, or selling. This is more fully covered in Chapter 2.

Insight 4. Improved Leadership Leads to Increased Performance Outcomes

The more data we have gather the more evidence we have that better leaders generate better results. While it is true that the worst leaders pull performance down a bit more and the best leaders drive it up, even small improvements in a leader's effectiveness can have some impact on critical organizational outcomes such as customer satisfaction, engagement of direct reports, and turnover. While there is some payoff for smaller changes, the goal for leaders is not to be good. Good leaders only generate good results. The goal for leaders should be to become extraordinary.

Insight 5. Great Leadership Consists of Possessing Several "Building Blocks" of Capabilities, Each Complementing the Others

We have described the "building blocks" of:

- Character
- Personal capabilities
- Focus on results
- Interpersonal skills
- Leading organizational change

Each of these consists of several fairly distinct competencies or sets of behaviors. These are described in some detail later in the book, but a key insight is that possessing only one of them is not likely to have you perceived as an effective leader. In fact, leaders possessing one competency as a strength at the 90th percentile would not be rated at the 90th percentile in terms of overall leadership effectiveness. Chapter 3 elaborates on this concept.

Insight 6. Leadership Culminates in Implementing Change

The highest expression of leadership involves change, and the highest order of change is guiding an organization through a new strategic direction, changing its culture, or changing the fundamental business model. Thus, change is an important and ultimate criterion by which to measure leadership effectiveness. Chapter 3 discusses this.

Insight 7. Some Competencies Differentiate Extraordinary Leaders from Those Who Are Not

There has been an enormous amount of money spent, mostly by large corporations, to define competencies. The implication of these lists has often been that all of these were of equal importance and that the wise manager would devote time to being good at all of them.

Our research, on the contrary, suggests that some competencies tower above others, and which ones are most important often depends on the organization. For example, in one organization we studied, the data showed that the single most important competency for a leader was to be seen as technically competent. Conversely, the quality that put leaders into the bottom rung was their lack of technical competence. This one characteristic was far more important than the second or third distinguishing capability. Many senior executives, in a desire to improve leadership effectiveness, decide independently or in a group discussion with other executives which competencies are most important for their organization.

The point is that if people seek to be perceived as great leaders, it behoves them to know which competencies really make a difference in their organizations. Our research identified 19 competencies that actually separated the top 10 percent of all leaders from the rest. This comprises Chapter 4.

Insight 8. Leadership Competencies Are Linked Closely Together

Although an effort has been made to make them appear unique and specific, the fact of the matter is that leadership competencies are highly intertwined. Several forces appear to be at work to make this happen. One is that becoming good at one competency appears to make people better at another. This is the "cross-training effect." The second way they become linked appears to be from "attribution" or the creation of a "halo effect." If a leader is perceived as being highly effective in working with people, then it is easy to attribute to that person the skills of being committed to the development of subordinates. See Chapter 4.

Insight 9. Effective Leaders Have Widely Different Personal Styles

Military leaders provide some of the clearest contrasts in leadership behavior. General Dwight D. Eisenhower was an able administrator and builder of coalitions and generally self-effacing. General Douglas MacArthur was strategically focused, sensitive to the culture of the enemy, and highly flamboyant. General George Patton was impetuous, passionate, and a "lone ranger." We now have solid research evidence of these widely different styles, especially viewed from one organization to the next.

Our data support the conclusion that effective leadership is incredibly complex and diverse. Providing one simple key to leadership is just not workable.

Our inability to find these universal issues was in many ways one of our most profound findings. The research suggests that extraordinary leaders come in all shapes and sizes. Chapter 5 elaborates on this principle.

Insight 10. Effective Leadership Practices Are Specific to an Organization

Countless leaders who were successful in an organization switch to another and then fail. This is compelling evidence that leaders must fit the organization. Our research showed wide variations between organizations regarding the specific competencies that were valued the most by each one. Leadership always occurs in a context. See Chapter 5 for further information.

Insight 11. Strengths Practiced at a High Level Do Not Become a Weakness

Some have argued that a strength taken too far becomes a weakness. Our research contradicts that conclusion. Genuine strengths cannot be practiced in excess. Chapter 5 elaborates on this conclusion.

Insight 12. One Key to Developing Great Leadership Is to Build Strengths

When people are challenged to improve their leadership effectiveness, they almost automatically assume that the best approach for improvement is fixing weaknesses. In fact, most leadership development processes result in leaders developing an action plan that focuses primarily on weaknesses. Our research has led us to conclude that great leaders are not defined by the absence of weakness, but rather by the presence of clear strengths. Great leaders, as seen through the eyes of subordinates and peers, possess multiple strengths, and our research shows a relatively straight-line progression. The more strengths people have, the more likely they are to be perceived as great leaders.

These strengths are not always the same ones. Of the 19 differentiating competencies that we discovered, great leaders did not have the same five strengths.

In general, in examining all of our data, it is clear that the greater the number of strengths you have, the more likely you are to be considered a great leader. This has enormous implications for executive selection processes, which seem often to be seeking people who possess no flaws. It seems that the emphasis should be on seeking people with remarkable configurations of strengths. This also has enormous implications for leadership development. In the past, we have often focused our efforts on patching over weaknesses. It is as if strengths are givens, and the thing to work on is weaknesses or less positive areas. Increasingly we are convinced this is a mistake. Chapter 6 expands this idea.

Insight 13. Powerful Combinations Produce Nearly Exponential Results

Being good at one thing is sufficient for some athletes or musicians, but seldom for leaders. Our research confirmed that a combination of competencies is the key to being highly effective. For example, the person who is focused only on getting results often fails to obtain those results. Why? It is akin to a person attempting to row a boat with one oar. Instead, good results come from a combination of skills, especially those joining the emphasis on results with strong interpersonal behavior and relationships with people. Neither one, by itself, takes you very far. Together, they produce spectacular outcomes.

Whether you are working with complex organizations or with one subordinate, there is seldom any one thing responsible for producing a positive outcome. Instead, it is the combination of several forces that produces desired outcomes. In general, leaders are most effective when they possess strengths in each of the major clusters of competencies. Chapter 6 provides further insight into this finding.

Insight 14. Greatness Is Not Caused by the Absence of Weakness

Our data reveal that a large percentage of leaders, approximately 70 percent, do not possess any severe weakness, and yet many are not perceived as strong leaders. They are "blah." Subordinates do not single out any one weakness as the root cause of the leader being weak. Instead, the combination of being in the "midrange" on a number of dimensions is the pattern of the mediocre manager. In sum, the absence of profound weaknesses combined with the absence of any pronounced strengths commits you to being no better than average.

Our research shows that the self-evaluation of most leaders in this category is highly distorted. They feel like they are good leaders, possibly because they are not really bad at any one area of leadership.

Chapter 6 elaborates on this important idea.

Insight 15. Great Leaders Are Not Perceived as Having Major Weaknesses

No one is perfect, so great leaders must some have highly visible flaws. We were fully expecting to find that notion confirmed by our data.

To our surprise, there is no hint of that. Instead, our data indicate that the leaders who are seen as highly effective by their subordinates are often seen as not having serious flaws. Their scores across all competency categories were remarkably similar on the high side. Chapter 6 explains further.

Insight 16. Fatal Flaws Must Be Fixed

Although our focus will be on developing strengths, there are some circumstances when a focus on weaknesses is warranted. Indeed, fatal flaws seem to most frequently be caused by things the leader does not do versus those the leader does. Chapter 7 covers this.

Insight 17. Leadership Attributes Are Often Developed in Nonobvious Ways

Our research has helped us uncover a new approach to behavioral change that we have arbitrarily called "nonlinear development." We will argue that the vast majority of action plans created by leaders use a linear philosophy regarding behavioral change. But, the perception of a competency may be strengthened in nonobvious ways. We will argue that competencies are not reality but are the perceptions of others about a given leader.

There may be several nonobvious ways to improve how leaders are perceived. We have called these "competency companions," and these are behaviors that always rise or fall with another competency.

Understanding the competency companions gives the leader additional ways to improve how they are perceived.

The more linear, "hit-it-straight-on" development seems best geared for moving people from bad to neutral. It may also be of some help in moving people from neutral to the "good" range. Companion behaviors provide the means for a leader to move from being quite good to being excellent. Chapter 8 elaborates on this idea.

Insight 18. Leaders Are Made, Not Born

This controversy continues. The question has not gone away. We attest that leaders are made. Although this is certainly not a new point of view, we go on record declaring this to be a fact. We contend that strong evidence exists to support this conclusion.

We readily acknowledge that some people start with advantages of intellect or personality. Studies of twins separated at birth gives convincing evidence that roughly one-third of a person's behavior as an adult is strongly influenced by genetics. However, that means that two-thirds is not, which leads to the conclusion that leaders are mostly made, not born. What we have not done in the past is to acknowledge that one-third of leadership behavior is genetically hard-wired. Chapter 9 provides research on how leaders can improve their leadership effectiveness.

Insight 19. A Leader's Self-Development Requires a Deliberate Plan

Left alone and cut adrift of any external encouragement, most leaders have no organized plan or effort to improve their leadership effectiveness. They nearly always lack data about their current performance. They rarely see a model of an executive who is personally engaged in self-development and who is focused on improving personal leadership abilities and behavior. This topic is introduced in Chapter 9 and continues to be addressed in Chapters 10 through 15, as the individual's contributions become combined with the organization's involvement in their development.

Insight 20. Leaders Can Improve Their Leadership Effectiveness Through Self-Development

In Chapter 9 we discuss the implications of our research to leadership development undertaken by the individual. These ideas apply to any people in leadership positions who desire to improve their own leadership skills and effectiveness.

A relatively small fraction, approximately 10 percent of leaders, have a personal development plan to which they give regular attention. Twice that number have something on paper, but one half of those are not doing anything to follow up on their development.

Insight 21. Leaders Must Take Responsibility for Their Own Development

Responsibility for a leader's development cannot be assumed by the organization, human resources, nor their immediate manager. They must own their own development if it is going to occur. Organizations should send the signal that leadership improvement is ultimately in the hands of the individual leader, with the organization and the immediate manager playing supporting roles. The individual leader must be in charge. Reference to this is made throughout the book, and Chapter 9 emphasizes the importance of individual responsibility.

Insight 22. The Organization Can Provide Significant Assistance in Developing Leadership

The individual leader occupies center stage in the development process, but there are enormous contributions that the organization can provide to make that happen more efficiently, consistently, with greater focus and economically. Some organizations are known for only using and consuming people, while others become known for growing and developing their people. The necessary elements for any corporation or public agency to incorporate into their culture in order to have greater success in filling their leadership pipeline are presented in Chapters 10–15.

Insight 23. Organizations Are Waiting Far Too Long to Begin Developing Leadership Skills

The average manager functions for nearly a decade in the role of managing people before receiving any formal development teaching them valuable leadership skills. Bad habits are acquired in that time. Worse yet, subordinates have endured a less than optimal boss. The organization, the subordinates, and the leader have all been negatively impacted by not beginning earlier. Chapter 11 provides data and insight on this important challenge.

Insight 24. Leadership Is Needed and Occurs at All Levels Throughout the Organization

Ideally, the behavior and thought processes of effective leadership permeates the entire organization. Some effective leaders do not have the words "manager" or "director" in their titles, but they influence many others. Some organizations invest the lion's share of their development investment in the most senior executives, leaving very little of their investment for the development of front-line supervisors or managers who are early in their careers. If one of the objectives of improving leadership effectiveness is to have every employee enjoy the benefits of working for a good manager, then it becomes obvious that development must involve all levels of the organization. Expanding the scope of leadership development is a key element of Chapter 11.

Insight 25. Optimum Leadership Behavior Is Remarkably Similar at All Levels of an Organization

Some have argued that organizations need a different competency model for different levels in the organization. They would contend that the senior executives require one model, that middle management demands another, and that the supervisory level demands yet a third.

We understand that reasoning. The decisions made and the nature of the work might seem to be extremely different. Having different competency models, however, means that a leader is not being assessed with the same criteria through their career. The boundaries between these levels are always arbitrary. Our research concludes that the behavior required of those in middle management as compared to those at more senior levels is very similar.

The main exception involves strategic thinking and championing change. Those at senior levels are required to do this more and to do it more adeptly than those in the middle of the organization. It is also true that people at senior levels are usually expected to perform at a higher level on all of the competencies, but the nature of what they do is very similar up and down the organization, with the exception of strategic thinking and championing change. See Chapter 11 for greater insight on this topic.

Insight 26. Filling an Organization's Leadership Pipeline Demands Scale

We know organizations with 2,000 executives, managers, and supervisors that sponsor development programs that involve 30 people each year. That is clearly better than doing nothing at all, but this is falling far short of what effective leadership development could and should be doing for the organization. Filling the pipeline demands impacting a far larger number. We recognize the need to balance cost, quality, and numbers of people involved, but there are ways to greatly improve the cost effectiveness of delivery to a larger number. Chapter 11 highlights this important conclusion.

Insight 27. Leadership Effectiveness Is Highly Contagious

Exceptional leaders appear to raise the bar for all around them. Poor leaders put an umbrella over all the leaders under them and subordinates seldom perform at a higher level than the leader above them. See Chapters 11 and 17 for further analysis of this observation.

Insight 28. Leadership Effectiveness in an Organization Seldom Exceeds That of the Person at the Top

In analyzing our many sets of data collected from multiple organizations, we observed that the scores of leaders in the organization rarely exceeded the scores of the most senior leader. That person was the cap on leadership effectiveness. See Chapters 11, 12 and 17 for further analysis of this observation.

Insight 29. Effective Leadership Development Requires Integration with Regular Job Duties

Nearly all the competencies required of an effective leader can be utilized in whatever position a person currently occupies. Expanding technical knowledge, learning to build stronger relationships, practicing good communication, sharpening the skills of being a good team member, or practicing the skill of getting feedback; these can all be learned in virtually any job. No one needs to wait until they have received a big promotion to consciously practice on a daily basis the capabilities of a good leader. Part of Chapter 14 addresses the importance of the leader's current position as both the classroom and laboratory for their development.

Insight 30. One Key to Effective Development Is Frequent and Long-Term Sustainment Activities

A big (and legitimate) criticism of leadership development has been the "one and done" nature of it. Bringing about change is a long-term effort. These sustainment activities range from articles being periodically sent, lunch and learn meetings, frequent coaching discussions, online courses, and virtual meetings to review participant's progress in implementing the skills they learned. Without meaningful sustainment activities, change is much less likely to occur. Chapter 15 is devoted to further analysis of this extremely important fact.

Insight 31. Women Are Better Leaders Than Men

On the 16 competencies that we have historically most often measured, women are statistically significantly better on 13 of them. Men are better on two and the other competency is alike. These differences are not miles apart. In fact, in absolute terms they are quite close. However, these statistically significant higher scores are true at every level in the organization, and also hold true in nearly every functional area of the firm. Women at the helm of traditional male bastions such as research, IT, and legal departments receive higher scores on leadership effectiveness than their male counterparts. Women continue to represent an untapped pool of talent for most organizations. Chapter 18 elaborates on this research and our conclusions from it.

Insight 32. Effective Leadership Development Demands Measurement

The process known as multi-rater feedback, or 360-degree feedback, is a powerful, economical, and valid method of establishing base line measurements, and to provide the opportunity to make repeated measurements in the future that verify whether an individual is making positive changes in their behavior. The benefits of this are obvious. It gives assurance to the organization and to the individual that progress is being made. It enables those who design and deliver the development with the means of fine-tuning what they provide, with an eye to constantly improving it. We have also found that a well-validated 360 assessment is the best predictor of leadership talent potential. In studies we have conducted we discovered a highly significant correlation between 360 scores and high potential ratings. Chapter 17 discusses the role of measurement in the leadership development process.

Insight 33. The Medium by Which Leadership Is Practiced Is Communication

This is a mixture of oral and written communication, one-on-one and in groups. While we often associate leadership with the leader running a meeting or giving a speech, the research is clear that an extremely important part of communication involves the leader's ability to ask questions and intently listen to the answers from others. In communication, it becomes clear that "catch" is more important than "pitch." This book does not address the specific content of leadership development initiatives. However, a high-level view makes clear that leadership is about behavior and the lion's share of that behavior is centered on communication via word and action.

Conclusion

Leadership has been shrouded with a "woo-woo" quality that drives our desire to make less mysterious something that has seemed so hopelessly baffling. Obviously, many more books on leadership will be written. We hope our research will help to push the study and understanding of leadership attributes and leadership development to the next rung on the ladder by removing some of that mystery.

2

GREAT LEADERS MAKE A GREAT DIFFERENCE

Good is the enemy of excellence.
Leadership is the challenge to be
something more than average.
—JIM ROHN

Good and Bad Leaders

In our research, we found conclusive evidence that leaders with poor leadership skills generate poor results. That finding will not come as a shock to anyone. It is quite intuitive to anyone who has worked in an organization for more than a few weeks. And our research is equally clear about the fact that good leaders tend to produce good results for their organizations.

What's more, most individuals do not need sophisticated measurement tools to tell the difference between good leaders and bad leaders. They feel the difference. They have experienced the effects at an exceedingly personal level. Poor leaders are a bucket of cold water on the people of the organization.

Great Versus Good Leaders

Our research, however, shows that there is another, even more dramatic, level of difference between good and extraordinary leaders. This is the central theme of this chapter and a major surprise finding of our research. We had failed to appreciate fully just what a significant difference there is between "ordinary" and "extraordinary" leadership.

In examining the relationship between leadership effectiveness and desirable outcomes, the consistent finding in all our research was the impact of the best and worst leaders on achieving bottom-line results. Figure 2.1 isolates the results on an employee engagement measure (high percentile scores indicate greater satisfaction/engagement) by the results of individual leadership effectiveness broken into 20 levels. Each level represents 5 percentile points on the leadership effectiveness measure. The leadership effectiveness measure is the overall average score from all the differentiating competencies. This is an aggregate study composed of hundreds of different companies and 90,252 leaders across the globe. Approximately 35 percent of the leaders were from outside North America. Note the dramatic change involving leaders at both the top and bottom of the rankings.

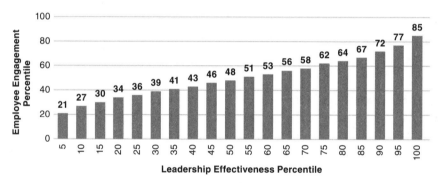

Figure 2.1. Impact of Leadership Effectiveness on Employee Engagement

The characteristics of the graph in Figure 2.1 are extremely significant in describing the relationship between leadership effectiveness and bottom-line outcomes. We see poor results at the lower percentiles, substantially more positive results at the higher percentiles, and with each increase in a leader's effectiveness we see an improvement in engagement. This graph presents several important findings:

1. Leaders have a dramatic impact as they move from "bad" to "good."
2. Poor leaders have an adverse impact on the groups they attempt to lead.

3. Any improvement a leader can make has an impact on the outcome of engagement.

4. Keep in mind that these results represent individual managers and their direct reports. If a senior leader is highly effective, then the direct reports of that leader are highly engaged. But if a lower level leader in the same organization is a very poor leader, then their direct reports are unengaged and dissatisfied.

5. One of the best predictors of high or low engagement is the effectiveness of the manager of that group. Poor leaders produce dissatisfied, unengaged employees, while great leaders produce highly engaged, satisfied employees.

Impact on Engagement by Geography

To demonstrate the consistency of the data we did studies that show results by geography (Figure 2.2). What is most interesting in these data is the consistency of the effect of improved leadership effectiveness. Regardless of geography or industry the better the leaders the better the results. To date, we have not found a place in the world or an industry where the impact was not profound.

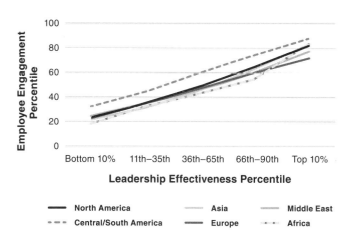

Figure 2.2. Impact of Leadership Effectiveness Across the World

Impact on Net Profits at a Mortgage Bank

From measures on subordinate commitment to the organization, we now turn to measures of financial performance. At a mortgage bank, we collected data on its measure of profitability, or net profits, for a series of leaders. Figure 2.3 shows the results of our study.

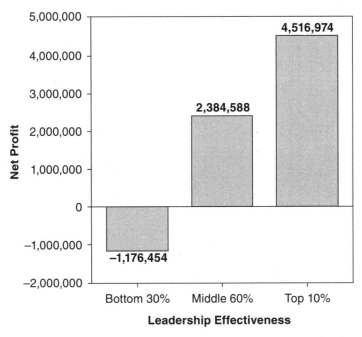

Figure 2.3. Impact of Leadership Effectiveness on Net Profit

What we found in this study was that the poor leaders actually lost money for the company. Their performance was so ineffective that it appeared to drive customers away or to create severe internal inefficiencies. The good leaders, on the other hand, made a reasonable profit for the company. Their performance, compared with that of the bad leaders, represented a substantial change. However, the extraordinary leaders nearly doubled the profit generated for the company by the good leaders. Imagine the impact of transitioning 10 or 20 percent of leaders from the "good" to the "extraordinary" category. It would add 10 to 20 percent to the bottom line of the entire company.

The retail industry has long known that there is a relationship between employee commitment, customer satisfaction, and store profitability. Common sense tells you that when an employee is happy and engaged, they will treat customers more positively, which in turn causes the customers to purchase more, return to the store more frequently, and recommend it to friends.

More than 30 studies confirm that elevated levels of employee engagement result in higher levels of customer satisfaction. Additionally, there have been studies that answer the question that has been raised regarding whether higher levels of customer satisfaction increased employee engagement, or whether employee engagement was the driver of elevated customer satisfaction. The research confirmed that employee engagement comes first and is followed by higher levels of customer satisfaction.

The implications of our research are that another link needs to be added to the chain; it should be the "leadership-employee-customer-profit chain."[1] Figure 2.1 showed the impact that leaders have on employee commitment and satisfaction, which ultimately translates into the direct impact of leaders on profitability.

The new chain of cause-and-effect events is:

Leaders → Employees → Customers → Store Profits

One should also keep in mind that the additional insight this research adds to the profit chain of events is that great leaders have even more impact on employees who affect customers and therefore create even greater profits for the organization.

Impact on Sales

A retail company in Mexico contacted us with a desire to help them improve the effectiveness of their store leaders and regional managers. The company provides goods and services to the poorest people in the country. They had been very successful but knew that there were significant differences between the sales revenue of different stores. One of their theories was that the effectiveness of the store manager could be a source of much of the variability. We created a customized assessment and gathered 360-degree assessment data on 95 store managers. The store managers typically did not have any formal education beyond high school and were promoted from within.

On average leaders were evaluated by 16 evaluators including managers, peers, direct reports, and internal customers. We noticed in the data there was a significant range in the overall effectiveness (overall average of all survey items) ratings of managers going from 2.89 to 4.55. On each of the stores we were able to collect sales results for the current year along with the previous year. We calculated the percentage growth in sales versus prior year. Overall there was a 5 percent year-over-year sales growth. Figure 2.4 shows the results demonstrating the impact of leadership effectiveness on sales year-to-year in the stores. The poorest leaders had only a 0.7 percent increase while the leaders in the top 10 percent had a 7.4 percent increase.

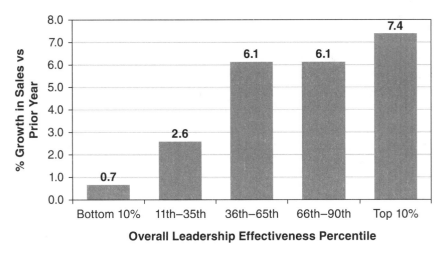

Figure 2.4. Impact of Leadership Effectiveness on Sales

To understand what caused the differences in sales between leaders, we looked at the leaders who were in the bottom third on their effectiveness and then calculated their employee turnover in stores. Those leaders in the bottom one-third had 81 percent annual employee turnover while those in the top one-third of leaders had a 68 percent annual turnover. Both numbers are high, but 81 percent is much higher than 68 percent and appeared to be one of the factors responsible for the differences in revenue. It appears that better leaders were able to retain more of their best employees, which helped the store run more efficiently and improved customer relationships.

Impact on Turnover at an Insurance Company

Turnover costs companies millions of dollars every year. John Sullivan, chief talent officer at Agilent Technologies in Palo Alto, California, put the cost of turnover for a software engineer at $200,000 to $250,000 per departing employee. He went on to say, "One firm I work with just calculated the cost of an engineer vacancy in lost revenue at $7,000 per day."[2] Although there are many reasons for turnover, our research consistently bears out that the relationship an employee has with his or her manager substantially influences the employee's decision to stay with a company or move on.

Figure 2.5 shows the results from a study conducted at a large insurance company. Leadership effectiveness was determined and matched up with yearly turnover rates within each leader's group. In this study, higher turnover (19 percent per year) was created by leaders in the bottom third in terms of their leadership ability as seen by their subordinates and peers. These leaders presumably did nothing to force people to leave, but their style and approach did not encourage them to stay. Better retention came from good leaders, who experienced 14 percent annual turnover. Extraordinary leaders, however, cut the average turnover rate in their groups by another 5 percent. Reduced turnover had a direct impact on profitability, customer satisfaction, and claim-resolution speed.

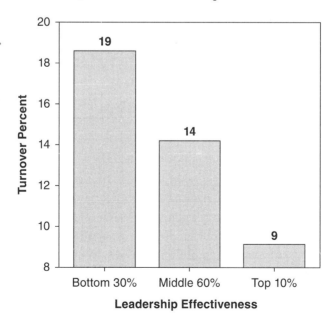

Figure 2.5   Impact of Leadership Effectiveness on Turnover

Intention to Leave the Organization

In another study conducted with more than 90,000 leaders from hundreds of different organizations, we examined at the relationship between leadership effectiveness and intention to stay with or to leave the company. These results were extremely consistent with an organization's actual turnover data. In most organizations, actual employee turnover is about one-half of the number of those who express an intention to leave. (In other words, if 50 percent of employees intend to leave, turnover is typically 25 percent.) In this study, high scores indicated a greater intention to leave, whereas low scores indicated a greater intention to stay. As is apparent from Figure 2.6, the employees of the extraordinary leaders were significantly more committed to stay with the company.

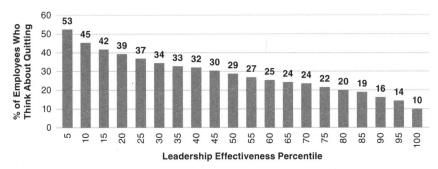

Figure 2.6. Impact of Leadership Effectiveness on Employee Retention

Impact on Customer Satisfaction

In a study done with a high-tech communications company, we studied the relationship between leadership effectiveness and customer satisfaction (Figure 2.7). Once again, extraordinary leaders have substantially better ratings on customer satisfaction. In this study, high scores indicate higher customer satisfaction. Again, we assume that in most cases the leader does not have direct contact with most customers, but it is the leader's influence on the level of commitment of the front-line employees that makes the dramatic differences in customer satisfaction.

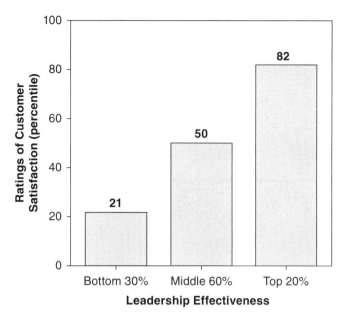

Figure 2.7. Impact of Leadership Effectiveness on Customer Satisfaction

In a related study conducted by our colleague Larry Senn, he was asked by a retail client to change the behavior of store employees to be more customer service oriented. The company began an intensive program aimed at changing the behavior of store employees. After months of work, it became apparent that some stores were being successful in creating a more customer-friendly atmosphere, whereas other stores were not. Employees in both the successful and unsuccessful stores had received the same training, and the employees did not appear to be any less capable or experienced in unsuccessful stores. As the researchers studied the unsuccessful stores to understand the reason for their failure, they found that managers in unsuccessful stores tended to be operationally oriented, whereas successful store managers were customer oriented. The operationally oriented store managers reinforced the importance of tracking money and time. Customer-oriented store managers, on the other hand, reinforced the importance of customer satisfaction. After going through the experience, the researchers came to the conclusion that efforts to change employee behavior had to start by making sure that their managers' behaviors were in alignment.[3]

Impact on Percentage of Highly Committed Employees

We performed a study looking at the percentage of highly committed employees in a work group. Each person who directly reported to a leader was asked the extent to which they felt that the work environment was a place where people wanted to go the extra mile. We selected only those employees who answered "5" on a 5-point scale. This is the kind of employee that is enthusiastic about the job. He or she is excited to take on challenging assignments and will do whatever is necessary to get projects completed on time and in budget. Every leader can identify a few employees that fit that description. What would be the impact of having more of this kind of employee on the success of any work group? Productivity would increase, morale would be higher, projects would get done faster, and therefore profitability would also go up.

What impact do these employees have on other employees? When people are walking or running and someone passes them, what do most people tend to do? They speed up. It is almost an automatic response. In work groups, when a high percentage of employees are highly committed and giving their best effort, the remainder of the group is usually not far behind.

Figure 2.8 shows the percentage of highly committed employees based on aggregated results for hundreds of organizations. Once again, leadership effectiveness is divided into 20 levels.

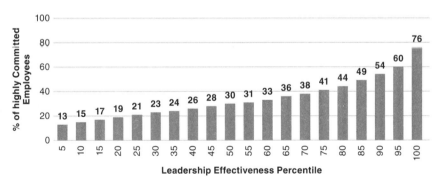

Figure 2.8. Impact of Leadership Effectiveness on Commitment of Employees

It is interesting that 13 percent of the employees of the worst leaders continue to be highly committed. Evidently, that is what nature produces. As you look at the chart, you will note a steady increase in the percentage of highly committed employees with the increase in leadership effectiveness: 44 percent of the employees of leaders who are at the 80th percentile are highly committed, whereas 54 percent of employees of leaders at the 90th percentile are highly committed. Those leaders who were the most effective in the top 5 percent, had 76 percent of their employee who were highly committed. If you were a leader of a work group where 40 to 50 percent of your employees were highly committed, would it have a significant impact on the bottom line? When we have asked that question to leaders around the world, the answer was always a resounding "yes."

Leadership Has an Impact on the Bottom Line

Our purpose in presenting these studies is to impress on the reader that the impact of leadership:

- Affects every business outcome dimension or organization performance
- Is substantial, not trivial
- Is extremely consistent

The more data we gather the clearer it becomes that every increase in a leader's effectiveness generates some outcomes that contribute to the organization's success. Continuing to find ways to improve the effectiveness of leaders will have a great bearing on the success of an organization.

Some senior leaders worry about the cost of leadership development, failing to factor in the impact poor leaders have on contributing to low morale, decreased sales, poor customer satisfaction, employee turnover, and an increasing number of employees who are unwilling to give their full effort. A careful analysis shows that those costs substantially outweigh the expenditures for leadership development.

Is "Good" Good Enough?

Though the results for extraordinary leaders are much better than those for poor leaders, the current problem is that too many good leaders feel that being "good" is good enough.[4] They are satisfied that they are not poor leaders and, therefore, remain unchallenged to go to the next level. Many of these good leaders do not recognize that continued improvement in leadership would make a substantial difference in the outcomes they are attempting to produce. Many "adequate" leaders stay where they are because they fail to understand the differences between good and extraordinary leaders.

What Causes Good Leaders to Be Unchallenged to Change?

As you look at the previous studies on the impact of leadership it is very clear that improving leaders would have a significant impact on an organization's success and yet, most leaders assume they personally are an above-average leader, have an above-average intellect, and are an above-average driver.

1. When you mention that there is a leadership effectiveness problem, many people automatically believe that the problem is poor leaders. There exists a natural human tendency to blame problems on low performers. We like to assign a scapegoat as the source of any problems. This can turn into witch hunts for the "bad" leaders. Frequently, many of the "bad" leaders are new, inexperienced supervisors who need time and training to develop. It is more tempting to ferret out the bad leaders than to face a different reality. This troubling tendency was most aptly expressed by Walt Kelly's comic strip character Pogo when he often observed, "We have met the enemy and he is us."[5]

   Blaming bad leaders is a simple solution. It is much more difficult to accept that the problem with leadership is the need for everyone to undertake some level of improvement. Those who are good could have a substantial positive impact on the organization if they moved from good to great.

2. Training programs often send a false impression. When organizations sponsor training programs positioned to take bad leaders and make them into good leaders, it unwittingly sends the signal that those leaders who are currently in the "good" category can coast. Beyond that, most supervisory and management training courses are designed to develop basic leadership skills. The focus is on acquiring and understanding the fundamental skills required in a leadership role. Many leaders act as if the introductory course in a series is the only course that exists or is necessary for them. We are aware of only a handful of corporate development programs targeted specifically to make good people truly excel.[6]

3. Many 360-degree leadership assessments compare leaders' results and show how they compare with the average. The unintended message that most leaders get from the assessments is that if you are in the midrange, "You are okay, and okay is good enough."

Figure 2.9 (see next page) shows the results from a 360-degree assessment. The dark background area is the norm, which is the average of all others taking this assessment. Looking at the results for Pat Brown against the norm gives the impression that Pat is viewed in a generally positive light by the respondents and is a good leader. The results for Pat are more positive in several areas than the norm. Even after informing leaders that a norm is the average of the best and worst leaders, most people continue to look at areas where they are slightly more positive than the norm as areas that are strengths; only areas considerably less positive than the norm are viewed as serious weaknesses requiring any remedial action.

Figure 2.10 (see next page) depicts the same results for Pat Brown, but this time the standard represents the 90th percentile score on each of the competencies. Showing this new target tends to change the focus of the feedback. Pat Brown is doing well but still has a long way to go to move from a good leader to an extraordinary leader. By contrasting results with a mean average, the message communicated is, "The goal is to be better than average." Contrasting results with levels of extraordinary leaders shows people the distance that they need to move to achieve a higher level.

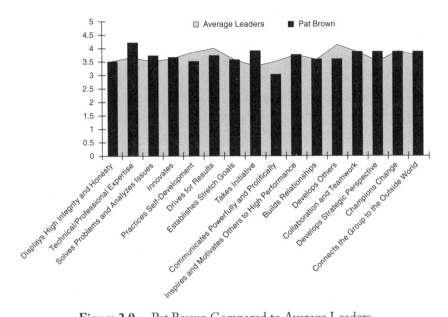

Figure 2.9. Pat Brown Compared to Average Leaders

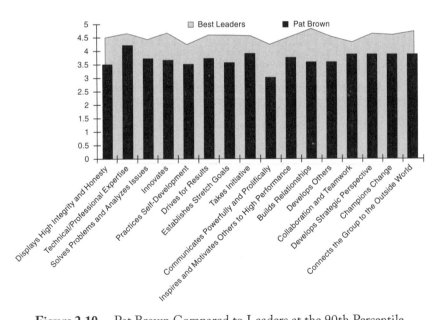

Figure 2.10. Pat Brown Compared to Leaders at the 90th Percentile

4. Good leaders often fail to appreciate and understand the differences between good leadership and outstanding leadership.

It is always interesting to watch diving competitions during the Olympics. When observers witness the first dive, most are usually impressed. The observer's point of comparison is often amateur diving, and compared with the dives of amateur competitors, the Olympian's dive is beautiful, graceful, and executed precisely. Then the scores come up and they are "5," "6," "6," "5," "7," and the commentator says, "Did you see that splash?" or "Notice how the knees were bent and the feet pointed in different directions." You are often surprised and chagrined because you had not noticed any of those problems. As the competition continues, the judges and the commentators train everyone on the finer points of competition diving. After an hour of watching diving competition, the ability of people to judge great diving skills has moved from nonexistent to rudimentary. If a diver makes a huge mistake you notice it, but you are still frequently surprised when you judge a dive as excellent and the judges mark it down because of a fine detail that you missed.

Judging leadership is much the same way. Too many have remained casual observers of leadership rather than becoming trained judges. They experience leadership from others and feel the effects (that was great leadership or that was terrible) but lack the insight of how the effect was created or what its longer-lasting consequences will be.

People frequently confuse personality traits for leadership. They assume that assertiveness, or the ability to make a compelling speech or give people crisp orders, is leadership. It is not.

In order for people to improve their leadership ability, they need to become astute observers of leadership. They not only need to understand some basic concepts and be reasonably well read but also need to be able to judge everyday interactions and understand what is missing.

5. Many good leaders believe that extraordinary leaders are prodigies, having been endowed with some unusual gifts from birth. Most recognize that people with exceptional leadership talents exist, but it is difficult for others to understand the path in their development that brought them from being good leaders to being extraordinary leaders. The bar set to achieve extraordinary

leadership seems too high to achieve, and the path to develop extensive skills is not clear. This is akin to watching a great concert pianist and aspiring to play the same way he or she does. The fantasy is fun, but given the reality of looking at what it would take to accomplish such a feat, most don't even start. One music student described her experience completing her degree in music pedagogy. She indicated that there were a few students who had exceptional natural ability but lacked discipline. Watching the professors interact with these students, she observed that the professors were not very excited about working with these students with natural talent but poor discipline. Professors chose to mentor students with strong discipline. When asked about their choices regarding which students they chose to mentor, one professor commented, "Discipline is always more important than some natural ability. With some dedicated practice, those with discipline will surpass those with natural ability in a few semesters. Without discipline and the ability to learn, those with natural ability will never progress above their current ability."

A great deal of research has been done on individuals who achieve high levels of individual performance. The researchers, Anders Ericsson and Neil Charness, described having exceptional ability or talent as "expert performance." These researchers have produced a great deal of empirical research on the question of whether people are born with "innate talent."[7]

Most people believe that there are individuals possessing superior intelligence and aptitude who distinguish themselves and are referred to as gifted. The philosophy of gifted individuals dates back to periods of time when kings and rulers were called "royalty." The implication of royalty is that there is some genetic or inherited difference between individuals. The idea that many individuals can develop exceptional ability is inconsistent with the idea that "only my son is qualified to be king." A review of the literature reveals that appropriate training can have a dramatic impact on performance. Research in music performance revealed that children who showed little sign of musical talent but who were trained with the Suzuki method achieved equivalent levels to those of musical prodigies. A common conception is that most child prodigies show innate abilities at a young age.

Research into the backgrounds of those with exceptional talent shows a great deal of evidence toward the personal interests of children but very little evidence of any innate ability.

The reality is that people who are considered prodigies in music, chess, athletics, or other areas all had a very consistent pattern. All showed interest in their talents, and all practiced from between two to four hours a day for 10 years. The 10-year mark was an amazingly similar finding regardless of musical, mathematical, or athletic talent. There is very strong research to show that expertise as a violinist correlated almost exactly with the number of hours of practice. Experts practice more than 10,000 hours, the next level about 7,500 hours, and the next level 5,000 hours. Ericsson and Charness concluded their analysis by stating, "The traditional view of talent, which concludes that successful individuals have special innate abilities and basic capacities, is not consistent with the reviewed evidence." They went on to say that more plausible explanations of individual differences "are factors that predispose individuals toward engaging in deliberate practice and enable them to sustain high levels of practice for many years."

Another characteristic of expert performers was that they typically had coaches who encouraged them to practice intensely. Suppose that a person decides she wants to learn to play golf. She begins by signing up for several lessons, and then she hires a personal coach to play with her. After a few months of lessons, she is performing at an adequate level and so she begins to "play" golf with friends. Playing is inherently more fun than intense practice, but the learning curve goes down considerably. To continue to improve, people need to take the time regularly for intense practice, and that is most effective when accompanied by an experienced coach.

Most individuals, as they become managers for the first time, go through an intense learning period. They receive a great deal of training and personal coaching, and are open to ideas and suggestions from experienced managers. They take time to plan meetings, performance reviews, and how they will give feedback to direct reports. They also pay close attention to others, watching to understand techniques and skills. They are practicing leadership with an intent to get better. Their learning curve is high. Once they get reasonably competent at being managers, they do something very similar to the previous golf example. They switch from practicing to playing. While playing, the intensity of their learning goes down. Playing leadership is inherently more fun than practicing leadership, but skill development is very slow and sometimes stops altogether. In a recent meeting at a large oil company, we asked a group of executives if they were focused on playing or practicing leadership. The consensus of the group was that everyone was busy playing and nobody was practicing getting better. That is, there was no deliberate plan that involved conscious effort to improve an important behavior.

One implication of this research is that some great leaders are not born with, but acquire at an early age, the desire to make things happen with other people. We believe that other leaders can acquire increased leadership ability with practice at any age. The real key is that they engage in intense practice. Bad leaders assume that deliberate practice makes no difference, so they continue to perform but never improve.

6. Leaders are only willing to be as effective as those who in turn lead them. Tom Watson, Jr., is often credited as the key architect of IBM's culture. One manifestation of that culture was that men wore white shirts, dark suits, and wing-tip shoes. He once remarked that if he wore a pink shirt to work, he was sure that the following day he would see hundreds of executives wearing pink shirts.

Leaders cast a significant shadow in the organizations where they work. A colleague, Paul McKinnon, did some research several years ago to measure the shadows of leaders with several of his clients. In a follow-up study we conducted to analyze the shadows of leaders, we found that employees who have worked for the same boss for several years tend to share not only the strengths but also the weaknesses of their boss. In the study, we examined the 360-degree results for a manager and identified areas of strength and opportunities for improvement. The 360-degree results were then analyzed for all of the direct reports of the manager (who were also managers).

Managers with a large shadow showed the exact same list of strengths and opportunities for improvement as their direct reports. The analysis calculated the percent overlap between managers and all of their direct reports. The percentages varied from a small shadow (e.g., 25 percent overlap) to a large shadow (100 percent overlap). This "shadow" can cut both ways. If you work with an extraordinary leader, the tendency is that your leadership effectiveness will be close to that of your leader. On the other hand, if your boss is an ineffective leader, the tendency is that you won't be much better. In the study, we found the length of a leader's shadow to vary. The length of time people spend with the same boss can increase the size of the shadow.

In the study, we found that some leaders and their direct reports had a 100 percent overlap between strengths and weaknesses. By their nature, people think their approach to work is best, and bosses tend to hire employees who have a similar style. Over time, bosses reinforce their positive as well as negative traits by unconsciously rewarding some employee behaviors while discouraging or ignoring others. As a result, employees are conditioned to mimic those to whom they report.

For example, assume a leader who is very detail oriented, task focused, and technically proficient, but not sensitive toward coworkers reporting to him. More often than not, this person's subordinates generally share his skills and are also not regarded as especially considerate of others. Most of the time, bosses do not actively encourage brusqueness, but the managers saw their boss get away with it and felt they could, too. The process of mimicking the strengths and weaknesses of one's boss is an unconscious process.

Possibly, one of the most startling pieces of research that validates these findings is the study of child abuse. It is well established that children who are abused have a high likelihood of becoming abusive parents. It seems almost impossible to comprehend why children who detest and suffer from the way their parents treated them often treat their children exactly the same way. Many adults have exerted great effort to successfully break their child-rearing practices from the past and start a new legacy of positive child-rearing. Many parents have had the experience as a child of promising themselves that they would "never treat their children that way," only to find themselves doing exactly the same thing to their children.

A by-product of the phenomenon is that employees are rarely more effective than their bosses. That is good news if the boss is an extraordinary leader. The direct reports tend to rise to that level. But we observed over and over that employees are only as good as their bosses. Bosses set the standards, high or low. The findings have implications:

- The extent to which leaders merely encourage subordinates to be their clones becomes problematic. Indeed, it may demonstrate a lack of appreciation for different styles and approaches, which ultimately may be detrimental to the organization's goals.
- Leaders in the organization should be made cognizant of the ways they reinforce their own behaviors in their direct reports. Superiors should think more consciously of the role they play in people's lives and careers and the legacy they will leave once they are gone.
- Superiors need to be reminded to recruit employees with a diversity of skills and work styles that would enrich and contribute to the organization.
- Organizations seeking a culture change should begin with an intervention at the senior level, as the best way to bring real change is usually to change the leaders. (As one comic suggested, "You have to change the leaders, or you have to change the leaders.")
- It takes great leaders to develop great leaders. The idea of "Do as I say, not as I do" just won't work with leadership.

Imagine the impact on any organization if 20 percent of the good leaders could move on to become excellent. Fast-forward in your mind to the organizational results that change would produce. Consider the profound impact on culture and the motivation level of employees. Imagine the transformed work experience of all inside the organization.

The research is clear regarding the impact of leadership on desirable outcomes. Good leaders are substantially more effective than bad leaders, but great leaders make a great difference.

The Proper Measure of "Greatness"

For the sake of convenience, we have selected "great" leaders by examining the top 10 percent from a population of leaders from well-respected organizations. However, we are the first to acknowledge that this is merely for convenience. The proper measure is against an objective standard, and there is no reason why an organization could not have 90 percent of its first-level managers or supervisors who were great, versus the arbitrary 10 percent that we analyzed.

Indeed, our definition could probably be reverse engineered. When you could identify a leader who produced . . .

- High productivity
- Low turnover
- High customer satisfaction
- High profitability
- Innovation
- Positive relationships with suppliers

. . . then you could, by definition, say this was an extremely effective leader. Effective leadership is best defined and measured by the results produced, not by simply taking a certain number from the top of a distribution.

The Organization's Objective

The more "great" leaders an organization can develop, the stronger it will be. This is true for multiple reasons, but some of those are the following:

- The contribution these leaders make to the units they manage
- The example or role model they set for the entire organization
- The cumulative impact their performance has in creating an entirely new culture for the organization
- The elevated standard of performance that is set within the organization

We have advocated strongly that individuals focus on their strengths. By doing that, they greatly increase the likelihood of being perceived as great leaders. That same principle applies to the organization. By increasing the number of high-performing leaders, the organization gains great strength. It is always tempting to attempt to fix the low-performing ones, but the greatest gain appears to come by helping more leaders become truly excellent.

One downside of any organization doing that is the target they become for headhunters. Any company that produces great leaders may become a target for executive recruiters. However, that is a relatively small price to pay for the enormous gains to be achieved by successfully developing great leaders for the firm.

Good Versus Bad Thinking

As a teenager, one of the authors had the opportunity to hear an astronaut describe the challenges of going to the moon. His analogy was that the accuracy of going from Earth to the moon was equivalent to shooting a bullet in New York and hitting a gumball in Los Angeles. It was a very dramatic example of the importance of correct aim and midcourse corrections. If the aim was off just a little in New York, the target would be missed by a state or two, barring major corrections. The more we work with individuals and organizations, the more it becomes clear that small, even barely noticeable, actions can have huge consequences over time.

One of the small, barely noticeable philosophies that most people hold today is binary thinking about good versus bad. We are constantly amused that when trying to uncover problems in organizations, there is a search to identify the "bad people." One of the most common tendencies is that when a mistake occurs in an organization and there is a search for the cause, frequently a person or group is sought to be the source of the problem. The "fall person" is blamed for everything. This is rarely the truth, but most people find it much more convenient.

On the other side, we have the search for "good." Having conducted a variety of studies to identify characteristics of high performers, what inevitably becomes a difficult task is to determine the criteria for identifying high performers. This would appear to be a simple task, but as the different measurements are laid out it becomes a challenge. Organizations search for some simple criteria to easily and quickly pinpoint the good from the bad.

In this chapter, we have presented a new philosophy about leadership. This philosophy expands a person's thinking from "Leaders are either good or bad" to "Leaders are bad, good, and great." This may seem like a small change from what many currently believe, but we believe this small philosophical difference can have a huge impact on the success of both individuals and organizations. For individuals, this philosophy should help good leaders understand that good is not great. It never was and never will be. Good is good, but the ultimate target is extraordinary leadership.

For organizations, this philosophy ought to clarify the competitive advantage of great leadership. When discussing their leadership talent, executives will sometimes state, "I don't think we have a problem with our leaders" (which when translated means, we don't have bad leaders). The problem is not an abundance of bad leaders; the problem is the universal acceptance of good leaders and assuming that they don't need to be any better.

3

THE COMPETENCY QUEST

*Many writers on leadership take considerable pains
to distinguish between leaders and managers. In the
process, leaders generally end up looking like a cross
between Napoleon and the Pied Piper, and managers
like unimaginative clods. This troubles me. I once
heard it said of a man, "He's an utterly first-class
manager but there isn't a trace of the leader in him."
I am beginning to believe that he does not exist. Every
time I encounter utterly first-class managers they
turn out to have quite a lot of the leader in them.*
—JOHN GARDNER

The most prevalent approach to leadership development in recent years
has been the competency movement. The fundamental premise is simple. Identify and define the competencies of effective leaders in a specific
organization. (Competencies are the combination of knowledge, skills,
traits, and attributes that collectively enable someone to perform a given
job.) Then, when selecting leaders, choose people who possess those competencies because they will have a much higher likelihood of success. If
you want to develop leaders in the organization, design activities that
directly expand or strengthen those competencies for the leaders in the
organization.

For example, if Ajax Manufacturing decided to embark on a
competency-based system, it would need to study its leaders to determine
what the best leaders had in common. To accomplish this, Ajax might
retain a firm experienced in this research, and that firm would follow one
of several paths to determine the appropriate competencies. Alternatives
could include:

- Conduct extensive field research within the firm by analyzing the requirements of various leadership positions, studying 360-degree feedback reports, and observing leader behavior.
- From their extensive experience, provide the organization with a list of competencies, basically derived from past work they had completed in other similar organizations.
- Assemble a group of senior executives in the organization and elicit their views of the competencies required to succeed.
- Assemble groups of people who work with leaders and obtain their collective views about the knowledge, skills, traits, and attributes required for success in Ajax.
- Try a more scientific, statistical approach. This is a three-step process:

  1. Gather a large number of items that describe behavior, traits, and characteristics. Administer the items with a large sample of individuals across different companies, cultures, and geographies.
  2. Apply a rigorous statistical technique that identifies those items that most powerfully differentiate those individuals who received the highest aggregate scores on all the items from those who received the lower scores.
  3. From this group of items, select those that have the highest correlation with important business outcomes, such as employee engagement, customer satisfaction, productivity, innovation, and profitability.

After having followed one or more of those avenues with the help of the outside consultants, Ajax might conclude that the best leaders commonly share a group of competencies:

This list of competencies then becomes the "touchstone" by which further leadership is selected and around which all development programs are structured.

This competency approach swept through human resource departments. It has been estimated that at least 80 percent of companies have created such competency lists. The competency movement promised to bring scientific objectivity to employee selection and development. Indeed, we think it brought greater rigor than previously existed and helped to improve the hiring process. And for the past two decades, companies have focused their people development efforts around these defined competencies. In sum, the approach has impeccable logic to it.

The Challenge of Competency Models

So, why has the competency movement not borne more fruit? Why has it not been successful in helping organizations produce higher-caliber leaders? As John Gardner wrote, "Why do we not have better leadership? The question is asked over and over. We complain, express our disappointment, often our outrage; but no answer emerges."[1]

We think the competency movement had several major flaws.

Our objective is to help the reader understand what has gone wrong, but more important, how this basic approach can be fixed and made more effective.

The Problems

The problems with the competency movement begin with the challenge of balancing simplicity and complexity. In the quest for rigor the solution can become wearisome and tedious. Beyond that some of the seemingly logical assumptions that have surrounded competencies are flat-out wrong.

1. Complexity

One large public-sector organization had an outside consultant create a list of competencies for each of three pay bands in the organization. Each pay band (or salary group) had 173 to 175 specific behaviors defined for it, which in turn were organized into 15 general competencies. Imagine a list of 175 behaviors that you were expected to understand and somehow apply to your work. It is patently ridiculous. Few people could ever comprehend the meaning of this amount of complexity, let alone put it into action.

Although that is an extreme example, it is not unusual to see organizations with lists of 30 to 50 competencies for their leaders to be evaluated and developed against. Complexity has become a major deterrent to effective implementation.

2. Some Faulty Assumptions About Competencies

There are several important assumptions underlying the focus on competencies. They were seldom stated overtly, so let us try:

1. Each organization possesses its own unique set of attributes or competencies.
2. Competencies within each person are distinct and separate from each other. They can be isolated and studied as if they were separate chromosomes in a person's genetic makeup.
3. The more similarity or congruence between an individual and the organization's unique pattern, the better leader he or she will be.
4. Competencies are all of roughly equal importance.
5. The best way to develop any competency is to focus directly on that specific trait or behavior. Working harder and longer at it will make you better at it, and therefore make you a better leader.
6. Competencies are static.

Unfortunately, it now appears that most of these assumptions do not coincide with the current reality, nor are they reinforced by our current research.

Correcting the Assumptions

Assumption 1. Competencies Are Unique to Each Organization

Fact: Despite the efforts to create distinctive lists of competencies, there is a remarkable sameness about them from one company to another. Several explanations for this come to mind. The first is that the requirements to work in one company or public organization are not that different from those in another. People are people wherever they work. What makes for success in one firm is a carbon copy of what causes success in another.

The authors have long felt that the differences between people within any one organization are certainly as large or larger than those between organizations in the same industry, and probably between all organizations. That is, the differences between the people who work for Ajax Manufacturing in quality assurance and sales, or those in accounting and marketing, or between the people in research and development in contrast with those in maintenance—those differences are usually large, and every bit as large as the differences between the people from Ajax Manufacturing and those from its competitor, Behemoth Manufacturing. And these differences are probably as large as the differences between Ajax and the Carthage Corporation in the neighboring state.

Another explanation is that the same consulting firms are doing the competency analysis, and their processes ferret out the same things wherever they go. Much of the research on competencies has been done by a relatively small group of consulting firms.

Finally, it is probable that there are a handful of factors that will always account for overall leadership effectiveness. Lyle Spencer writes in his book *Competence at Work* "that the competencies of achievement orientation, influence and personal effectiveness will likely account for 80–98 percent of all competency models."[2]

Assumption 2. Competencies Are Unique and Distinctive Traits or Qualities Possessed by an Individual

Fact: One of the most dramatic discoveries of our analysis is the massive linkage between competencies. The linkage we are talking about does not consist of a handful of competencies that are slightly linked to each other. Instead, nearly every competency we studied was highly correlated with many others. Rather than being separate and distinct, each organization's competencies were like a three-dimensional spider web, in which any place you touch is linked to countless other strands in the web.

It appears that the researchers who were driving the competency movement wanted to make competencies appear unique and distinctive. So, the research was done in a way that gave the appearance of separation between the competencies. Nothing is further from the truth. With such complex, strong links between competencies, it becomes problematic even to give them individual labels.

Later in this chapter we present our views of why competencies are linked together. Later chapters present other important findings about the importance of multiple competencies, and insights about how leadership effectiveness increases when competencies are strategically positioned in different clusters of behaviors.

Assumption 3. The More Congruence There Is Between the Organization's Defined Competencies and the Individual's, the Greater Is the Likelihood of Success

Fact: This is the only one of the assumptions that our data do not challenge. However, the validity of the assumption hinges on whether the organization has empirically derived its own list of competencies and whether there are good ways to measure an individual's competencies. Our data confirmed that leaders whose profiles were compatible with the high performers in the organization were much more likely to be highly rated than those who were not.

Assumption 4. All Competencies Have Roughly the Same Importance

Fact: There are huge differences between competencies' importance. As described earlier, we began by identifying the top tier of all leaders as seen by their peers, subordinates, and bosses, and comparing that group with the lowest-rated group. The question was, "What separates these high and low groups from each other?" The result was the identification of 19 competencies that actually separated the high and low groups. These competencies, selected from a pool of 50 or more, can be grouped into the same categories as the model we introduced in Chapter 1, and are treated more thoroughly later in this chapter.

For example, some believe the myth that effective executives are prompt and punctual. They arrive at meetings on time and don't keep others waiting. Our data show, however, that the lowest-rated executives were as apt to be punctual for meetings as the best. So, while we are in no way advocating that everyone shows up late to the next staff meeting, we think it is also important to point out that punctuality will not elevate you above other people. Simply put, ineffective executives are also highly punctual.

If you want to work on improving your leadership capabilities, we advocate focusing on behaviors that truly make a difference. So, what are they? We present these in Chapters 4 and 9.

Assumption 5. Competencies Are Best Developed by a Direct Focus on That Specific Competency

Fact: Our research suggests that one competency is developed in the process of developing another. They appear to be, in many cases, by-products of one another. That means that the direct linear method is not the only way to develop or strengthen a competency. Indeed, there may be better and easier ways that come in from the sides and the back, rather than merely hitting it straight on. Chapter 8 expands on this concept.

Assumption 6. Competencies Are Static

Fact: As society changes and business evolves, new competencies emerge. We began our research in 2002 and by 2019 we could clearly identify new competencies that had emerged. For example, the requirement for managers to practicing inclusion and value diversity had gained much traction in North America and other developed countries over that time period. We see it becoming more widespread.

3. Unintended Consequences

The largest drawback of the competency movement may have been its unforeseen by-products. We think that the competency movement has sent a series of implicit messages to leaders. These include:

- Competencies are a checklist, and the leader's objective is to check each one of them off. You either have it or you do not.
- Everyone needs to be adequate in any given competency. Chapter 2 emphasized that "adequate" is not the correct target. The target needs to be "extraordinary," not adequate.
- The emphasis has been almost exclusively on those competencies on which you are perceived as being deficient. The implication is that the greatest value comes from moving a weakness to a middle range where it no longer stands out.
- No emphasis has been given to taking a relative strength and making it "off-the-chart" strong. Unwittingly, this has contributed to our general pattern of "aiming low."
- It has driven out other powerful and practical techniques for developing people. Management experts ranging from Peter Drucker to Thomas Gilbert have proposed an extremely effective way to improve productivity and performance in an organization. They advocated identifying top performers and then carefully determining what they do differently from everyone else. In every activity in an organization being performed by a number of people, one person figures out extremely efficient ways to get the job done. That may consist of clever shortcuts or streamlined work processes. Or, it may consist of more efficient ways to work with colleagues in other departments. Research on the productivity of workers shows huge differences between the people doing essentially the same tasks.

To discover what these star performers are doing differently requires careful observation of them, along with interviews about their thought processes and techniques. Then, using these same people (or other trainers), teach everyone in the firm to adopt the best techniques of these top performers.

This extremely obvious and logical method for improving performance has met with great resistance. Few organizations use this obvious means of lifting performance to the rafters. That resistance comes in part from the "mindset" many managers have that sets major boundaries around what the average person is capable of becoming or producing. Executives just cannot believe that nearly everyone can perform at a high level. Many executives think that peak performance is reserved for just a few. These executives believe that we simply cannot expect or attain high performance from the great majority of our people—including our managers and leaders.

Rigidly defined competencies also may have the unintended consequence of creating cookie-cutter people inside the organization. If the competency system was implemented, would everyone appear to be cut from the same mold? How, then, does the organization attract and retain the maverick who is so valuable in challenging the status quo? Are the wild ducks killed just after they hatch? The concern is that, over time, sameness creates a homogeneity that becomes mind-numbing, and the culture devolves into one of anti-innovation.

4. Poor Execution

The basic premise of competencies was that they would be created from extensive analysis of hard data, not senior executives' personal speculations. However, that has not occurred. Indeed, as one writer observed, "Most of the current activity going on under the banner of competency modeling is really only list making."[3] The empirical, data-driven approach that was earlier described as the last alternative way to create a competency model is rarely used. It requires data and analysis and is more difficult to execute than simply gathering opinions, sorting cards, or deferring to one executive.

What had promised to be extremely rigorous has evolved into a process of compiling the collective beliefs of some senior managers regarding the important attributes of leaders in the firm. Maxine Dalton, of the Center for Creative Leadership, writes, "Seventy percent of the competency models I see are just lists of positive attributes that may or may not have anything to do with management effectiveness. They reflect a half-day, off-site meeting with senior managers in which a list is made with the underlying implication, 'If the CEO says it's a competency, it's a competency.'"[4]

To be applicable to the entire firm, the competencies of necessity are quite broad and encompassing. The more general the competencies become, the less accurate they are. In recent years we have seen a trend where many companies want a competency model with fewer competencies. In one company the executive who was charged with the assignment of coming up with a new competency model was given the parameters that there should be no more than five competencies in the model. The push for fewer competencies was fuelled by the feeling that most competency models are too complex so having fewer competencies would simplify the process. The resulting product was five very broad attributes that combined four to six different competencies together into one description. In a quest for simplification, the organization achieved something that was impossible to assess presenting five different competencies as one attribute. Most of the competency models that attempt to have just a few attributes make the same mistake. They smash a variety of behaviors together and imagine that they are simplifying a process only to make it more complex and confusing. Feedback from models such as this are so general that individuals can rarely find anything specific to improve.

Another execution issue is that competencies are focused on past requirements for effectiveness, and not what the future will require of leaders. This tendency to "look in the rearview mirror" tends to create leaders who look and act like the current group, which may be exactly what kills the organization in the future. To the extent that competencies are used for developmental purposes, the competencies should reflect abilities and behaviors required in the future, not only the past or present. They should also describe the ability to learn those skills required for future success.

The competencies are not being used for selection and promotion purposes. Many organizations complain that although Human Resources has the list of approved competencies, they are not finding their way into the other day-to-day HR systems, such as hiring, onboarding, compensation, performance management, and promotion Some have likened a firm's competency model to owning an expensive automobile. It is easy to forget that it needs to be maintained, and its true value only gets realized if you use it.

- Competency models are expensive to do well and need maintenance over time, as organizations evolve, merge, divest, globalize, and change their activities.
- Development programs have not been tailored around them to any large measure. It is complicated to find developmental activities for many of the competencies. Plus, the competency lists give little help in guiding ways in which people might attain these skills.

Why Competencies Are Linked Together

We readily confess that we do not completely know the answer to this question. Our current research methods do not give us the visibility or evidence needed to answer this question fully. We are rather confident, however, that there are four plausible explanations. We think all are at work, but it is impossible to define precisely how much of the linkage is attributed to one of these forces versus the others.

The four explanations are the following:

1. A strength in one competency creates a powerful "halo," so that colleagues, whether subordinates, peers, or bosses, perceive the individual as being effective in a number of other areas because of a strength in one.
2. In the process of developing any one strength, the individual develops other skills. Getting good at something enables you to be more proficient at several other related activities. We have labelled this the "cross-training" effect.
3. Self-confidence is increased when any skill is acquired and produces success. People often possess skills but do not use them because they lack the self-confidence to try them. Success in developing one competency increases confidence, which leads to trying another.
4. Aspiration level increases when people succeed in any one dimension. It encourages the individual to set his or her sights higher and higher in other realms.

Let's look at each of these in more detail.

1. The Power of the "Halo Effect"

Solomon Asch in 1946 did experiments on how people form impressions of others.[5] His theory was that perceptions are formed from our view of an entire person rather than by focusing on individual traits and characteristics. In other words, people's perceptions are created from our view of the whole person rather than a rational evaluation of each individual piece. To prove this theory Asch devised an ingenious experiment. He generated lists of attributes that described an individual. The lists were read to two different experimental groups. Table 3.1 shows the characteristics on each list.

Table 3.1. List of Personal Attributes

List A	List B
Intelligent	Intelligent
Skillful	Skillful
Industrious	Industrious
Warm	Cold
Determined	Determined
Practical	Practical
Cautious	Cautious

As can be readily noted by reading through the two lists, they are identical except for two words. List A has the attribute "Warm," whereas List B has "Cold." After being provided either List A or List B, each group was then given an additional list of attributes and instructed to indicate other qualities an individual might have. Substantial differences were found between attributes marked by groups who had List A and those from groups that had List B.

Groups given List A would choose additional qualities such as happy, imaginative, good-natured, generous, humorous, wise, humane, popular, altruistic, and sociable. Groups given List B did not select those same attributes. There were, however, some attributes, such as serious, strong, reliable, persistent, honest, and important, that were equally likely to be chosen on either list.

From a brief list of a few attributes, people generalize to a broader set of attributes. Once again, this reinforces the belief that people form an impression of a person as a whole, and therefore they attribute additional characteristics even though they have been given no specific information about the person.

It is intuitive to most people, just based on their experience working with others, that certain traits and behaviors go together. The Asch experiments confirm that, and we suspect that the reader will easily think of many examples of this. People's dress, facial characteristics, country of origin, or manner of speech all trigger stereotypes that we have in our minds. Stereotypes persist because there is just enough truth in them to make them continue to live.

Another researcher tested Asch's basic theory only this time that researcher had subjects actually come in contact with a person. H. H. Kelly, in a follow-up experiment, had students evaluate teachers.[6] Before attending a brief lecture, the students were provided a brief biographical sketch of each teacher. The descriptions were exactly the same except that for some students, a teacher was described as warm, whereas for other students, the same teacher was described as cold. The instructor then gave a 20-minute lecture. After the presentation, students rated the instructor. The students who had "warm" as part of the instructor's biography evaluated the instructor more positively than did those for whom "cold" had been listed. This showed that the students' perceptions were strongly influenced by the written biographical sketch and that these perceptions were not altered by subsequent interactions with the person.

The Asch and Kelly research reinforce a powerful conclusion. Some attributes, such as "warm" or "cold," are central traits. When a person is perceived to possess that characteristic, others immediately impute tag-along characteristics. These are glued to the central trait.

We invite the reader to participate in a quick experiment that illustrates this point. In Table 3.2, draw lines between the traits that go together. Match one from the left-hand column with one from the right-hand column. This example comes from research conducted by three psychologists, S. Rosenberg, C. Nelson, and P. Vivekananthan, who conducted a study in which people were asked to indicate the relationships among 64 different traits.[7] The researchers found that various traits cluster together in groups. That is, if I have quality A, then people are very likely to believe I have quality B.

Table 3.2. List of Personal Attributes

A. Honest	1. Serious
B. Intelligent	2. Wasteful
C. Irresponsible	3. Modest
D. Stern	4. Critical

From their research, they found that the following traits tended to be clustered together:

    A. Honest and (3) Modest
    B. Intelligent and (1) Serious
    C. Irresponsible and (2) Wasteful
    D. Stern and (4) Critical

Their research showed a regular and consistent pairing of traits. The powerful finding of this research was the consistency with which people linked one trait with another.

In their research, Rosenberg and his colleagues also measured issues that clustered on four dimensions:[8]

- Bad social (e.g., unpopular, unsociable, boring, cold, moody, dishonest)
- Good social (e.g., honest, happy, popular, reliable, modest, warm)
- Bad intellectual (e.g., foolish, unintelligent, clumsy, wasteful, irresponsible)
- Good intellectual (e.g., scientific, persistent, skillful, imaginative, intelligent)

If people know you have a trait in one dimension, they assume you also have other traits within that dimension. However, people would not assume, for example, that if a person is moody, that person is also clumsy. Moody and clumsy are on different dimensions.

Takeaways from this research include:

1. Perceptions are colored by small pieces of information, which may or may not be correct. (The way the instructor was perceived was colored by whether he had been described as "warm" or "cold.")
2. Initial impressions are used to create an overall view of a person. Knowing a few things, we then fill in the missing pieces in our minds. It is like seeing fragments of a picture and immediately filling in the blank parts of the canvas. (If I find you to be unsociable and boring, that is enough for me to fill in many other blanks. Until you prove otherwise, I assume you are cold, moody, dishonest, clumsy, wasteful, foolish, and irresponsible.)
3. We do not form an overall view of someone by painstakingly assembling all of the pieces.
4. Certain characteristics or attributes are consistently linked together.
5. Attributes are clustered into various dimensions in the minds of most people.

Fitting Theory to Our Data

Basic links or companionships between traits are well established in people's minds. They are generalized across all people within a culture and are not specific to individuals. Therefore, when a person observes a leader displaying a specific competency, there is an immediate assumption that this individual possesses a number of other characteristics, despite the lack of any specific evidence to support that.

Many, if not most, impressions others have of our leadership abilities are not totally accurate. People are influenced by their experience, and because of that, they form a general impression (*gestalt*). Rather than being a totally accurate accounting of each of our competencies and abilities (e.g., Competency a, Competency b, Competency c, Competency d, Overall Leadership Ability), people form their impressions based on an unequal weighing of competencies from bits of knowledge. Even though these impressions are not totally accurate, people cannot be talked out of their impression by a rational, precise accounting of our competencies. People have strong attachments to their impressions.

Many observers react to this and say that it is unfair that others are not accurate in their perceptions. However, this sword definitely cuts two ways. If others have a general impression that a person is a poor leader, then they will probably be negatively biased in their evaluations of specific competencies and underrate the person's real abilities. On the other hand, if others have a general impression that a person is an extraordinary leader, they will overestimate this person's skills and abilities. Though being underrated is unfair, being overrated, though still unfair, is something leaders can use to their advantage. The key is to get the attribution process to work for you rather than against you.

This helps to explain many of our research findings. For example, we found many leaders with extremely high scores on all competencies and with no perceived weaknesses. The tendency for everyone to attribute positive social behavior and positive intellectual capabilities to someone who possesses one positive attribute sheds light on this phenomenon. The combination of creating an overall picture or *gestalt* about someone, combined with the strong linkage between traits and attributes, provides insight into this.

Why do we present this research and theory about how perceptions are formed? Understanding theory helps in planning a successful strategy.

Understanding how others formulate their perceptions helps us to understand why leaders are successful at times and why they fail.

2. Cross Training

The second explanation for the strong linkage between competencies is simply that in the course of becoming good at one thing, you get better at something else.

We see evidence of this in many other areas of life. A musician who plays the saxophone will often easily switch between the clarinet, alto saxophone, and tenor saxophone. Learning one instrument increases the ease of learning and performing with a somewhat different instrument. The athlete who is a runner parlays the endurance and strength gained through running to become a long-distance swimmer and cyclist. Similarly, piano players are often extremely fast typists.

Skills Are Transferable
It is logical to believe that acquiring the skill of conducting effective meetings helps the leader to also be more effective working one-on-one with peers. Developing the skills of communicating powerfully and prolifically provides many of the same skills required to inspire and motivate others to high performance.

The skill of setting stretch goals for your team is related to the skills required to initiate action and focus on results.

3. Success Increases Confidence

When people experience success in one arena of life, it increases their confidence and willingness to try something new.

One of the authors' granddaughters became interested in diving. Jumping off a board in a typical backyard pool was easy. Then came the three-meter board, which seemed frightening to an 11-year-old. Finally, the team went to a diving pool that included a six-meter-high diving board. (That is, jumping roughly from the height of a two-story building into the pool.) As she went to the end of the board, she started to turn back, and the coach said, "You can do it—just jump." She did. Success at previous levels gave her confidence to try. She wanted to be able to dive from the high board, and it was no longer frightening except to her parents and grandparents.

4. Success Increases Aspiration Level

We know that success increases people's aspiration to try and do more. Any growth in one area gives us new skills and the confidence to seek growth in another. The late Andrall Pearson was a high-visibility executive, having been a senior director of McKinsey & Co., then head of PepsiCo for 14 years, then a teacher at the Harvard Business School who published frequently in the *Harvard Business Review*. In a 1980 *Fortune* magazine article, he was listed as one of America's toughest bosses.

At age 76, he became chairman of Tricon Global Restaurants, Inc. (now renamed Yum) and learned an entirely new set of leadership skills. He learned to inspire rather than control. He gained an appreciation for the power of human emotion. In earlier years he would display his own intellect and overpower people with his ability to grasp issues quickly. In an earlier leadership role he had told his colleagues, "A room full of monkeys could do better than this."

Late in life a new Pearson desisted from issuing orders to people and began asking questions and soliciting ideas. He became a mentor to many in the firm. Pearson acknowledges that many of these leadership methods were new to him, and that his experience was a capstone of an already remarkable career.[9]

Jacob Bronowski wrote, "We have to understand that the world can only be grasped by action, not by contemplation. . . . The most powerful drive in the ascent of man is his pleasure in his own skills. He loves to do what he does well, and having done it well, he loves to do it better."[10]

As we ponder the ways that competencies are linked together, we have no way of tearing apart the impact of these many forces. Is it a halo effect, or is it the result of cross training? What role does increased confidence play, or escalating aspirations? We may never know the answer, but we are convinced that the answer lies in some combination of the four.

Assessing Individual Competencies

After discovering these differentiating competencies and understanding the impact of developing strengths, we examined typical approaches used in assessing a leader's effectiveness using 360-degree feedback. Our evaluation of common practices identified several consistent problems with the design and approach of most 360-degree assessments:

1. Many assessments give leaders a false positive impression of their ability. Leaders assume that they are doing fairly well when in fact they are only average.
2. Most assessments emphasize identification of weakness rather than building strengths.
3. Many compare one individual's results to the mean averages, thus reinforcing the notion that average leadership was the target.
4. No assessments provided an evaluation of the impact leaders have on important organizational outcomes such as employee engagement or commitment. They made no pretense at having predictive value.
5. Open-ended comments requested suggestions for improvement. These reinforced the focus on weakness because they generated long lists of suggested improvements.
6. No assessments directly asked for identification of fatal flaws or significant weaknesses. This made it difficult for leaders to identify the difference between a skill that was rated as less effective and a skill that if not corrected would have a substantial negative effect on their success.

Based on these insights we designed a unique assessment that addressed these issues. We created items that best differentiated poor, good and extraordinary leaders and that could be completed in approximately 15 minutes. We sought to give leaders a more accurate view of their strengths or insights into a potential fatal flaw that would crater their effectiveness. Rather than compare leaders to a mean average of all others, we showed them how their scores compared with leaders at the 75th and 90th percentile. This comparison to the best leaders tended to automatically reset an individual's target.

We incorporated five questions that assessed the level of employee commitment and engagement of the people that reported directly to each leader. All of our research has indicated that these two dimensions are highly correlated. Using these data each individual leader could get an understanding of how their leadership impacted the engagement, commitment and expected turnover of team members. We have come to the conclusion that this approach provides a stronger platform for change and improvement.

One of the keys to helping leaders improve starts with measuring the right things. Too many organizations have created competency models by simply having a group of senior leaders arbitrarily decide on a set of competencies. If a group of general practitioner physicians decided on a cure for cancer, would you bet you life on that cure without any scientific testing? Our guess is you would want some evidence that the cure really works. There is a set of competencies that have been scientifically tested to have the greatest impact on leadership ability. In the next chapter in this book we will provide an overview of the 19 differentiating competencies.

4

HOW THE
EXTRAORDINARY
LEADER BEHAVES

We have to understand that the world can only
be grasped by action, not by contemplation.
—JACOB BRONOWSKI

Leadership is ultimately about behavior. To truly understand leadership is to define and describe what a leader does. In Chapters 1 and 3, we presented many of the dimensions that create the extremely complex nature of leadership. In this chapter, we wish to reduce that complexity to a model of leadership that is more easily understood.

We will present compelling evidence in this chapter that:

1. Not all competencies are equivalent to each other. Some are far more powerful in separating highly effective leaders from the rest.
2. Leadership behaviors are knit together, much like the complex network of the human brain. There is a great deal of interdependence between them. Each of the 19 competencies that are most powerful in separating leaders are highly correlated to all of the other 19 competencies.
3. Effective leadership demands a balance of competencies from five different sectors.
4. Combinations of competencies, not any single one, produce great leaders.
5. The more people have of the 19 competencies that truly make a difference, the more likely they are to be perceived as great leaders.

Tents

One model of leadership is represented by a large tent, as depicted in Figure 4.1, with the three-dimensional space under the canvas representing the leadership effectiveness of the individual. The poles of the tent are laminated, so that each pole has up to five elements, glued together to give it extra strength. To complicate the matter a bit, imagine fiber-optic strands connecting each of the five tent poles to every other one, which obviously creates a highly complex network inside the tent. The best leaders have the greatest number of cubic yards of space under their tent. This occurs when each pole grows longer. We think this view helps to illustrate the true nature of leadership and how it is developed.

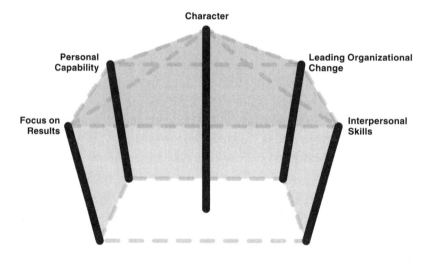

Figure 4.1. The Leadership Tent

The distinguishing characteristics of this model are:

1. Leadership behaviors are clustered into five areas.
2. Strength in a cluster becomes a "tent pole" that lifts the leadership of that person to a higher level.
3. Effective leaders possess skills in each area; so multiple poles are necessary to lift the tent. While some poles are longer than

others, one cannot be extremely short or missing lest the tent dramatically shrink.

4. Statistically significant correlations exist between most of the important competencies (the canvas is in one piece).

The key to lifting more of the tent (becoming a more effective leader) is to get multiple poles higher in the air. If you have only one tent pole, it pulls the entire tent around that one pole. Our metaphor unfolds as follows. Allow us the liberty of having modern tent poles that extend themselves like the antenna on a car. As a pole is extended, one section of the tent is lifted up, and a broad expanse of canvas is raised. The more the pole is extended, the higher the canvas is lifted. (Remember, the length of the tent pole is the degree of strength and the number of competencies with great strength that an individual possesses.) So, assume that this first tent pole comes up from the cluster we have labeled "Character."

A second pole (assume this one is created by the cluster "Focus on Results") elevates a new section of the tent, and in so doing, it raises the canvas that is directly above it but also raises the canvas that is between this new pole and the first one. The canvas that was initially around the first pole moves closer to the full height of both tent poles. With each succeeding tent pole, large expanses of canvas are lifted until ultimately there is a huge volume of space under the tent.

The poles in our metaphor represent key "strengths" of the individual leader, especially those that have been shown to make a difference in separating the great from the good. The canvas represents all of the behaviors and competencies possible to be displayed by a leader. (We noted earlier having seen a competency model from one organization in which there were 173 behaviors defined for the leaders to assess themselves against. That seems to us to be a more behaviors than most humans can keep track of on a daily basis.)

Making a Leader

We will now more thoroughly describe these five major elements of leadership attributes and the 19 competencies associated with these five areas of leadership.

I. Character—the Center Pole of Every Leader

We begin with the component that is indeed at the core. Everything radiates from it. It is the center pole of the tent in Figure 4.1. It is so important that some authors have written about it as if it were synonymous with leadership. For example:

- Warren Bennis, one of the most respected writers and researchers on leadership, has talked about leadership being all about integrity.
- Max De Pree, the CEO of Herman Miller and a frequent writer on leadership, has equated leadership with personal character.
- Jim Kouzes and Barry Posner have written a book entitled *Credibility* and defined personal credibility as the foundation of all leadership.
- Jim Shaffer writes about leadership being defined by "telling the truth."
- Stephen Covey has written about the importance of leaders following fundamental principles in their daily behavior.

These are just a sampling of the many writings about leadership that emphasize the role of personal character in leadership. Our research confirms that personal character is absolutely at the heart of effective leadership.

Here are some of the ways character gets defined:

- Making decisions with the organization paramount in their mind, versus allowing a personal agenda to influence decisions
- Keeping commitments that are made
- Treating everyone the same—no "smiling up and kicking down" behavior
- Treating the waitress and bellman with dignity, as well as people of high status
- Trusting other people; assuming they have good intentions
- Not acting in an arrogant manner toward others

Many organizations have learned that finding people with the right character is the absolute requirement for long-term success of the organization.

A colleague asked a senior executive of Louis Vuitton, the maker of high-end luggage and personal accessories, how they went about getting people to produce such high-quality products. The executive's answer was, "You look for people who seek quality in their personal life, and in all the things they use and possess. You can't train that into people."

The retailer Nordstrom is currently working to regain the position that it once held as the leading provider of excellent service. Again, when the executives are asked about how they plan to do that, their answer is "Hire nice *people." It is much easier to teach a nice person the requisite selling skills and how to use "point of sale" equipment, than it is to teach "niceness" to someone who mostly knows how to complete the paperwork for a sales transaction.

However, our research shows that when people receive high scores on this important dimension of leadership, but this is all they score highly on, then the likelihood of them being perceived as outstanding leaders at the 75th or 90th percentile is 0.1 percent. And if people are given low marks on these "character" dimensions, they will absolutely not be perceived as great leaders.

We generally concur, therefore, with the people who have written of the importance of leaders being persons of high character. Without it, long-term failure is certain. Where we part company with some is our conclusion that character is a necessary, but not sufficient, element for great leadership.

To complicate the matter even further, there are some people who are perceived as effective leaders yet who seem to possess major character flaws. It seems more often to be reserved for political leaders than for those in business and industry, and we do not pretend to fully understand that anomaly. Our data show that fewer than 2 percent of leaders have one or more measured competency in the top 10 percent while also having one or more competencies in the bottom 10 percent. It is rare, but it happens.

In the aftermath of the attack on the World Trade Center on September 11, 2001, then Mayor Rudolph Giuliani stepped in to orchestrate the City of New York's response to the situation. Giuliani rose to the occasion with hands-on, calming, decisive behavior that earned him extremely high marks from citizens and the media. One commentator on National Public Radio said that "it was as if the situation erased all the negative images that had surrounded Giuliani." He had been through a sordid divorce, had been accused of racial slurs, had been tagged as "Mussolini on the Hudson," and was in general disfavor with New York voters.

Then, suddenly, an event and the way he handled it transformed him into a hero. Later, as President Donald Trump's personal attorney he found himself engulfed in controversy again. His hero status probably depends on the evaluator's political persuasion.

Apple cofounder Steve Jobs was an example of a person possessing extremely positive leadership qualities while at the same moment displaying equally negative personal behavior.

II. Personal Capability

The second important tent pole of leadership is the personal capability the individual possesses (Figure 4.2). This cluster of abilities and skills are absolutely crucial for people to be highly regarded by peers, subordinates, and bosses. These are not skills that would typically be described as leadership skills, and yet our research proves they must be in place for any individual to be perceived as a strong leader. Ideally these skills are acquired early in life.

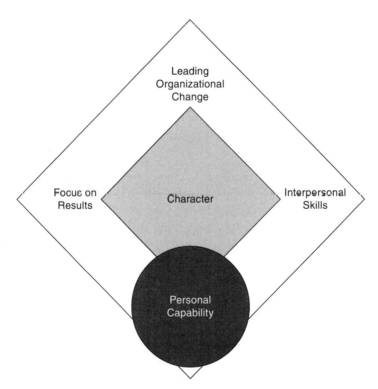

Figure 4.2 Personal Capability

Character was the first of the 19 competencies. The next four competencies are:

2. *Technical/professional acumen.* This has several branches. One is technical knowledge. Research with a large natural resources products company showed that the quality or attribute that had the highest correlation with being perceived as a great leader was technical competence. Those who were perceived as the best leaders always scored high on this dimension. Conversely, those in the bottom 10 percent of the overall scores scored low on technical competence.

A second branch of acumen is product knowledg*e*. This includes a thorough understanding of what the organization produces and why it is superior to competitive products. Another branch of acumen is general business knowledge, including an understanding of accounting and financial statements. That is the language of business. The final element could be described as professional skills. These include the ability to write an intelligent, concise report or memorandum; the ability to comfortably make a compelling presentation in front of a group; and the abilities to organize one's work in an efficient manner, to monitor progress, and to act without being told by someone in authority.

3. *Problem-analysis and problem-solving skills.* This competency is the ability to define a problem, analyze it, and come up with solid recommendations for resolving it. Effectiveness in this competency is often measured by others in terms of speed and accuracy. Those who quickly can come up with a solution that is correct get high marks.

4. *Innovation.* This refers to the ability to have a fresh outlook in approaching a problem, to shake loose of old methods and processes and see new possibilities. Innovation means being able to climb out of ruts and do things in a different fashion.

5. *Learning agility.* The willingness to ask for an act on feedback from others is a key characteristic of this competency. Our research has shown that younger employees are more likely to be skilled in asking for feedback but those who continue to ask throughout their career end up being significantly more effective leaders. Another key aspect of this competency is the ability to be agile. In order for organizations to survive they need to

be able to quickly change approaches, processes and products. Employees who are inflexible find themselves unable to survive.

III. Focus on Results

Our model for effective leadership now takes on a new dimension (Figure 4.3). It would be ideal if we could erect these next two tent poles simultaneously. These two elements, focus on results and interpersonal skills, require that character and personal capability be in place, but it appears to make no difference which of these two components comes after that. Indeed, there exists a remarkable relationship between these two components of leadership.

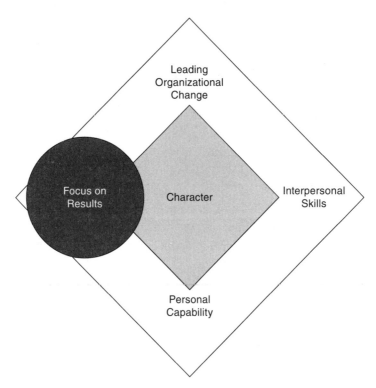

Figure 4.3. Focus on Results

How does a leader focus on results? Five competencies make up this tent pole. They are:

6. **Results driven.** Takes personal responsibility for the outcomes of the group and does whatever they can to achieve goals and objectives. We often describe this competency as PUSH. Setting deadlines, reinforcing the importance of hitting targets, and holding others accountable are key characteristics of this competency.

7. **Stretch goals.** Sets elevated targets for the group to achieve and has the ability to get team members to accept those targets. Some leaders resist setting stretch goals, but there is a surprisingly positive impact on the engagement and satisfaction of team members when stretch goals are achieved. Many people resist difficult targets but when people accomplish difficult objectives they thought were impossible, they start to believe in themselves and feel a strong sense of accomplishment.

8. **Initiative.** Personally sponsors an initiative or action. Initiates new programs, projects, processes, client relationships, or technology. Many leaders can create a list of things that need to get started in order for the unit to function more effectively. Those who wait to be told what to do are rated poorly on taking initiative.

9. **Making Decisions.** With new information technologies organizations and leaders have never had more information but one would think that all this information would make it easier to make decisions. Unfortunately, that is rarely the case. Leaders who constantly put off decisions to gather more data will fail. Decisions need to be made and organizations need to move forward even in the face of ambiguity.

10. **Risk taking.** In the past organizations could survive by playing it safe but with all the extensive disruption in the marketplace leaders need to disrupt themselves before their competitors disrupt them. Organizations are in need of leaders who are willing to take acceptable risks.

Producing results is a key outcome of effective leadership. As Dave Ulrich, Jack Zenger, and Norm Smallwood noted in their book *Results-Based Leadership*, leadership is ultimately about producing results.[1] What we have described in this section are some of those behaviors, skills, and competencies that lead directly to the production of positive results in an organization. The authors of *Results-Based Leadership* described these as the "attributes" necessary to produce spectacular results.

Notice the pattern of taking action, causing things to occur, pushing forward, and continual improvement. The image that comes to mind is leaders with their foot on the accelerator—most of the time, pressed to the floorboard.

IV. Interpersonal Skills

The companion set of skills to Focus on Results required for effective leaders is "people" skills or Interpersonal Skills (Figure 4.4.). These are extremely important to the success of any leader, especially since the demise of "command and control" styles of leadership. This tent pole, along with the one in the center, supports the most canvas. Interpersonal Skills includes more "differentiating competencies" than does any other cluster, and they are the most frequently correlated with all of the other "differentiating competencies."

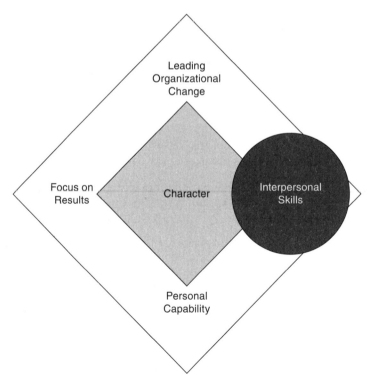

Figure 4.4. Interpersonal Skills

What are the specific skills required of a leader with strong interpersonal skills? Here are the six competencies:

11. *Communicating powerfully and prolifically.* One of the most frequent complaints of employees is that they were not adequately informed. Leaders who let team members know about the "where, when and how" regarding events and issues, and who do that in a way that is both efficient and interesting, end up being more effective leaders.

12. *Inspiring others to high performance.* We have discovered through our data gathering from more than 100,000 leaders, that this competency is the lowest rated competency of all in terms of effectiveness. Yet when direct reports are asked what is most important, inspires and motivates others is rated number one in importance. We often refer to Drive for Results as PUSH and Inspires and Motivates as PULL. Mastering this skill can have a significantly positive impact on the effectiveness of a leader.

13. *Building positive relationships.* Building strong, positive relationships with others is another critical competency. Those leaders who do this well show concern and consideration for others. One of the outcomes of building positive relationships is trust.

14. *Developing others.* This competency has two benefits. First, it increases the effectiveness and productivity of a team; second, it increases the engagement of team members. One of the key satisfiers team members look for in a job is having the ability to develop and learn new skills.

15. *Collaborating and teamwork.* For most organizations this is an essential skill that is often missing. Organizations have the capacity to create synergy between groups and teams but only when there is excellent collaboration and teamwork. Left to their own devices, teams hoard resources, fail to share critical information, and compete with other teams. Finding leaders who have a desire and talent for collaboration is critical in every organization.

16. *Valuing diversity.* This competency is becoming more and more critical as globalization increases and workforces become more diverse. In our research we have found that leaders who do not

value the diversity of others had a substantial damaging impact on the engagement and satisfaction of all team members. We have also found that many leaders who believe they do this well in reality need significant improvement. Getting good assessment data on this competency is critical.

Some writers on the subject of leadership have suggested that interpersonal skills are the major determinant of leadership effectiveness and that 80 percent of all organizations' lists of crucial competencies for success would be included in the dimension of interpersonal effectiveness. Our data show, however, that if leaders are good only at interpersonal relationships, they again have a fairly low probability of being in the top 10 percent of all leaders in a firm.

V. Leading Organizational Change

The final cluster of competencies is viewed by many as only relevant to those at the top of the organization, but in today's firms, leaders at all organizational levels need to be clear about the strategy. They are often intimately involved in change efforts. In a recent study we did on high potential leaders we found that one of the major skills lacking in many of the candidates was strategic perspective. Organizations are looking for individuals who have a strategic mindset before they are put in a position to formulate a new strategy.

What are the specific skills required for Leading Organizational Change (Figure 4.5)? Here are the three competencies:

17. *Develops strategic perspective.* Clarity about where the organization is going and how it is distinctive is essential for a firm to successfully compete. Senior leaders define the strategy, but lower level leaders need a deep understanding of the strategy along with the ability to translate strategic initiatives into meaning goals and objective for work groups and teams.

18. *Champions change.* Today organization are experiencing significant challenges around change. Technology, which has created greater efficiency, has led to the need to change almost every aspect of the way people function and work in organizations. Having the ability to help team members navigate change as opposed to resisting change is a critical skill.

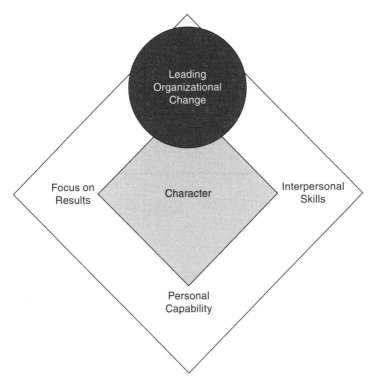

Figure 4.5. Leading Organizational Change

19. *Has customer and external focus.* Organizations that stay close to customers, understand their current and future needs, and are well informed about global trends are set up for success in the future. Providing customers with an experience they cannot get anywhere else provides firms with a significant competitive advantage.

Effective Leaders Champion Change

With most organizations today in a constant state of change—from dramatic growth to downsizing and restructuring—a critical skill for leaders is leading successful change efforts. A turbulent business environment puts leaders to the test: excellent leadership can turn a significant change into a pleasant journey, whereas poor leadership might be better described as a "trip to hell."

We know that the best leaders inspire their troops to rally around a change, whereas poor leaders have to push, persuade, or even threaten employees to accept change. Top-performing leaders become effective marketers of projects, programs, or products, gaining support for them along the way. Conversely, poor leaders fail to engage or commit others to the change.

Two Ways to Champion Change

A key learning from our research on leading change was that either of the two approaches (pushing and pulling) can be detrimental if used exclusively. Effective leaders used both approaches in a careful balance.

The metaphor that comes to mind is a person rowing a boat. For maximum control and speed, you need both oars. One oar alone causes you to go in circles, no matter which oar you choose.

For example, while directing may be a great way to maintain control, leaders who significantly favor directing change may end up with employees feeling that changes are being done to them but not with them. Consequently, employees may become resistant to change and begin to distrust management.

Additionally, those who have strong directing tendencies typically have a well-organized plan and communicate the change plan and provide feedback about what needs to be done differently. However, they often fail to have open discussions with their teams about the impact of the change.

Those who favor involving others in change often fail to provide sufficient direction, leaving employees confused about next steps, what their roles are, and what they need to do to keep the change moving forward. Also, a high involvement tendency may indicate an unwillingness on the leader's part to take risks or to be decisive.

Our research shows clearly that these two sets of behaviors are both necessary in order for a leader to manage change effectively. Leaders who direct change help their people know the specifics involved in the change. Involving others in the change efforts increases employee commitment rather than emphasizing employee compliance. The more significant the change, the more of both is needed in order for a change to work effectively.

How These Five Elements of the Model Interrelate with Each Other

As we noted earlier, much of past thinking about leadership has been the quest to find out, "Is the key to leadership having high integrity, or is it ambition? Is it developing trust in people, or is it being a good problem solver?" We hope that the reader will be permanently disabused of this thinking and will cease to view leadership in "or" terms but will instead think about it in "and" terms. We will attempt to describe why these leadership elements logically go together and why development efforts in one area is like flooding the pond and lifting all boats at the same time.

1. Character is at the heart of our model, and everything radiates out from it. It ties strongly to Interpersonal Skills. A person of questionable character is not usually effective interpersonally. In eyeball-to-eyeball conversations, you cannot help seeing deep inside the other person. We recoil from phonies. We do not enjoy being with toadies who butter up people in authority and abuse everyone else. Most people avoid those who are arrogant or condescending. Relationships with such people are distant and strained. If someone has broken his or her word to us, we deal with that person in a cautious and tentative way. The link between Character and Interpersonal Skills is an extremely strong bond. So is the link between self-development (personal character) and developing others (interpersonal skills). It is also clear that the ability to inspire and motivate others is strongly linked to how people perceive the integrity of the leader.

   We return to the question, "If leaders can be made, then how do you make them?" The linkage between character and interpersonal skills is a good example. Social psychologists confirm that the easiest way to change people's character, as expressed via their attitudes, is by getting them to behave in a new way. People make their attitudes conform to their behavior.

   Consider the case of an older supervisor in a manufacturing plant. He has received no training on how to manage people effectively. His behavior is patterned after the way he was treated by his supervisors. When an employee makes a mistake, this supervisor chastises the employee, sometimes in public. Often the erring employee may be threatened with potential discipline or termination if such mistakes continue. If a change needs to be implemented, the supervisor says what must now be done, but with no explanation of why. This supervisor would never solicit ideas and opinions from the employee group. Turnover is higher in this supervisor's area, productivity is below average, labor grievances are more frequent, and upper management recognizes that this supervisor must change. But how? Isn't this behavior part of this supervisor's character? Short of extensive psychotherapy, how could this be changed?

Our experience is that the most surefire way to bring about behavioral change is to have this supervisor participate in a training process that provides a new mindset or way of thinking and then teaches new behaviors and skills. The supervisor is not told how he must think and feel, but simply is told that there is good evidence of a better way to behave. He learns how to describe a problem in a calm, rational way to an employee, to ask for the employee's ideas about how to solve it, and to agree jointly on the best way to proceed. The supervisor discovers that this works wonders. The same or better results are achieved with a great deal less anger. His relationships with his employees improve significantly. They greet him like a friend, not the enemy. His attitudes toward his subordinates become less adversarial. He is open to new ideas that previously would have been instantly rejected. His character changes. Why? Because his behavior changed, and people make their attitudes conform to their behavior. That principle is extremely well documented in social psychology research. It is also true, however, that it becomes a circular phenomenon. As attitudes improve, behavior begins to change as a result.

2. Character also affects the cluster labeled Focus on Results, but possibly in a less obvious way. People around the leader are often sensitive to perceived motives for doing things. If the focus on results is for reasons of self-aggrandizement, to look good to a boss, to further a political career in the firm, or for any other perceived selfish reason, then personal character detracts from any successful drive for results.

David McClelland, a Harvard psychologist, did extensive research on the need for achievement and its role in people's behavior and effectiveness. His research showed that the success of nations depends on the presence or absence of this need for achievement. He developed ways to measure this quality, but many assumed that it was something with which people were born. McClelland decided to experiment with ways to increase people's need for achievement. One test he used was the game of quoits. Quoits is a children's game involving a wooden peg on a base, and several 8-inch hoops of rope called quoits. The game consists of attempting to toss the quoits over the peg from a distance of several feet. Participants were asked to place the peg anywhere they chose in a large room and then get the quoits onto the peg. People with low levels of need for achievement would either put the peg near their feet and drop the quoits onto it, or they would put the peg at a huge distance and fling the quoits toward the peg with little hope of success. People with high need for achievement would put the peg a reasonable distance away, so that a careful toss of the quoits would have a reasonable chance of success. McClelland took the people who had displayed little or no need for achievement and had them perform this exercise the "right" way. Over time, these people from Third World countries developed stronger motivations to achieve. By giving them an experience in feeling the success of attaining a positive result, their attitudes and character began to change.[2]

3. Personal Capability links to Interpersonal Skills. The respect and esteem with which anyone in the organization is viewed begins with his or her personal capability. The time when people are developing their professional and technical skills is the time when they should also be developing skills that will enable them to work effectively with others. Technical and professional expertise is tightly linked to developing others and building relationships.

4. Personal Capability links to Focus on Results. One of the key roles any leader plays is that of role model. When the leader is personally effective and highly productive, that example is viewed by everyone involved. Leaders cannot ask others to do what they are not doing.

5. Focus on Results is linked to Interpersonal Skills. We earlier noted the unusually close link between these two characteristics.

Many leaders think that the linkage between Focus on Results and Interpersonal Skills is an *or* rather than an *and*. They believe they can be one or the other but not both. Whereas each is highly desirable by itself, they are like a voice being amplified by a great sound system when they are combined together. The combination of the two ignites a power that catapults a person into the highest realms of effective leadership. Focusing on results and setting stretch goals have multiple links to the interpersonal skills of "inspiring and motivating to high performance" and to "collaboration and teamwork."

6. Character links to Leading Organizational Change. Organizations follow a leader who is perceived as being of high character. The greater the "connection" that is felt with the leader, the more likely the organization is to support the change being proposed. That support is tied to perceptions of the genuineness, caring, and integrity of the leader.

7. Focus on Results links to Leading Organizational Change. Leading organizational change is most often a long-term objective, and effective leaders are always balancing short-term and long-term objectives. A focus on results is a necessary balance to the longer-term emphasis on strategic change.

8. Interpersonal Skills links to Leading Organizational Change. Nowhere is there a higher requirement for consummate interpersonal skills than in the introduction of strategic change within the organization. Whether it is an attempt to change the culture or to implement a major new initiative, trust from others and the communication skills of the leader are absolute requirements for success.

The Power of Combinations

From an experience in his professional life, one of the authors recounts the following story. "Upon returning from a trip, I noticed that my administrative assistant had a severe rash on the inside of her arm. We worked for a pharmaceutical company, one of whose specialties was dermatology. I jokingly said, 'Kathy, you aren't a very good advertisement for our products.' She explained that she had been to three dermatologists, who had each prescribed a different medication. Nothing had helped. I said, 'Well, we have a consulting dermatologist downstairs who is considered to be one of the best in the world—let's go see him.' So, this eminent dermatologist looked at it, took a culture from it, and when I returned from another business trip, Kathy's rash was gone. I asked what had happened, and she said, 'Dr. Scholtz discovered that I had both a fungal and bacterial infection on my arm. Two of my previous doctors had treated the bacterial infection, and the other doctor treated me assuming I only had a fungal infection. He treated them both simultaneously and it cleared up.' I learned from this experience that doing two necessary things together can work magic, while doing one alone accomplishes nothing."

In a study, we analyzed more than 100,000 leaders and identified those managers who were in the top quartile on Focus on Results but were not in the top quartile on Interpersonal Skills. The likelihood of those leaders being perceived as a great leader was 9 percent. If we did the opposite and took people in the top quartile on Interpersonal Skills and not in the top quartile on Focus on Results, there was an 8 percent probability of them being perceived as a great leader. When we found leaders who were good at both Focus on Results and Interpersonal Skills, the likelihood of that person being perceived as one of the top 10 percent leaped to 82 percent probability. This fact powerfully reinforces the idea that effective leaders are not one-celled people who focus maniacally on just one thing. To the contrary, we have learned that great leaders do at least five things well.

Similarly, success in changing the culture of an organization comes from doing several things simultaneously. No one thing, by itself, does much. But the combination of training programs, surveys, team building, and coaching initiatives is extremely powerful.

5

GREAT LEADERS POSSESS MULTIPLE STRENGTHS

*One shining quality lends a luster to
another, or hides some glaring defect.*
—WILLIAM HAZLITT

An Approach to Improvement

Imagine that you were working to improve your leadership effectiveness. To start the process, you participate in a 360-degree assessment of your skills and competencies. The assessment is given to your boss, several peers, and direct reports. The results of the assessment are compiled and create the profile shown in Figure 5.1 (see next page).

The profile shows a series of leadership competencies based on the assessments of others. For your convenience, each of the leadership competencies is sorted from the most positive competency to the least positive. This gives you a quick overview of your results. If this were your leadership profile, which issues would you select for change? Mark the ones that would be your focus of attention for the next six months.

In this profile, some of the leadership competencies are more positive than others, but nothing stands out as being extremely positive or negative. No competency stands out as either a profound strength or a terrible weakness. In our experience, when people get feedback like this, they always seem compelled to focus their attention on the least positive items. Things that have been said earlier in this book may have prompted you to consider some of your strengths. But that would be an extremely rare event in the absence of receiving this apparently "counterintuitive" or contrarian message. Something in our culture says that you pass over the higher scores and go directly to the lowest ones.

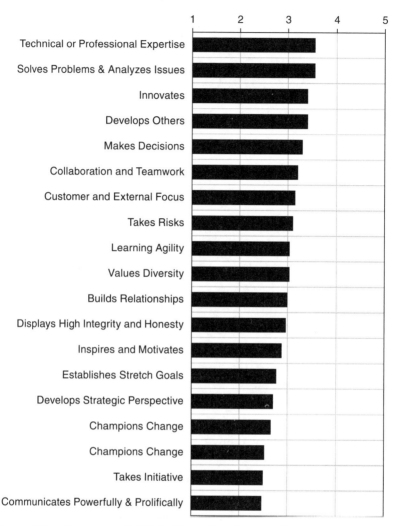

Figure 5.1. Summary of a Multi-Rater (360-Degree) Feedback Assessment

In this example, one of the areas for improvement would likely be communications. Typical plans for change would have the person systematically tackle the lowest scores, get those fixed, and move on to the next-lowest scores. That logic assumes that it is the areas of lower effectiveness that hurt this person's performance. People seem more satisfied with a fairly consistent profile, with all competencies at about the same level.

Philosophies of Effectiveness

Most people, whether consciously or unconsciously, adhere to a philosophy that their effectiveness is substantially hurt by lower performance in any area. The solution is, of course, to fix the weaknesses. We are not certain of the genesis of this belief. Possibly it stems from our educational experiences. The recollection many have of school is a focus on what they did wrong. Think back. Can you remember taking a test and having the teacher or professor spend additional time emphasizing the answer that everyone in the class got correct? On the other hand, do you remember reviewing the answers the class got wrong? (You could argue that there is a certain logic to focusing on the problems missed, or the information that no one could recall.)

We argue, however, that time spent emphasizing the success people had would also have been extremely valuable.

Another explanation is that we all seek to be well-rounded "Renaissance people." The assumption is that we should be good at everything. There is something inherently weak or inferior about acknowledging that there are some things I do well, and there are some things I don't even try to do. We admire the "iron man" who swims 2.4 miles, rides a bicycle for another 112 miles, then runs a marathon.

Whatever the source, there is a pervasive belief that I should eliminate my weaknesses, and by so doing I will become a more effective person. A growing number of voices, however, convey a different message. For example, the respected research psychologist Martin Seligman writes: "I do not believe that you should devote overly much effort to correcting your weaknesses. Rather, I believe that the highest success in living and the deepest emotional satisfaction comes from building and using your signature strengths." He continues, "[T]he good life is using your signature strengths every day to produce authentic happiness and abundant gratification. This is something that you can learn to do in each of the main realms of your life: work, love, and raising children."[1]

In work situations, performance appraisals most often search for some deficiency. The approach of telling people some good news, then focusing on areas where they need development or improvement, and finishing up with a positive comment or two is standard procedure in many organizations. (Is it any wonder that people begin to wince when they hear the positive comments, knowing that it is often the precursor to the important message of their deficiencies?) It is best to have frequent conversations that focus only on the positive aspects of the person's work.

The research, in fact, suggests that the positive dialogue should occur five times more frequently than negative conversations if you want optimal performance from your team. Medium-performing teams had a ratio of just under two to one, and the poorly performing organizations had a ratio of roughly three negative comments for every positive one. Kim Cameron, a leading scholar at the University of Michigan, writes, "The single most important factor in predicting organizational performance— which was more than twice as powerful as any other factor—was the ratio of positive statements to negative statements."[2]

It is perfectly understandable that managers who can give only 4 people out of the 20 in their group a superior rating will focus discussions on deficiencies rather than strengths. This provides the rationale for why some get a raise whereas others do not. If the manager were to focus only on positive issues and give a "meets expectations" rating, that might be very confusing to the direct reports. Even those who get an "exceeds expectations" rating will often be provided feedback on areas where their skills are not quite as positive.

You're the Coach

To understand this basic belief more objectively, we propose jumping to an entirely different realm. Imagine that you have agreed to be the soccer coach for a competition soccer team of 12-year-olds. You are excited to work with the team. After agreeing to be the coach, you learn that 20 children have signed up to try out for the team, but the team can only field 15 players. Because this is a competition soccer program, it is necessary for some children to be cut from the team. On the first day of practice, you explain that you only have 15 slots on the team and that everyone is going to have to try out.

You proceed to run the children through a series of drills. On each drill, you select the two or three children who were superior and two or three who did not perform as well. After an hour of intensive drills, three-on-three "shoot-outs," and races, your roster becomes increasingly clear. Three of the children are clearly not at the same level. They should be moved to a less competitive league. Two additional children were close but did not perform well on several of the drills.

Now comes the tough part. You make out your team list. You gather the children together in a huddle and thank them for their effort. You tell them that you are proud of everyone and that it takes a lot of guts to try out for competition soccer. You then read the names of the children who made the team. Fifteen children are elated. Five of the children look quite dejected, though they keep a "stiff upper lip." Luckily, they have kind and supportive parents who bolster their children. As you begin to gather the equipment and jerseys, one of the children who was cut approaches you with a dejected look. This was one of the two children close to making the team. She gets your attention and says in a quivery voice, "Coach, why was I cut? What can I do to play next year?" You desperately want to make this child feel better. You look at your notes. There was one drill where the child's name was jotted down as superior but two other drills where the child did not perform well. What's the most constructive answer?

If you tell the child about what was done well, that makes her feel good, but starts her wondering even more, "Why was I cut?" The typical recommendation from most people on how best to approach this situation is to start with the positive, but then help the child understand that your decision was justified because of some failing on the child's part. Many coaches would describe the child's performance on the two drills where her performance was low. That will enable the child to understand that your decision was fair. A good way to close the conversation would be to say something like, "You are almost there, if you keep practicing I think that you will be playing competition soccer next year for sure."

As the child walks away and takes that long drive home with her parents, she will probably keep asking herself the question, "Why was I cut?" To which she will answer, "Because I blew it on two drills." In other words, failures come because of mistakes. But what would have happened if this child had been an extremely accurate kicker, or had been extremely good at playing goalie? Would the mistakes on the two drills have been irrelevant?

The reality of this situation is that the child was cut because there were no outstanding strengths, and above that, her performance was poor on two drills. Which of those is more important? We think most coaches would overlook flaws on two drills if they saw tenacious determination and competitive spirit or if they saw strong kicking ability or skill at playing goalie. The question here is not only what to tell the child about why she was not chosen this year, but more important, what to tell her about how best to prepare for next year.

Our belief is that emphasizing the child's weak performance on two drills is the wrong message. It would be far better to acknowledge that as of now you did not see important strengths, and that is what this child should work on in preparing for next year. What a terrible year it will be for her if her entire focus is on "not messing up on the drill." How much better it will be if her focus is on getting really good at some specific skills that make players valuable to the team. Most coaches are looking for raw talent and believe they can teach children to correct mistakes.

As they think about this short scenario, most people can replay several real-life situations about themselves that are very similar. Through this reinforcement and conditioning, people have come to the common belief that it is their mistakes, weaknesses, and poor performance on tasks that keep them from being successful.

In our research, we have found that leaders with very negative ratings on competencies were perceived less positively overall. We call these issues fatal flaws. Fatal flaws need to be corrected. There is, however, a significant difference between fatal flaws and areas that are slightly less positive than others. Let us call these rough edges. A person performs at an adequate level. For many leaders, we have noted their tendency to focus their efforts for improvement on rough edges, using the same logic as if it were a fatal flaw. Most people believe that lower-scoring competencies tend to hurt more than profound strengths help.

Look at Figure 5.2. Which person do you believe would be perceived as being more effective as a leader? Surprisingly, in a study we conducted with more than 8,000 leaders, Person B was perceived to be more effective.

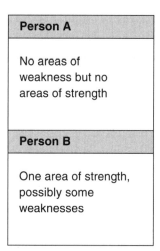

Figure 5.2. Who Is Likely to Be Perceived as the Better Leader?

Most people are more concerned with eliminating any perceptions of weakness than they are focused on developing strengths. This approach is reinforced by organizational practices that punish people for either weaknesses or rough edges but frequently fail to encourage people to develop strengths.

Rethinking the Personal Development Plan

Look back at Figure 5.1. Let's reconsider the best development plan for this individual. Rather than drilling into the less positive scores and attempting to elevate them to a higher level, we strongly contend that this person would be far better off selecting one to three of the higher scores and striving to push them to the highest quartile. Doing that will propel this person's career forward far more sure-footedly and rapidly than trying to fix the lower scores.

What Is a Strength?

A strength is something we do well. The question is how well. Many managers seem satisfied when the results of a 360-degree assessment show slightly above-average scores on all competencies. But that same person would be highly disappointed if his or her child came home from school with all C+'s on a report card.

A strength is also something that is used in a wide variety of situations and possesses an enduring effect. It lasts over time. We associate good outcomes with strengths. There is something inherently valuable about those qualities we deem strengths. The use of a strength does not detract from or diminish another strength.

Strengths are generally the outcome of some extremely natural ability with which a person is endowed, or they are the result of intensive practice and effort. Our society reveres the classic strengths, and thus there are proverbs and parables that support such strengths.

Our research led us to define 19 differentiating strengths or competencies that are described earlier in the book. As a reminder, these include qualities such as:

1. Possessing high character
2. Technical competence

3. Problem-solving skills
4. Initiative
5. Focus on results
6. Collaboration and teamwork
7. Communicating powerfully and prolifically (and 12 others)

In our research, we found a dramatic effect that strengths could have on the overall perception of a leader's effectiveness. That effect was present only when a competency stood out. Leaders with a variety of competencies that were positive but with none that stood out did not show that same impact on overall leadership effectiveness.

In a relative sense, we have defined strengths in most of our studies on leadership as a skill or competency at the 90th percentile. In an absolute sense, we define a strength as a 4.5 or higher rating on a 5-point scale. This rating requires at least 50 percent of the responders to mark the most positive response and the others to mark the next most positive response. If any lower evaluations are given, a majority of the responses on a 5-point scale need to be the most positive response.

Strengths are deeply rooted and are exhibited in differing situations over long periods of time. They consistently produce positive outcomes, but in those rare cases when there is not an immediate result, the strength is still valued.

Impact of Strengths

To understand the impact of strengths and weaknesses on overall leadership effectiveness, we researched results of assessments from 2,000 leaders and followed that with a second study of more than 100,000 leaders. The results of the two studies were remarkably consistent.

When asked, "What would you guess the overall effectiveness percentile would be for people with no strengths?" most people indicated they thought it would be approximately the 50th percentile. Figure 5.3 shows the results.

In our studies, leaders who had no perceived strengths were, on average, rated at the 34th percentile. Possessing no strengths plunges you to nearly the bottom third in terms of perceived overall leadership effectiveness.

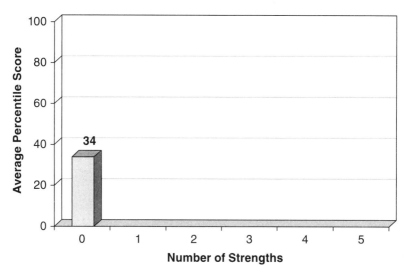

Figure 5.3. Impact of No Strengths

Why were leaders with no area of strength perceived on average to be in the bottom third for overall leadership effectiveness? They lack a redeeming quality, skill, or ability. They may not be ineffective at anything, but they also are not terribly effective at anything.

Figure 5.4 (see next page) shows the results for leaders with one strength. It is impressive that leaders with one strength move on average from the 34th percentile to the 64th percentile. Imagine, a 30 percentile point increase just for possessing one strength! This shows the powerful influence of being good at any one competency. Consider a hypothetical situation where you are asked to choose between hiring two employee candidates. Candidate A has no areas of weakness, but nothing stands out as a strength. Candidate B has a few minor weaknesses but a profound strength in an area critical to accomplishing the job. Whom do you hire? Most people admit that the candidate with the strength would most likely be more successful. The data in our studies clearly demonstrate the profound influence of having one thing that you do extraordinarily well. This is also consistent with the research about leaders presented in Figure 5.2.

Figure 5.5 (see next page) shows the influence of having multiple strengths. Note that the results in Figure 5.5 show that leaders with three strengths are at the 81st percentile on average.

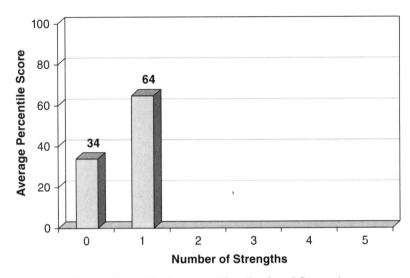

Figure 5.4. The Impact of One Profound Strength

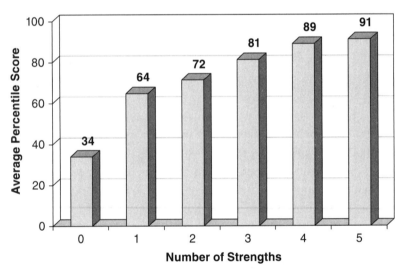

Figure 5.5. The Impact of Multiple Strengths

Leaders with five strengths are at the 91st percentile. When we have challenged leaders to move from the 50th percentile to the 90th percentile, their response was most often that it seemed impossible. Their perception was that they needed to be perfect in almost every competency in order to be at the 90th percentile. That clearly is not so, but it is a hard concept for many to absorb. To be at the 90th percentile simply required a leader to be highly skilled at five competencies! This seems achievable to most aspiring leaders.

For example, we have been working with a large financial services company and determined that in one large group, of the 150 most senior executives, one-third of them had six or more competencies at the 90th percentile. That was the good news. On the other hand, 46 percent of them had no competency at the 90th percentile. This provided a huge opportunity for development within this executive team.

After presenting this research at a conference, one conference participant asked, "What is the most significant finding from your research?" The answer given was a bit academic, carefully including many of the various insights covered in this book. The participant's response was, "No, that stuff is all important, but the thing that is most impressive is your research on the impact of strengths on overall effectiveness." The participant went on to explain his answer: "When I saw the research that showed the impact leaders can have on bottom-line results, I was both impressed and depressed—impressed that the impact occurs and depressed because I thought there was no way to develop those kinds of leaders. Those leaders are born, not made. Then you showed me the strength research. When you understand the key to being at the 80th percentile is having three strengths, it seems possible. Developing four strengths also seems possible for a large number of our people. It also seems clear to me that our managers have invested all their energy in trying to fix a nit here and there rather than concentrating on developing three strengths."

How Much Should I Bite Off?

If a person has a strategy for personal improvement that relies on incremental improvement of weak areas and moving all competencies to higher and higher levels, this seems like an overwhelming, maybe impossible task. Our research indicates that people can only be successful at change if they focus efforts on change in a few areas. Ideally, people would work on building one strength at a time, make progress that is observable by others, and then move on to the next opportunity.

Sometimes leaders want to fix something that is very specific and relatively easy to correct. For example, a leader received feedback about his lack of respect for other people's time when he came late to meetings and had the entire group wait while he was briefed on what had happened prior to his arrival. He also wanted to work on becoming more inspirational and motivational. We observed that there are little things and big things. Being on time to meetings is quite easy to fix if you are serious about it. Becoming more inspirational is more complex and a far bigger issue.

Can Strengths Be Pushed Too Far?

There is a commonly held belief that strengths carried too far become a weakness. Robert Kaplan and Robert Kaiser expressed this viewpoint in their article titled, "Stop Overdoing Your Strenghts"[3] They divided leadership behavior into two categories. They label these behaviors as being "forceful" versus "enabling" and have defined those two categories as strengths. They observe that if a leader overuses what they have labeled a "strength" by being constantly directive, always taking charge, making every decision, and pushing people, the leader's effectiveness diminishes.

That conclusion is one most would accept. However, these behaviors do not fit the usual definition of strengths. Earlier in this chapter we gave our definition. We see being forceful or enabling as behavioral tactics, not strengths. They are not valued in their own right. Using one invariably diminishes the other. Neither one is revered for its inherently good qualities. No proverbs and parables support them. Our conception of strengths is very different.

As we review our list of 19 potential strengths, we cannot envision a situation where doing less of any one of them would be better than doing more. Can someone be too honest or too skilled at solving problems? Can a person be too technically competent or excessively innovative? In all of our data analysis, we found no evidence that extremely high scores ever had negative consequences.

Different Way to Optimize Strengths

Kaplan and Kaiser suggest that backing off strengths is the right solution. The person seen as "too forceful" should be more moderate. The "too enabling" person should be less empowering or less sensitive to others.

Balance is important, but our remedies for getting balance differ. For example, our data clearly show that a leader who gets extremely high scores on "drive for results" will be more effective if those scores are balanced with high scores on interpersonal relationships. We frequently coach leaders who have extremely high scores on driving for results. They often catch flack from colleagues about the impact they are having on the organization. But asking this leader to ratchet down a passion for results is not the best advice. That is probably a big part of what got this leader into his or her current position. Our recommendation is to hang tight on high standards and lofty expectations, but balance it with a greater emphasis on "people" skills.

In short, we find no evidence that what we and others have identified as strengths can ever be overdone. Therefore, we can't envision a time when we would advise a leader to tone down a strength.

Powerful Combinations

Brett Savage, a long-time colleague, told the secret of his success playing high school football. Brett was 6 feet 4 inches tall, fairly slender, and a strong runner. Brett's physical appearance was more like that of a basketball player than a football player. But Brett had another talent: he could catch anything thrown anywhere close to him. At 6 feet 4 inches, Brett towered over the defensive backs who attempted to cover him. His success in football came from a simple play. Brett played the end position. He would sprint out for a pass, get to his predetermined destination, and wait for the quarterback to throw the pass high. Brett would jump to catch the pass, but no defender could come close to the ball because they could not touch him while the pass was being thrown without drawing a penalty. There was little they could do but wait for him to catch the ball and then tackle him. The strategy was flawless, and as Brett explained his success he said, "The combination of height and good hands was powerful."

When considering strengths and the impact of combinations of strengths on leadership, we were interested to see if the most effective leaders had consistent combinations of competencies. To research this (Figure 5.6), we examined leaders who had very good skills at building relationships (e.g., this competency in the top quartile) but were not rated positively in terms of drive for results. Of these leaders, only 8 percent were at the 90th percentile in terms of their overall leadership effectiveness. Next, we looked at leaders who were in the top quartile on drive for results but were not at the top quartile on relationship building skills. In this case, 9 percent of these leaders were at the 90th percentile in terms of their overall leadership effectiveness. We then studied those leaders who were in the top quartile for both drive for results and building relationships. In this case, 82 percent were at the 90th percentile in terms of their overall leadership effectiveness. Clearly, this is a powerful combination. Both skills are valuable and lead to success, but the combination of being very good at both skills substantially increased the probability of overall effectiveness.

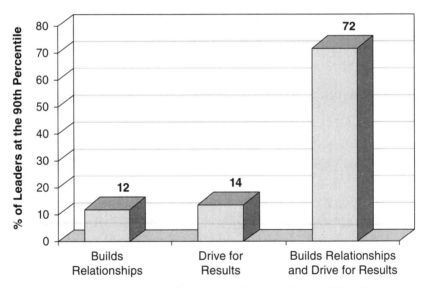

Figure 5.6. Combined Impact of Relationships and Results

This research led us to the conclusion that it is not strengths that hurt a person's effectiveness, but rather strengths standing alone without counterbalance. That is what creates the perception of a strength pushed too far becoming a weakness. The more we researched this phenomenon the more it became clear that this powerful interaction effect is created because a person's ability to do one competency well improves the other competency. Think of a person who is very driven to achieve results. Having a strength in building relationships improves trust and the sense that the leader does not just care about the results, he or she cares about each member of the team. Another person may be very effective at building relationships. Having a strength in driving for results helps them to deliver on their promises.

Powerful combinations do not require that people back off one competency in order to do another well. The secret to building success as a leader is to be excellent at powerful combinations of skills. We have found that there are many such powerful combinations. The more differentiated the combination, the more potentially powerful is the combination.

The effect of powerful combinations is to erect and lengthen the tent poles that lift the overall leadership tent to new heights. Powerful combinations also demonstrate the interconnections between all of the different competencies.

The Halo Effect

As we noted in Chapter 4, a halo effect occurs when our perceptions of others are distorted either positively or negatively. After studying results from thousands of leaders, it became evident that strong positive and negative halo effects occur. Results for the best leaders showed that the perceptions of others rated almost all competencies at the 90th percentile (they can do no wrong). Results for the worst performers showed that the perceptions of others rated almost all competencies at the 10th percentile (they can do no right). We have come to believe that both are a distortion. When leaders perform extraordinarily well on a few behaviors, they begin to be viewed in a very positive light, and others' impressions of them on other competencies tended to be distorted in a positive direction.

The opposite effect seems to occur for those with a few profound weaknesses. Consider our day-to-day experience with people who have achieved some measure of fame. How many times have you been disappointed to hear a speech by a star athlete? Why did you believe that he would have something insightful or even interesting to say? Just because a person performs an athletic feat well does not mean that that athlete has the ability to speak, write, or communicate well. The notion of product endorsement by famous people provides validation for the impact of the halo effect. Having a famous person endorse a product creates more sales of that product. This is the direct impact of the halo effect. We see the effect on the negative side when we demonize people who have made serious mistakes.

The halo effect is very real, and everyone has experienced its impact. The important issue for leaders is to get this effect to work for you rather than against you. We believe the key to getting the halo effect to work for you is to build up a few profound strengths.

L. A. Festinger wrote *The Theory of Cognitive Dissonance.*[4] In the book, he describes the idea that people have a different set of beliefs or knowledge elements to which they hold. A belief might be as simple a thought as "I like ice cream," or "My manager is a terrible leader." Dissonance is created when there is psychological conflict between different beliefs (i.e., "My manager is a terrible leader" and "My manager is very good at solving complex and difficult problems"). Through hundreds of experiments, Festinger and other researchers have demonstrated that when dissonance occurs, people will do whatever is necessary to reduce the dissonance. When leaders improve their abilities on a few competencies, this can create dissonance in the minds of others. People ask themselves, "How can this leader be so effective on some things but less effective on others?" The tendency is for others to close the gap on the dissonance, and typically this involves a positive halo effect for leaders who develop extraordinary strengths.

The implication of the halo effect is that when strengths are pushed to higher levels, the halo effect tends to push up competencies that are not as positive. This creates a fairly level profile. For those who worry that they need to improve on their weaknesses because that is what their manager will focus on in performance discussions, the halo effect can help them. Rather than trying to incrementally improve a few less positive issues, focusing efforts on substantial improvement in a few key strengths will create a positive halo effect in the way a person's manager perceives him or her. A few less positive issues fail to show up because of the presence of a few profound strengths. Most managers focus on less positive issues when they fail to see any real strengths that draw their attention. The extraordinary strengths are the keys to guaranteeing promotions, bonuses, stock options, and high performance appraisals for two reasons. First, those strengths help to produce tangible results. Second, they create a powerful "halo" that settles in around the person.

Focusing on Strengths Transforms a Leader's View of Subordinates

A client from a telecommunications company shared the following story with us. It illustrates the power of focusing on strengths as a way to change basic boss-subordinate dynamics. This person was an assistant vice president in the compliance arena of the organization. She wrote:

> A manager on my team had been struggling with her performance. I had initiated several coaching sessions with her. The focus of the sessions previously were the areas where I felt she was weak and together we developed strategies for her to improve. After a year of seeing very little improvement, I felt I had no choice but to sit her down and tell her that she needed to seek a position elsewhere as she was just not making it on my team. I went as far as to consult with human resources to try to get her placed outside my group.
>
> Unrelated and purely by coincidence, someone told me about your book *The Extraordinary Leader*. I bought the book and read it cover to cover. I was intrigued by the idea of focusing on a person's strengths as a way to become a more effective leader. While my intent in reading the book was self-development, I could not help but wonder what effect it might have if I went beyond focusing on my own strengths and focused on the strengths of this subordinate manager. I began looking for the things that she did well and began to acknowledge her for those behaviors and assign her projects that utilized those skills. Within a few months I noticed an incredible turnaround in her performance. Not only did she help the team by taking on the projects that played to her strengths, it created a "halo effect" and I began to see improvement in some of the areas that I had previously identified as being "weak."
>
> Previously I had coached her several times about not communicating with me about issues she was working on— by focusing and assigning her projects that aligned with her strength, which was her ability to gain consensus on difficult issues, she began to send me unsolicited emails weekly recapping her activities that week. I also noticed by focusing on her

strengths I began to change my view of her and began to see other strengths that had previously gone unnoticed.

Thank you for educating me about this very powerful tool. It goes beyond positive reinforcement. It caused a shift in my management style, which has allowed me to better utilize the skills on my team, and as a result, the entire team is now more productive.

6

LEADERS MUST FIT
THEIR ORGANIZATION

Old thieves make good jailers.
—GERMAN PROVERB

Bruce worked in administration for a large university, and because of an excellent referral from a university professor, he landed a position with a small consulting firm. His role was to start out as the office administrative manager, but he was slated to move quickly into the role of managing director of the firm. At the university, Bruce had been a shining star. He was extremely meticulous in his work and paid a great deal of attention to detail. He always made sure to ferret out all the information before making a decision. These were valued traits at the university. As he began his role in the consulting firm, he found the environment to be extremely different. At the university, the proposals moved slowly through committees. Ample time was allowed for study and debate.

The small consulting firm moved quickly. Partners, all of whom felt they had decision-making authority, controlled the firm as a group. However, one partner would make a decision one way and then a second partner would reverse that decision. The partners would meet occasionally to hammer out the decision and resolve the disagreement. Partner meetings would be hardball discussions where differences were debated openly. The partners, rather than staying in the office to implement decisions, were constantly away on consulting assignments. They assumed that the decisions they made would be implemented.

Bruce approached his new assignment warily and decided that what the firm needed was more deliberate decision making, clear lines of authority, and a committee structure to consider various decisions. He worked for six months to implement these changes. After six months, the only thing Bruce accomplished was convincing every partner that he needed to leave the firm. The partners ultimately recognized that this new role for Bruce was not working, nor was it likely that he would ever succeed. They provided a severance package to Bruce. He quickly landed a job in administration at a hospital. During the next several years, Bruce was promoted in the hospital and enjoyed an excellent reputation with the staff and the physicians.

Was there something wrong with Bruce? Why was he so successful at the university and the hospital but such a failure at the consulting firm? Was there something wrong with the consulting firm? The consulting firm continued to grow and prosper.

What this series of events illustrates is that leadership is specific to the organization. Some combinations of individuals and organizations just do not work out well. Although it was certainly true in this episode that neither was without a share of responsibility for the failure, what becomes evident to everyone with a variety of work experiences is that some organizations fit certain individuals better than others. Individuals have unique competencies, beliefs, and experience. Organizations have extremely different cultures and needs. Although there can be some accommodation by either the individual or the organization at some point, people are more effective when they are they are true to themselves.

Keys to Success and Failure

One of the primary focuses early in our research was to discover if there were some competencies that are absolutely essential in order for a leader to be considered great. In other words, "Great leaders always do _____ well." In addition, we looked for competencies that, if done poorly, were a cause for failure. Surely, there must be some behaviors that catapult leaders to success; conversely, there must be others that drag leaders to failure. In the research process, however, it appeared that whenever we found a rule, we always found exceptions to that rule. We found much greater similarity in the causes of failure than we found in the reasons for effectiveness. Rather than identifying a consistent profile or style that always worked for every person, what we found was a tremendous variety in the style, approach, and makeup of extraordinary leaders. What started out as a disappointment in our research soon turned out to be valuable insight on leadership. Extraordinary leaders are unique. Some have one cluster of attributes, whereas others have a different cluster of attributes. This isn't to say that each of the

19 competencies was equally powerful in predicting overall effectiveness. Indeed, one competency, "inspires and motivates others to high performance," is the single most powerful competency, and this has prompted us to write a subsequent book about it, *The Inspiring Leader*.[1]

The commonality we could find in extraordinary leaders is that they are extremely effective at a few things. Having the necessary leadership skills for success all be the same would make life simpler for those responsible for leadership development, that is not the reality. We suspect most people are glad that this is not the way the world works. It would be mind-numbingly boring.

The good news of our research is that it reinforces the notion of individuality and the power of developing individual talents and gifts. For the authors, this comes as a great relief. Whereas both of us hope we possess some strengths, our strengths differ markedly from each other. This fact has been of great benefit in researching and writing this book. The strengths of one author balanced the flat side of the other author. After many years of personal change efforts, being extraordinarily talented at some competencies continues to evade us. It is just not in our bones. (This does not mean we are totally incompetent at these skills, but clearly we are not extraordinary.)

The Leadership Paradox

Leaders are both unique and alike. They are unique in that each one has a different set of competencies that ideally fits the organization in which he or she works. They are alike in that, to be highly effective, they need to have strengths in the different sections of the tent. The net effect is that leaders do not appear to be alike. Just as nearly all vehicles have four wheels, a power source, and electrical and braking systems, at the same time they have very different body styling (SUVs, sedans, pick-up trucks, and limousines). In the end, leaders appear extremely different on the outside, with several fundamental similarities under the surface.

Discovering Your Genius

A psychologist once observed that the secret to life is discovering what "instrument" you are, and then learning how to play it. Woodwinds are no better than brass, nor are cellos superior to kettledrums. Each does something extremely well, and different musical scores call for that unique contribution. Some people seem to spend their entire lives searching for what that instrument is for them. Others, fortunately, discover their instrument quite early in life.

As individuals, we all have competencies and abilities that come to us more easily than do others. We are drawn to some tasks and resist others. It is difficult to know if our being drawn to some activities results from possessing a unique, inherent skill, or if being good at something causes us to try harder at some skills versus others. Whatever the reason, it is not difficult to observe any group of leaders in any organization and notice marked individual differences. All seem to have both a combination of unique competencies and also other skills where they fare well, but are not necessarily great. A handful have pronounced weaknesses in a few areas.

In an effort to help people discover their genius, a former colleague, Kurt Sandholtz, has conducted research with thousands of people.[2] His quest was to determine the method whereby individuals have a "career best" experience, or a time that constituted the high point in that person's career. Understanding these "career best" experiences helps people understand their genius.

Gene Dalton and Paul Thompson first developed the core of this idea when they wrote, "If individuals don't understand their unique strengths or interests, they don't have any basis for deciding whether a job or an assignment makes sense for them. They are vulnerable to attractive external rewards or organizational pressures. They have little basis on which to form enough conviction to say no to an apparently attractive opportunity. Answers to career questions come from within one's self."[3]

To help people discover what they do best, Sandholtz asks them, "What is the best job you've ever had?" After examining the results of these studies, he discovered that "career bests" have some common characteristics.

First, "career best" taps into a person's talent or competencies. Competencies, as noted in Chapter 4, are skills and behaviors that a person performs well. Second, a "career best" experience tends to highlight what people are passionate about. Passions are things that we love to do, independent of how well we do them. Some love to sing in the shower, despite being told they are not always on key. Third, a "career best" activity inevitably adds value to the organization. When people describe their job, they don't say, "I was very competent at doing this job, I loved to do it and nobody in the organization gave a hoot."

A basic requirement of a "career best" activity is doing something that is valued and provides benefit to the organization. According to Sandholtz, activities and jobs mentioned were frequently a "product of luck rather than planning." Rather than having planned out each stage in their careers, individuals tended to say of their "career best" that they were "just in the right place at the right time."

The CPO Model

In an attempt to increase the frequency of career bests and make them more of a planned event rather than a stroke of luck, Sandholtz and Ron Cutadean came up with a model that describes the primary drivers of a "career best" experience.[4] We have adapted that model and call it the CPO model, where C is Competencies, P is Passion, and O is Organizational needs. In Figure 6.1, we display the CPO model graphically using a Venn diagram with three intersecting sets.

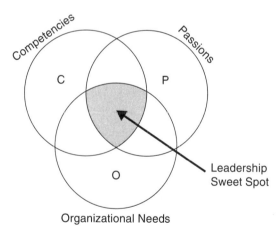

Figure 6.1. Finding Your Career Sweet Spot

A leadership sweet spot occurs when there is an intersection of competencies (e.g., skills or behaviors a person performs well), passions (e.g., activities people love to do), and organizational needs (e.g., outcomes that an organization values).

Competencies

Competencies are those skills, behaviors, and abilities that a person does extremely well. Our research on the impact of strengths arbitrarily defines these as behaviors rated at the 90th percentile by other people. A competency can also be an area of knowledge or expertise. As you think about yourself and your abilities, some of these competencies are behaviors that you tend to be naturally good at, whereas others have been developed over years of steady growth and practice. They may be skills at casual conversation, writing, understanding complex problems, conceptualizing models, listening, giving direction, or staying calm under pressure. To understand your competencies, you might ask yourself: When people talk about my strengths, what do they mention first? Where have I been successful in the past? What abilities do I seem to possess more than most others?

Passion

Just because we have competence around a skill does not mean that we will have passion. I might have a great voice but decide that there is no future in singing, or I might detest getting up and performing in front of others. Competence, yes, but passion (I love to do this, I want to do this, doing this gives me a personal high), no. The result is an undeveloped competency. Passion and competence can function independently of each other. People's passions may be in sports but physically they are uncoordinated, slow, and weak. People in general have an interesting attitude about passions. They feel that what they love is naturally given to them. Some people seem to be controlled by their passions and rarely attempt to broaden them. Other people see that the things that we become passionate about can change over time. We can develop passions for things that we did not really like at one point in our lives.

To help understand your passions, Dalton and Thompson suggest you might ask yourself the following questions:[5]

- What do I really enjoy doing?
- What events bring me a great deal of personal satisfaction?
- Which activities energize me in such a way that they hold my interest? When do I lose all sense of time?
- What activities do I daydream about or imagine myself doing?

Organizational Needs

The O in the CPO model stands for organizational needs. In order for leaders to be successful or for an individual to find the "leadership sweet spot," the competencies people have and the passion for what they want to do have to be valued by the organization. Typically, organizations value competencies and passions of individuals that have a fairly direct impact on the success of the organization. Many organizations seem to have a narrow set of competencies and passions that they value. People can argue about whether the organization "ought" to value particular competencies when it does not, but the fact remains that in order for people to find the "leadership sweet spot," there needs to be an intersection of competencies, organizational need, and passion.

Research on People in the Sweet Spot

Contrasting people who are experiencing the sweet spot against others in the organization reveals substantial differences in both performance and attitude. Those who are in the sweet spot:

- Add more value than do their colleagues
- Are ranked as higher performers
- Usually work more hours per week
- Are not looking for another job
- Are more engaged and motivated
- Are learning and developing new skills
- Are having fun . . . and are fun to work with

Barriers That Get in the Way of Finding Your Sweet Spot

Competency Plus Organizational Needs but No Passion

In Figure 6.2 (see next page), a person has the competence and the organizational need is present, but there is no passion for the job. This person will often feel bored, stuck, or "pigeon-holed." In this situation, a person might have been working at a job for a long time and have great competence, but that person has been in the position for so long that he or she fails to see any challenge or excitement.

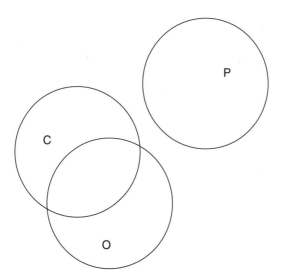

Figure 6.2. When Passion Is Lacking

Organizational Needs Plus Passion but No Competence

In the situation depicted in Figure 6.3, a leader works in an organization that has a need and where the leader has a great deal of passion, but not a high level of competence. Passion and desire can never make up for competence. This person is sometimes viewed as incompetent, but more frequently viewed as average. In this situation, the organization needs a particular competency, and the individual has a strong desire to attempt the competency but lacks the ability to do this skill with above-average expertise. In our research, we found several examples of this. One was an organization that engaged in upstream exploration for oil, and the organization's most prominent need was technical competence. The organization was composed of geophysicists, engineers, and geologists who had extensive expertise and ability. Leaders who lacked the level of technical knowledge to "keep up" were most often viewed as the poorest leaders.

Competence Plus Passion but No Organizational Needs

Figure 6.4 shows a situation where a leader has the right combination of competence and passion, but all are built around skills and competencies that are not needed in the organization. There is a fascinating philosophy that many people have that an organization ought to accommodate the needs and passions of an individual. Having coached people in this

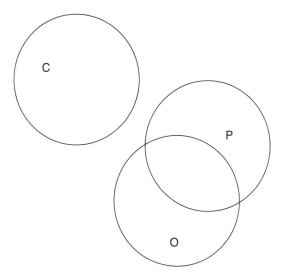

Figure 6.3. When Competence Is Lacking

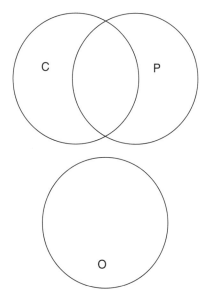

Figure 6.4. When Organizational Need Is Lacking

situation, they often respond with something like, "Well, this company needs what I have to offer, but it is just too dense to understand and appreciate how I can contribute." This is a bad fit. Not every person is going to have a satisfying and productive career in every organization. Frequently, individuals get a job in an organization and when they discover that their contribution is not valued, they push back and try to change the organization in an effort to make things work. They assume that their inability to be successful in the organization says something about them. In reality, all it says is that the organization does not value or need their contribution. They feel like they are a failure rather than a bad fit. So often we see individuals who have struggled and been miserable in one organization move to a different organization, only to find themselves being valued, contributing, and making a real difference.

Using the CPO Model

When your competence and passions intersect with organizational needs, the outcome is always positive for the individual and the organization. The individual is doing something he or she is competent at and has energy or passion about the tasks to be accomplished. The organization is getting good results in return. Our research has helped us understand that some competencies are better at creating leverage and success in an organization. Chapter 4 showed the research on 19 key competencies that have a higher likelihood of leveraging overall leadership effectiveness. These 19 competencies provide a great deal of latitude in terms of selecting competencies that a person can develop into extraordinary strengths.

Organizational Competency Drivers

When competence and passion intersect with an organizational need, this creates an opportunity for an individual to show extraordinary leadership. Displaying exceptional skill on a competency where there is no organizational need fails to provide much clout in terms of leveraging leadership effectiveness.

Imagine you are a member of a small team in a high-technology company that has the unpleasant task of downsizing a group of people by half. Each person is discussed. Strengths and areas of needed improvement are reviewed for each one. All of the people are selected for dismissal except one. It is difficult to choose between two employees. There is a fair amount of disagreement in the group about the two people. Finally, the person sitting next to you, who has been a strong advocate for keeping one of them, says, "She is a great pianist." What would be your response?

Probably, "What difference does that make?" Although being a great pianist is a very nice skill to have, unless it fills an organizational need, it does not benefit you at work.

In this chapter, we have avoided being prescriptive about skills that everyone needs to do well to be a great leader. Our advice is to build a high level of competence in three to five skill areas, balanced across the major areas of the tent we described in Chapter 3.

In researching the profiles of different companies, it is apparent that different organizations have specific profiles that point to key competencies absolutely required to be successful. Organization profiles reveal one, two, or three dominant characteristics that tend to define a key competency for that organization. Doing well on this skill or competency places you in good company with most other members of the organization. However, doing exceptionally well on this competency does not tend to leverage overall leadership effectiveness. The reason for this is that everyone does the competency well so it is almost impossible to differentiate yourself from most others. Doing poorly on these competencies, however, would be a certain path to failure. These organizational competency drivers tend to hurt more than help. To be successful in an organization, it is critical for people to understand what these competencies are and to possess a reasonable level of skill in them.

What Organizations Value

An implication of the CPO model is that to be successful in an organization, people need to combine their competencies with their passions and then find an organization that needs what they have to offer. In the same way that people come with different and unique personalities, so do organizations. No two are exactly the same. In the same way that one has courtships with a variety of different people to find a partner that best fits one's own personality, so should people find a match between themselves and the organization for which they work. Many people try to accommodate their own personal style and desires to the needs of an organization. Although this can be done successfully, frequently this leads to frustration, job dissatisfaction, and failure to be promoted and advanced. Finding an organization where there is a good fit often allows people to truly excel.

One of the authors recently visited a large bank. Upon looking through their aggregated leadership assessment data, it became evident that they were an "avoiding mistakes"/"customer emphasis" organization.

Both issues were very strong and positive for 80 percent of the leaders. If you work for an organization that has a profile of being an execution organization, you need to be good at executing (e.g., getting projects done on time and within budget—no excuses). A mismatch hurts a person's chance of success, and everyone needs an environment where he or she has a reasonable chance to succeed.

Organizational Culture and Prized Competencies

Based on research on 22 different organizations, we found 20 profiles of competencies and organizational capabilities that may be valued by or define an organization. In most instances, organizations had two or three of the characteristics that described what the organization valued, though one appeared to dominate. In an effort to help readers assess what are their own organization values, here are some of the more pronounced organizational characteristics. The opportunity here is to judge the "goodness of fit" between what your organization truly values and your own pattern of competencies. We will divide these into three unequal buckets. First, we will identify different behavioral styles, then we will describe what the organization emphasizes, and finally we will recognize some external realities that shape organizations.

I. Preferred Behavior

1. The Genteel Organization

Leaders in this organization focus on developing a kind and considerate organization. Confrontation never occurs. Serious issues are usually swept under the carpet. Performance reviews are avoided or couched in extremely gentle terms.

One of the authors recounts, "I was working in a company in Minnesota and asked an internal employee what it was like to work in the company. His response was, 'We are all Minnesota nice.' 'What is Minnesota nice?' I asked. The employee explained that people in the company were extremely polite with each other. They were always pleasant. They never said negative or demeaning things about other employees. After hearing all this I commented, 'Sounds like a great place to work,' to which the employee responded, 'It is, but you never know what people really think of you.'" Some organizations have created a culture that encourages people to play nice.

2. The Candor Organization

Leaders in this organization "tell it like it is." Typically, there is a strong feedback culture, in which feedback flows rather freely both up and down the organization. Those who thrive in this company need to be not only good at receiving feedback but also effective at giving others feedback. While listening to a conversation between two leaders in a candid organization, one author heard a leader comment that a direct report did an ineffective job of presenting her findings. The other leader immediately asked, "Did you give her that feedback?" "No." The other leader replied, "Well, then, you're in more trouble than she is."

3. The Learning Organization

In a learning organization, people learn from mistakes rather than hiding them. Development of skills and talents is valued, and people are constantly looking for different or unique learning opportunities. There is typically a strong value for innovation. People are constantly collecting feedback and looking for a better understanding of what happened and why.

4. The High-Integrity Organization

Doing the right thing is valued by leaders in high-integrity organizations. There is a very strong emphasis on honesty and ethical behavior. Many voluntary organizations focused on noble causes have this strength. People have strong desires to promote the cause of the organization, and typically there is a high level of congruence among organizational members about what is appropriate and what is not.

5. The Fair Organization

One of the most frequent complaints coming out of organizations is that promotions and advancements are biased. Whether it is a "good old boy" network, a bias toward MBAs from certain schools or a preference for golfing friends, this issue is frequently a source of dissatisfaction in many organizations. Organizations that have developed fairness as a key strength have figured out how to create an organization relatively free from bias. Leaders who have a strong desire to treat people with fairness learn to pay careful attention to their biases. Frequently, these organizations have fewer levels and greater equity in pay and benefits. There is often a push to treat everyone the same rather than have one tier of benefits for people at one level and different benefits for those at another level. These organizations eliminate executive parking and boondoggles along with a propensity to hire people of a certain gender, race, age, or school background.

6. The Political Organization

The political organization is often referred to as a "good old boys" club. Politics and connections are among the most critical factors in determining who will be promoted and who will get a raise. The hierarchy is greatly respected. People follow the chain of command. For people who work in these kinds of organizations, there is a fair amount of predictability. For those who know the rules and enjoy playing the game, this organization can be a good place to work.

7. The Bureaucratic Organization

The bureaucratic organization has established strong bureaucratic processes and procedures and sticks to them. Many but not all government or utility organizations fit this model. There are clear norms to uphold. There are manuals that describe what must be done and how difficult situations are handled. There is great adherence to processes and precedents.

8. The Clan/Club

This organization emphasises bringing people together who have much in common. The emphasis is on nurturing and mentoring people. People believe in and practice collaboration, and the organization often uses the metaphor that "we're a family."

9. Lofty Standards Organization

People in this organization are held to an extremely high standard of conduct. The biggest mistake possible to make is to do anything that would besmirch the reputation of the organization. People hold each other to an extremely high standard of conduct.

10. Fun/Celebration Organization

These organizations relish the opportunity to find success and celebrate it. They put a high priority on making work fun. Work is characterized by frequent commendations in public.

II. What Is Emphasized

11. Technology Emphasis Organization

In the technology organization, leaders need to be highly knowledgeable and viewed as having technical expertise in the core activity of the firm. Although you would imagine that these firms were high-tech companies, we have found this characteristic to be very strong in construction companies and natural resources organizations as well. In a technology organization, people thrive on technical knowledge and expertise. A frequent sign that you are in a technology company is that people often talk in code. New employees frequently need a translator or lexicon to understand what people are saying. At HP, the best technical experts were called "Graybeards." These sages had spent their lives inside HP, developing new and exciting technical innovations. They were looked upon as heroes in the organization.

12. Excellent Execution Organization

In this organization, there is a substantial need to drive forward and achieve results, to get done on time, stay in budget, and always make your numbers. Leaders enjoy challenging results, and they often run on adrenaline. There is constant energy in the air. People inevitably come to work early and stay late. This organization attracts or encourages people who aspire to climb the corporate ladder of success. Goals are always aggressive and challenge everyone's abilities. Frequently, these organizations have high rewards for the best performers and a process to constantly "weed out" the bottom 10 percent.

13. Error Avoidance Organization

In this organization, there is a critical need to do things right. Excellence, quality, and conformance to standards are the organizational bylines. However, the reward for taking on a new project or taking some initiative is not as great as the punishment for making a mistake. So, there is an enormous emphasis on checking every written document two and three times. Presentations are rehearsed and re-rehearsed. Every column of figures is added and re-added to make sure there are no mistakes. This is a frequent phenomenon in organizations that have large corporate staffs. Their role often evolves into one of "cop," where the emphasis is on catching mistakes made by an operating company.

One of the authors was reviewing a presentation with a client to be presented before their chairman. After seeing the presentation, she said, "I have some feedback for you." "Great," I commented. Her feedback was, "You need to be a bit more buttoned up." At first, I wasn't quite sure what she meant. "What do I need to do less of?" I asked. Her reply, "Don't ask so many questions. Just give the chairman the facts. And keep the presentation short. The more information we give the chairman, the greater the chance for his disagreeing with something you say."

The emphasis on avoiding mistakes leads to a general practice of micromanaging.

14. Customer Emphasis Organization

Leaders in this organization are totally focused on satisfying customer needs and responding to their requests. Leaders take pride in knowing customers, working personally with them, and solving their problems. Customer interests are often placed before those of the employees or the shareholders. If there is ever a problem between a customer and an employee, the customer is assumed to be right and the employee wrong.

One of the authors thought he knew what it meant to be customer focused, but then was asked to build an assessment tool for a company that was obsessed with customers. Some of the items that were created to assess the intensity of their desire to understand customers included:

1. Continually seeks information about customers' underlying or future needs
2. Can describe the customer's business from the customer's viewpoint, not the company's point of view
3. Spends enough time in the marketplace to understand the underlying, unmet needs of customers
4. Makes other people get inside the customers' world

A major part of leaders' evaluations were based on the results to these questions.

15. Personal Commendation Organization

The commendation organization is built on individual efforts and opportunities for rewards. Organizations with this strength find ways to reward people well for strong individual efforts.

16. Adhocracy Organization

This organization values being fast and being first to do things. Traditional organization structure is de-emphasized. People are encouraged to be entrepreneurial. The motto is "just get it done." An organization chart is often nonexistent.

17. Sales Organization

Some organizations are driven by their revenue engine. Everything revolves around sales and business development. Their perspective prevails in all discussions and decisions. The people who are most highly valued are those who are the lifeblood, the ones bringing in revenue.

18. Process Organization

The process organization emphasizes efficiency, and the way to obtain greater efficiency is to slavishly define and follow work processes. Building relationships and emphasis on interpersonal connections are secondary to the work processes that are at the heart of the organization.

III. External Realities

19. The Virtual Organization

The virtual organization is a new type of organization that is emerging. In these organizations, people are combined together to form a group but work independently. The group may only meet together physically in a rented conference room, and the interconnection might be through a website. This organization attempts to leverage the power of the group, but each person acts as an independent entity.

20. The Start-Up

These organizations are often in a fast growth mode. Roles and responsibilities are not nailed down. People are value to can see what needs to be done and you instantly dive into doing without being told. There is high energy and excitement. People generally work long hours and sacrifice any work–life balance. These are not the best places for a person who needs predictability and structure, but they are ideal for those who thrive on excitement and change.

Implications

It is critical for leaders to understand their individual areas of competency, the things that bring them passion, and the needs of their organization. The "leadership sweet spot" that is the intersection of these three elements holds great promise for both individual and organizational success. It is rare to find a perfect match between individual competence and passion and organizational needs. We know that individuals can develop new competencies to fit the needs of an organization. We also know that organizations can change their culture, which requires leaders with different leadership competencies.

We find the idea of the CPO model compelling, but we also find people rationalizing the lack of intersection in their personal situations. Individuals will complain that the organization really ought to value what they do and that organizations are narrow-minded in terms of what they need. These rationalizations do not help the individual or the organization to become more successful. A key to success for leaders is to find their own personal "sweet spot." For each person, there is something that he or she can do extremely well. There is a competency with which he or she can make an enormous contribution. The late Gene Dalton spent most of his career researching how people achieve success in their careers. He found that people who are successful are constantly focused on how they can make a contribution to the organization.[6] It may take time to develop a competency. Organizations need to be patient and assist with that individual development, but ultimately organizations need to be successful or they cease to exist. When an individual can provide an extraordinary competency that an organization needs, the only other component that is required is passion. This is the element that is most underrated and yet potentially the most critical part of the model. Love, desire, motivation, inspiration, and passion are in the final analysis the greatest differences between good leaders and great leaders. For additional tools with which to diagnose your organization's culture, visit www.zengerfolkman.com.

FATAL FLAWS MUST BE FIXED

The bearded lady at the circus said,
"Everybody's got something wrong with them.
With me, you can tell what it is."
—RICHARD NEEDHAM

Maturity is coming to terms with that other part of yourself.
—RUTH TIFFANY BARNHOUSE

Magnifying strengths to the fullest has been one of the main messages thus far. In doing so, we may have implied that weaknesses should never be the focus of a personal development plan. If that is the case, it should be corrected. In many cases, focus on a weakness is absolutely the correct thing to do.

A Natural Place to Begin

As we have already observed, people challenged to improve their leadership effectiveness or, for that matter, effectiveness at almost anything have an amazingly similar plan for improvement:

- Step 1: Assess areas of strength and weakness. Being really good or even moderately good at something means you don't have to worry about it, so immediately look at your low scores.
- Step 2: Decide which weakness is most significant, usually because it has the lowest score.
- Step 3: Develop some plan of action to fix the weakness.

In fact, in some cases, working on a weakness is the best approach to improving. Those cases involve a category of attributes that we will call fatal flaws. For example, while looking at a data set of 103,510 leaders who were assessed on the differentiating competencies we found that 29 percent of the leaders had one or more potential fatal flaws. We defined a potential fatal flaw as a competency at the 10th percentile. When we looked at the impact of fatal flaws we found that those with one or more potential fatal flaws as a group scored at the 19th percentile in terms of overall leadership effectiveness. Leaders with just one potential fatal flaw scored at the 33th percentile, those with two at the 25th, and those with three at the 20th percentile. Weaknesses have a dramatic negative impact on perceptions of overall leadership effectiveness.

A second test must be met, however, for a behavior to truly qualify as a fatal flaw. Not only must this competency receive a score that is at or below the 10th percentile, it has to be important to the person's current job. Different positions have varied requirements. Having a low score on a competency that is irrelevant to your job nullifies the need for defining it as a fatal flaw.

Fatal Flaw Profile

Suppose that the profile in Figure 7.1 was an assessment of your leadership effectiveness as reported by your subordinates. The profile shows their perceptions of your effectiveness on a variety of leadership competencies, A through P. The longer the bar, the greater your perceived effectiveness.

Competency J is perceived by others as an area of significant weakness, and for the sake of illustration, suppose item J is "Capable of learning from mistakes." An extremely low score on this dimension is a fatal flaw. In our research, we found that people with this profile, if they improve their behavior on item J, will experience a dramatic improvement overall in the way their subordinates perceive them. That improvement lifts everything with it. If the fatal flaw is not corrected, it will act as a drag on the overall perception of leadership effectiveness. It is impossible to prove, of course, but we believe that even one extremely low score has a negative halo effect. The extremely poor performance in the one competency drags down the perceptions on all other competencies.

Our data show that a leader who is perceived poorly on any single, important leadership trait pays a high price. If one score is in the bottom

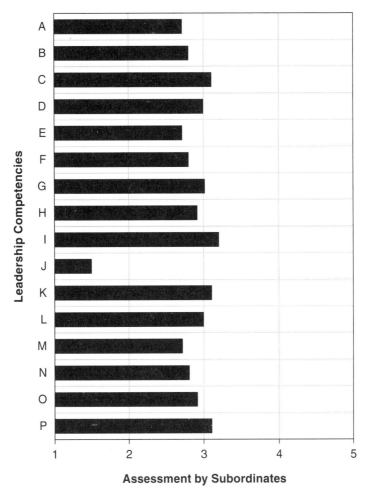

Figure 7.1. Summary of Multi-Rater Assessment Results

decile on one key skill, he or she will be ranked in the bottom fifth overall when compared to other leaders—*no matter how positively other strengths are rated.*

Frederick was the director of research for an international pharmaceutical company. A brilliant chemist, he towered over others in his grasp of the technical aspects of the research process. But his personal manner was curt and abrupt. He cut people off in meetings. He rejected suggestions or ideas for procedures that were not his own.

The other disciplines of molecular biology, pharmaceutical science, and clinical medicine felt that he failed to listen to their input. After extensive feedback from other people and through surveys, Frederick began to change the way he treated others. Making changes in this one specific arena caused his overall ratings to escalate to much higher levels. Conclusion: If you have a fatal flaw—fix it.

Frequency of Fatal Flaws and Strengths

In our research we discovered that nearly all leaders fall neatly and rather equally into three or four categories:

1. Those who possess one or more flaws—Our data confirms that 29 percent of all leaders fall in this category.
2. Those who have neither flaws nor strengths—Approximately 38 percent of leaders fit here.
3. Those who possess one or more strengths—Our data shows that 33 percent fall in this category.
4. Those who have both profound strengths and fatal flaws—Only 2 percent of leaders simultaneously have profound strengths and potential fatal flaws. These people are double counted because they have both fatal flaws and profound strengths.

Consequences of Fatal Flaws

Leaders with fatal flaws have the lowest employee engagement, customer satisfaction, employee retention, and productivity. Bottom line, the organization pays a high price for keeping them in leadership roles. And from a personal point of view, they have serious limitations on their career progress, along with having minimal enjoyment from their work.

Finding the Most Common Fatal Flaws

To understand what might cause people to fail, we analyzed results from two studies that used totally different approaches. In our first study, we collected 360-degree feedback data on more than 450 executives. Three years after the collection of that data, we found that 31 of the executives had seriously derailed to the point that they were asked to leave the company. We compared the results of the 31 failed leaders with the remainder of the data set to understand if there were early identifying signals that predicted their lack of success. Indeed, a clear set of factors emerged.

In the second study, we analyzed the 360-degree feedback data pertaining to more than 11,000 leaders and identified the bottom 10 percent and the bottom 1 percent of those leaders. We then looked for the largest differences between those who were perceived to be less effective and average leaders and another comparison with those at the 90th percentile or higher. Looking at the results of both studies, we found highly consistent themes. By combining the conclusions from these two studies, we were able to identify 10 fatal flaws that consistently contribute to a leader's failure.

Multiple Flaws

As we have worked with leaders over the years, we have found that while any single behavior can be fatal, some are more common than others. The purpose of this research was to identify those that were most common and noticeable. It appears they travel in groups of three or four. One problem usually creates other problems, which in turn causes many of the behaviors to appear to be linked.

Ten Fatal Flaws That Consistently Lead to Failure in Leadership

Following are the 10 most frequently identified failings that leaders displayed, listed in descending order of the frequency with which they were observed.

1. Not Inspiring Due to a Lack of Energy and Enthusiasm

The most noticeable difference in leaders that failed was their lack of energy and enthusiasm. One leader was described as "having the ability to suck all the energy out of any room." We all have periods of time when our energy is low and we are dragging, but their energy level stays low. Many were deliberately unenthusiastic and passive. Their lack of energy caused them to perceive any additional assignment or initiative as a huge burden.

Visualize a person that is floating on the sea with a life preserver that barely keeps his or her head out of the water. New initiatives, challenges, and changes are all like lead weights that drag the person underwater. Naturally, this person resists new and challenging assignments. The leader's lack of energy affects the whole team, including the boss and peers. This leader pushes hard for consistency, regularity, and conformity, which in the right circumstances can be good things. However, the leader's motive is to ensure not being overwhelmed or overburdened. Because such leaders fear having too much to do or being overwhelmed, they never volunteer and rarely make suggestions for change.

2. Accepting Mediocre Performance in Place of Excellent Results

This is another visible shortcoming and it has a high probability of leading to termination. When leaders fail to achieve agreed upon results, there is a high probability that an unpleasant conversation will follow. Every leader is clear about this, but what many leaders are not as clear about is their tolerance of mediocre performance. Some leaders find a way to sandbag their goals and targets, convincing their boss to agree to minimal expectations, to ensure they will be achieved. They justify this by repeating the phrase, "I believe in 'underpromising and overdelivering'!" These leaders have convinced themselves that their mediocre performance is completely acceptable and hence never look for opportunities to improve.

3. Lack of Clear Vision and Direction

Some leaders believe that their job is merely to execute the objectives of their organization and let other people deal with strategy, vision, and direction. They argue that their direct reports have all the necessary information to be fully productive. People know what to do and when to do it, they don't need to know why it's being done. But this leader fails to understand that subordinates, while not needing to know, want to know why something is required and how their work contributes to the success of the organization.

Much like a hiker who cautiously stays on the trail, everything is fine until there is a fork in the trail. Without a clear picture and insight into where the hike is going, the probability of success is reduced at each juncture.

Failure in this arena appears to have two components. It begins with the leader's murky view of the future and precisely what direction to take. It is compounded by the leader's unwillingness to take the time to communicate.

4. Loss of Trust Stemming from Perceived Bad Judgment and Poor Decisions

When leaders lose the trust of others, it becomes difficult for them to succeed. Loss of trust occurs several different ways. People begin to distrust a leader because of poor decisions. They also lose trust because promises made are not kept. Often, they feel that they were taken advantage of and misused.

Robert Galford and Anne Drapeau created a powerful formula to describe trust:[1]

$$\text{Trust} = \frac{\text{Credibility} + \text{Reliability} + \text{Intimacy}}{\text{Self-Interest}}$$

This formula expands the elements of trust and helps to explain why trust is so easily eroded. Credibility describes the degree to which people believe their leader to be technically competent and to have adequate knowledge about an issue. Reliability describes the consistency and predictability displayed by the leader. Intimacy defines the warmth and closeness of the relationship. (Trust diminishes when subordinates feel an icy, distant aura around the leader.) Finally, the formula suggests that the three main components all get divided by the self-interest displayed by the leader. If decisions are made for personal gain and glory, rather than the organization's welfare, then trust plummets.

5. Not Collaborative or a Team Player

Many of the leaders who derailed had a difficult time cooperating with other leaders. They viewed work as a competition and other leaders as opponents. Rather than developing positive relationships with peers, they avoided them and looked for ways to act independently. Their lack of collaboration caused them to be set adrift without the help or insights of others.

Virtually every study that has been conducted on the impact of competition versus collaboration has shown that competition loses. Why? Success in today's world demands the sharing of information and resources. Competition erodes and finally destroys that. Competition breeds suspicion and hostility that in turn actively discourage any sharing of information and resources. Furthermore, trying to do well for the overall organization and trying to beat an internal competitor are two totally different objectives. Both cannot be met at the same time.[2]

6. Not a Good Role Model (Failure to Walk the Talk)

A highly predictable path to failure is to behave in ways that are clearly opposite to the values and culture of the organization. Unfortunately, examples of this abound. The leader announces that everyone needs to control expenses and then proceeds to book the most expensive hotels and eat in the highest priced restaurants. Or the leader publicly declares that people are the most valuable asset and deserve to be treated with the greatest respect, and then proceeds to publicly berate a secretary to the point of tears. Beyond that, this is the leader who never thanks people for their contributions and hard work.

As a rule, organizations tend to choose as their leader a person who personifies the values of the organization. The leader of a street gang is chosen for being tough, fearless, and combative. The leaders of religious orders are chosen because they represent the values of the order—selflessness, compassion, service, and introspection. Similarly, we expect the leader of a business or public agency to represent the values it proclaims. When leaders fail to do that, this ultimately leads to their downfall.

7. No Self-Development and Learning from Mistakes

There is an extremely interesting body of research on derailed executives. Morgan McCall, Jr., and Michael Lombardo have written extensively regarding executives who were expected to go all the way to the top of their organizations, but who got derailed. These researchers compared those who were derailed with those whose careers took them to senior positions in their firms. Their findings contain some extremely valuable lessons. Derailed executives made about the same number of mistakes as did those whose careers continued onward and upward, but derailed executives did not use setbacks or failure as a learning experience. They hid their mistakes from others, not alerting colleagues to the consequences of how their mistake would affect the colleagues' activities. They did not take immediate steps to rectify what they had done. Finally, they tended to brood about the mistake, constantly reliving it for years afterward.[3]

Those whose careers continued to soar did exactly the opposite. They readily acknowledged what happened to those about them, alerted colleagues to the potential consequences, did their best to fix it, and then proceeded to forget about it and move on in their careers. Our research confirms that the inability to learn from mistakes is a major cause of failure. We can only speculate about the reasons for this. Is failure to learn from mistakes a symptom of not being willing or able to face reality because it is painful? Or is it symptomatic of arrogance and unwillingness to move across the emotional hurdle to accept the fact that "I" did something wrong? Or do these people genuinely not recognize the serious consequences of what they have done? ("That problem I had was no big deal. It doesn't really matter.") Or is it because they have never learned the skill of objectively analyzing their own behavior?

We know the reasons differ among people, but little research has been done on why some people learn from past experience, whereas others seem destined to repeat the same mistake over and over.

An executive with a brilliant mind and many accomplishments had one fatal flaw. He made quick decisions about people, dismissing some as being incompetent after a 20-minute interview.

Others were tagged as his "A" team because of one thing they had done or said. No amount of subsequent disconfirming information would change his mind. He selected one executive as his vice president of finance. Countless people in the organization warned the CEO of this person's reputation for backstabbing and sinister political behavior. Worse yet, this behavior was exactly the opposite of the culture the CEO was espousing that he wanted to create—a culture of openness, innovation, and trust. The pattern of hasty promotion decisions continued to other key appointments, with one mistake after another. Finally, the vice president of finance was successful in ousting the CEO, through an end run to the board. Several people commented, "We tried to tell him, but he would not listen."

8. Lacking Interpersonal Skills

This failure comes from two sources: sins of commission and sins of omission.

Sins of Commission. When leaders are abrasive, insensitive, browbeating, cold, arrogant, and bullying, this is a sure pattern that leads to failure in today's world. That behavior was often tolerated 50 years ago, but less often today. This cluster of behaviors, clearly interpersonal ineptness, is a major factor in the downfall of leaders. In the human resources profession there has been the saying, "We hire people for their technical competence and fire them for their interpersonal incompetence." No amount of other talent and ability is capable of surmounting this deficiency. No combination of intelligence, hard work, business acumen, and administrative skills covers over this lack of interpersonal skills. Being interpersonally bungling and ham-handed inevitably sinks leaders.

Sins of Omission. We are often stunned to see the number of people in middle-management positions in organizations who lack the most rudimentary of social skills. These basic human skills include:

- When you talk with people, look them in the eye.
- Learn and use people's names.
- When talking with people, say or do things that let the other person know you are listening and understanding.
- Do not dominate the conversation and take all the "air time."
- Sincerely inquire about others' ideas and activities.
- Laugh at others' jokes and attempts at humor.
- Praise others' hard work and efforts in furthering a good cause.
- Smile when meeting and greeting other people.

Many aspiring leaders fail to use these extremely fundamental interpersonal skills. Furthermore, these skills become the basic platform for the skills of leading group discussions designed to identify and resolve problems, giving and receiving feedback, coaching, making powerful presentations, and running effective work-team meetings.

9. Resistant to New Ideas, Thus Did Not Lead Change or Innovate

This cause of failure comes from rejecting suggestions from subordinates or peers, insisting on doing things the same old way, and being generally closed to new thinking. This is a major turnoff for subordinates. It produces two negative consequences.

One is the impact on subordinates. People feel ignored, their ideas unappreciated, and their contribution undervalued. This unwillingness to consider new ideas also creates a stultifying climate of stagnation. People's development is seriously curtailed. Morale degenerates, and turnover escalates.

A second consequence is that good ideas and solutions fail to get implemented. The organization becomes stuck. Because good ideas are squelched, people stop thinking about better ways to do things. The organization misses out on improvements that come from accepting new ideas from multiple sources. The total quality movement verified that the best ideas for process improvements came from the people who were working directly in that arena, not from outside experts.

Many consulting firms have developed a successful practice by interviewing employees and seeking their opinions about the serious issues the organization faces and what they would recommend as solutions. These ideas are then combined, bound into an expensive leather-bound report, and presented to upper management; the consulting firm then presents a hefty bill to the company for its services. The fact of the matter is that the employees would have been willing to tell the executives exactly the same things had they been asked. In fact, according to many we talk with, they have usually tried to pass on those messages, but no one was listening. Companies could improve the level of commitment of their workforce, get excellent ideas for improvement, and save a good deal of money if they would seek answers from their own people. Not doing so is a fatal flaw of leadership.

Many of us have worked for leaders whose automatic response to every idea or suggestion was a negative one. One company describes these people as their "abominable 'no' men." It is impossible to calculate the damage such a person does inside an organization, measured either in the number of good ideas that get permanently squelched or by the number of talented people who permanently exit the organization. They were completely turned off by this leader's behavior.

The one thing worse than a leader who constantly says "no" is the leader who pretends to listen and then does nothing about it. Pretending to listen raises the hopes of the employee, and these hopes are dashed when no action is taken. Leaders are often beset by twin demons—arrogance and complacency. The belief that your ideas are superior to everyone else's is an ultimate expression of arrogance. Unwillingness to listen to others' ideas and experiment with them is a further expression of arrogance. These leaders feel threatened by good ideas coming from others. Maybe they grew up with the mistaken assumption that because you have a formal title or role as the manager or director, it means you should have answers to all problems and that ideas for changes should all emanate from you.

Ralph was a senior executive in the research division of a semiconductor company. When anyone had an idea that was revolutionary or outside the normal way of doing things, they would go see Ralph. We asked why he thought that was the case, and he was exceedingly clear about the reasons. "I don't ever discourage a new idea. Ideas are tender and need to be nourished. So, I ask lots of questions and give the person encouragement to pursue it, unless I'm positive it won't work. If I have the slightest inkling it could succeed, I am enthusiastic about it. Over the years, that's paid off in some remarkable advancements."

10. Focus Is on Self, Not the Development of Others

In addition to being highly self-centered, these leaders perceive the development of their subordinates as an optional activity. It is "nice, when and if I have some time" but not a central part of their job. They assume that not spending time on the development of their direct reports does not and should not impact their own personal effectiveness.

The evidence, however, is very clear that those leaders who were not concerned about helping their direct reports develop and were not seen as coaches or mentors were more likely to fail. Clearly, they were primarily focused on themselves and were not concerned for the longer-term success of their employees, their department, or the organization.

What we know about leaders who are good at developing their direct reports is that they are able to generate a great deal of commitment and engagement by encouraging and supporting the development of others. The increased engagement typically raises the performance of the group. Building the capabilities of others also often allows leaders the opportunity to delegate challenging assignments. This provides the leader greater latitude to spend more time managing and leading the group. When people are learning and growing in their jobs, they feel positively about their work and their leader. Often, leaders who fail to focus on the development of their direct reports are primarily focused on their own career and their own success. They may even stoop to take credit for the accomplishments of their team. The disengagement of the team and lack of motivation by team members makes achieving difficult targets almost impossible.

What Fatal Flaws Have in Common

As we study these 10 patterns of behavior, three things stand out.

First, each is extremely obvious. They are observable by anyone with even the most casual of connections to the leader in question. Everyone close to these leadership behaviors feels their impact (or in many cases, their lack of impact). No one is immune. They have a huge influence on the organization because the leader has an enormous "ripple" effect in the organization.

Second, these fatal flaws tend to be mostly "sins of omission." Each case is marked primarily by an inability to do something. It is defined by failure to initiate activities, not discovering the causes of failure, ignoring obvious needs, not reaching out, not taking initiative, not seeking out new ideas, not connecting with people, and not exerting energy to make things happen. It could be summed up as complacency and general apathy. These are the people who are perceived as lukewarm and "blah" because they are not effective in making things happen.

Third, the fatal flaws are not intellectual deficiencies, but much more on the "emotional intelligence" or interpersonal side of the equation. These flaws arise from emotional and behavioral dimensions and seldom from a dearth of knowledge or technical incompetence. The person with these fatal flaws basically lacks the ability or discipline to initiate or get things going. In nearly every case, a serious effort to remedy that deficiency would result in some significant changes for the better.

One of the authors worked with a vice president of administration who had been responsible for all maintenance, new construction, personnel, public relations, and purchasing. He was a tyrannical leader and lacked effective interpersonal skills. His were the only "good ideas," and no one made suggestions for improvements because they were certain they would be "shot down." People inside his areas often used the phrase "Don't rock the boat." The result was the lack of any new initiatives.

One fascinating but tragic consequence was the devastating impact this person had on each of five subordinates. None was ever promoted. They had been so smothered by his leadership that they became incapable of taking initiative or embracing new ideas from other sources.

After the termination of the vice president and despite a new leader with a totally different approach, over the next two years each of the directors who reported to him ultimately resigned under some pressure or was terminated. They never recovered from their experience of working under this tyrant. This is an example of the grim impact of leaders with fatal flaws, and illustrates how fatal flaws often go together and amplify each other.

Why Are Fatal Flaws So Hard to Self-Detect?

Because most fatal flaws are sins of omission, they are harder to see in ourselves. The outcomes, after all, are not visible to the perpetrator. The flawed leader is not looking for or aware of the process improvement that never happens, or the project that never got off the ground. These leaders are simply not making things happen. They are not looking for what does not happen.

When they get their low scores back, these leaders often say something like: "But I've done nothing to deserve these ratings." To which their colleagues muse to themselves: "You are right. You've done nothing—and that's why you deserve these ratings."

There are some things anyone can do to identify fatal flaws. Start by finding a "truth teller," that honest friend who is a straight shooter. Our data confirm that there are usually several people who see the fatal flaw. Find a person who will tell the truth and let them know that you genuinely want their feedback.

If your company offers a 360-degree feedback process, volunteer to get involved. Ask to have a coach work with you. More and more organizations are recognizing the value of having their leaders spend time with a skilled, experienced coach. If that doesn't work, consider hiring outside help.

Can Fatal Flaws Be Fixed?

We all know the adage about not being able to teach old dogs new tricks. Luckily, that isn't true of humans. We recently analyzed a group of 545 leaders from three different organizations. Of the total group, 18 percent or 98 of them had a very low score (below the 10th percentile) on one or more competencies. When the total group was retested after 12 to 18 months, we found that 71 of the 98 showed significant improvement in the competency on which they received a low score. Their progress is summarized in Figure 7.2.

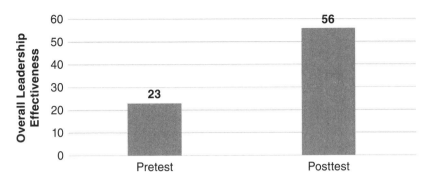

Figure 7.2. Fatal Flaws Can Be Overcome

Note the huge gains they made as a group. They moved from being below the 1st quartile in performance to now being above average, with a gain of 33 percentile points.

Fixing Fatal Flaws

If a leader possesses one or more of these characteristics, action should obviously be taken to remedy that deficiency, make that weakness irrelevant, or to move that person back into a role of being an individual contributor where that behavior is less necessary. (In fact, however, those 10 fatal flaws will also stand in the way of the "professional, individual contributor" being highly effective in the long run.)

People can overcome these characteristics. First, the organization can ensure that the person knows he or she possesses one of these "fatal flaws" and the serious career consequences the flaw will have. If willing to change, the person can often make significant contributions to the organization.

The organization usually has a sizable investment in this individual, and this now tests several fundamental convictions of the organization's leadership. These include:

- Can people really change?
- Are people truly valuable?
- Does the organization have a responsibility to help the person who is willing to change?
- Do people possess latent talents and abilities?
- Is it worth the organization's investment to help an individual fix a fatal flaw in their leadership skills?

We contend that the organization owes it to the leader to provide developmental experiences that will provide a positive path to remedy dysfunctional behavior. These may include external or internal programs or a coaching/mentoring relationship that provides ongoing feedback to help change the leader. Chapter 9 provides several avenues that could prove helpful to the individual wanting to change, and Part II of the book provides ways for the organization to help such leaders.

Prescription: Massive Doses of Feedback

This is a perfect use of the 360-degree feedback process. Once it has been established that a leader has a major deficiency in one of the areas described above, it should be made clear to the leader that change would be of benefit both personally and to the organization.

One powerful strategy is to indicate that 12 to 18 months from now, we will do a follow-up round of 360-degree feedback instruments with the subordinates and peers, and the expectation is that these areas will be remedied. The setting of a clear expectation for change, and the creation of a powerful sense of urgency about it, is the most likely way to erase fatal flaws.

Why Feedback Works

Inside everyone's head is a picture of how they see themselves. It describes what sort of person they are, what values they possess, their overall pattern of behavior, and sums up the image they have of themselves. In most cases, the leader with a fatal flaw is totally unaware both of the nature of the flaw, as well as it being fatal. For example, leaders who immediately reject others' ideas would in great likelihood describe themselves as being full of confidence and having such extensive experience that they know what ideas will succeed and which will fail. Such individuals are usually unaware of the perception that they reject everyone else's ideas. How can that be changed?

Feedback in the form of coaching, team discussions, or 360-degree feedback surveys (if honest and direct) provides "disconfirming information." The messages conveyed would be contrary to this leader's self-perceptions. This creates a dilemma and forces some action. The leader now has one of several choices to make.

First, the leader can deny the information. But if it comes from multiple sources that are clearly reliable and have no personal axe to grind, it becomes extremely difficult to deny this consistent pattern of feedback.

Second, the leader can choose to change his or her self-concept, saying to themselves, "Well, okay, I guess I am arrogant and think my ideas are the only good ones that exist." For the person possessing some general health of character and personality, this self-concept is unacceptable and illogical.

Third, the person can change behavior. For most people faced with a barrage of disconfirming information, the easiest course of action is to act differently. That is the power of feedback.

Clearly, some fatal flaws will be specific to the position the person occupies. For example, the director of research and development will not usually survive unless he is perceived as being highly technically competent. The head of sales will not survive if she is perceived as lacking important interpersonal skills. A partner in a CPA firm will not survive, regardless of how good an auditor he is, if he fails to take the initiative to generate revenue and develop customer relationships. In these cases, the person does not always need to transform the weakness into a strength, but the behavior needs to be taken from the liability column and made into a neutral characteristic at worst.

Different Responses to Feedback

People respond differently to feedback. That is something we have all observed. The work of one researcher may shed light on those differences. Tory Higgins, chairman of the Department of Psychology at Columbia University, has been honored for his distinguished contributions to the field of social psychology. His research concludes that people fall into one of two camps in their fundamental orientation on how they regulate their behavior. The first orientation is toward achieving positive outcomes. He labeled this a "promotion" orientation. This group wants to make positive things happen. Their focus is on achievement.[4]

Promotion Orientation
Higgins concludes from his research that this group of individuals is highly motivated by positive feedback. It reinforces that they accomplished what they set out to do. Positive feedback means that others have noticed what they did. Their intention to produce something or complete

a project met with success. Positive feedback is the reward for doing that. In the parlance of investing, this group sees success as achieving big gains. Yes, there might be periodic losses, but so long as the gains are there in the long run, the short-term losses are quite acceptable.

These people are devastated by negative feedback. It wounds their self-esteem. Their intention to do something worthwhile has not been recognized or their efforts were a failure. Negative feedback is exactly what they did not want to hear, and thus it becomes highly demotivating to them. They pull back and become deflated by criticism.

Prevention Orientation

The second group of people has a "prevention orientation." Their primary objective in life is to avoid negative outcomes. Averting failure is what life is about. The way to avoid failure is constantly to monitor what you do, and instantly head off any impending mistake or omission. Thus, someone mentioning to you that there is an error in your draft of a report to upper management is greatly appreciated. That enables you to avoid looking bad to those receiving the report.

As investors, this group is in the camp of "Don't lose anything." Success means never having a stock go down. It is perfectly all right not to have spectacular gains, or even gains that mirror the performance of the overall market, so long as nothing is lost.

Feedback for People with a Prevention Orientation

Any information that alerts this person to an impending problem or difficulty would be sought after and greatly appreciated. Individuals in this group welcome what others might see as "negative feedback."

In contrast, this group is not enthralled with positive feedback. For these individuals, it comes across at worst as phony and hollow praise; or at best as fairly useless. Positive feedback does not help the individual steer clear of failures, so it has little value.

The takeaway here is that one kind of feedback may be extremely helpful to some people, whereas it may be irritating to others. Much of that has to do with their orientation to life. Be aware that two people may respond very differently to exactly the same feedback based on their life-orientation.

Fatal Flaws in the Prevention Camp

Those people we described earlier with fatal flaws may be in either the prevention or promotion camp. For those in the prevention camp, their behavior is almost always characterized by a lack of openness to new ideas, because new ideas are risky. There is a much greater possibility of mistakes happening when you try something new, so they are thinking, "Reject new processes or approaches as long and hard as you can." Or, as one wag observed, "It is a good idea, but it is a new idea, and because it is a new idea, I must reject it."

Those in the prevention orientation group would also like to be divorced from any accountability, because that way they can avoid the negative outcomes attendant with poor performance. Their position: "Never have your fingerprints on a project that might fail." "Always get someone in between you and a risky program, so that if it does not work out, you can blame them." Much of life is spent in following the maxim: "It doesn't matter whether you win or lose, it's how you place the blame." They want someone to be the scapegoat in case of failure.

Finally, this group does not initiate new projects or programs. Why? The less you do, the less likelihood there is for error. The more things you get under way, the greater the chances are for something to go wrong. So, the key is to do as little as possible and survive. Keep your head down. Don't draw attention. Don't rock the boat. That is success. If someone gives me information that helps me to avoid failure, then I am forever grateful.

Higgins' research sheds light on why people respond so differently to feedback and helps all leaders to be clearer about the right type of feedback to give to others, depending on their basic orientation to life.

Another social psychologist, then at Columbia University and now teaching at Stanford, Carol Dweck, conducted extensive research with schoolchildren and developed a framework with some similarities to that of Higgins. Her research on feedback sheds further, but consistent, light on this fascinating topic.

Dweck's research showed that people fell into two categories that she called "improving" and "proving." The first category, "improving," views the world as an opportunity to learn and grow. Problems they encounter that are hard or highly time consuming are welcomed because that means they can "improve" themselves. Mistakes are viewed as useful feedback.[5]

The "proving" group of people view life as a process of justifying or proving themselves to others, particularly those in authority. Therefore, problems that are hard or time consuming become a threat because they show that the person was not as capable as others had thought. These people, therefore, tend to shrink away from difficult tasks and revert to tasks that are easily accomplished. They develop a helpless and dependent behavior.

We find much consistency between these two research models. The "improving" and "promotion" orientations seem quite analogous. Likewise, the "proving" and the "prevention" orientations seem similar. Dweck's research focused on the right and wrong kinds of feedback to give to anyone. It did not distinguish the feedback that would be more appropriate for one group than another.

Dweck concluded that the wrong feedback to give was anything that was global, was general, or could be construed simply as praise. If a well-meaning parent tells a child, "You are really smart" or "You are a gifted student," what is that child to think when a week later he is in agony in a class in which the teacher has given him a problem he cannot solve? Or, what is the employee to think after a manager has told her what an intelligent and talented employee she is, and now she has been given a report to write and she simply is not making any progress on it?

On the other hand, think of the positive outcomes from the parent who tells the child, "I really admire how hard you've worked on learning the multiplication tables" or "You have really been creative about looking for different ways to get the information for your term paper. When you combine that with how tenacious you have been, I know you will come up with a good paper."[6]

Or, consider the leader who tells a subordinate, "I want to compliment you on how hard you have been working and at your ability to overcome the obstacles in your path on this project. The progress you have made is a reflection on your focused effort."

The difference in these two approaches may seem subtle to some, but they are extreme opposites. The first is focused on the person and his or her innate abilities. The second approach is focused on the process he or she has used to tackle a project or a problem. That focus may be on the intensity of the effort, or on the innovative approaches to it, or on the ability to overcome obstacles, or it could be on the ability not to be distracted by other things. The benefit of the second approach is that anytime later, if this person is feeling a challenge in solving a problem or completing a project, his or her thought processes will be different. The question will not be, "Did my parent (or my boss) lie to me about being so capable?"

Instead, the thought process after the second pattern of feedback will be, "Maybe I'm not working hard enough." "Perhaps I haven't been innovative in looking for other ways to solve this problem." "I need to work harder to overcome some of the barriers that exist in our systems here." In short, the focus is now on the process that is being used, not on his or her fundamental intelligence or worth as a person.

These two bodies of research on feedback have given us better ways to understand the different reactions to the same feedback and also provide a good template for a better approach to giving feedback. First, examine the nature of the individual and whether positive or negative feedback will be of most value. Second, whatever the person is like, keep feedback focused on the behavior or process the person is using and not on him or her as a person. These two powerful ideas greatly enhance our understanding of the feedback process and how it can help leaders overcome fatal flaws.

Steps in Fixing Fatal Flaws

There are five steps to fixing a fatal flaw.

Step 1: Face Reality by Getting Accurate Feedback

Get honest and accurate feedback from people you trust.

Step 2: Accept How It Impacts Your Career

The second step is for people to accept the fact that they have a fatal flaw and that the flaw will eventually be fatal to their career (if it has not held them back already). Until a person acknowledges there's a significant negative impact that comes from the flaw, nothing will change.

Step 3: Create a Specific and Measurable Plan for Change

Once people understand a problem sufficiently, the next step is to formulate a plan for change. The plan should lay out goals and activities that will demonstrate a significant change to others. One of the major failings in generating a plan is that people start with a general notion of change, but in order for change to occur, it needs to be very specific.

Step 4: Seek the Help and Involvement of Others

Often people work on improving their fatal flaws without telling others of their plans or enlisting their help. Sometimes people are embarrassed by the fatal flaw. They believe that telling others they are working on change and asking for their assistance is a sign of weakness. The reality is that everyone is probably well aware of the problem. By enlisting help from others, the person will feel supported and uplifted from the ideas and encouragement they receive. They will also feel a greater sense of accountability to change since others are involved.

Step 5: Reward Progress

An important aspect of the change process that is often overlooked is to find a way to reward yourself for your progress and for achieving the goal.

Time for Your Check-Up?

The great benefit of periodic physical exams is that they discover a condition we didn't know about. Caught early, these problems can often easily be corrected.

We think every leader should have a periodic checkup on their leadership health. Everyone benefits. Roughly a third will be surprised to learn that some behavior is holding them back. Only by discovering what it is can they fix it. The rest will get a few tips to make them even better.

In conclusion we invite the reader to consider the following: Remembering that roughly one-third of leaders have a fatal flaw, if you are sitting in a management meeting, we invite you to look to your right and then to your left. Then, as the old joke goes, if in your opinion neither of these two colleagues has a really serious weakness, then statistical logic suggests there is a strong likelihood that you are the one.

8

ALTERNATIVE PATHS FOR LEADERSHIP DEVELOPMENT

*I dreamed a thousand new paths. I
woke and walked my old one.*
—CHINESE PROVERB

*There are always many choices, many paths to take.
One is easy. And its only reward is that it's easy.*
—ANONYMOUS

Warfare through the 1700s to the middle of the nineteenth century was characterized by rows of soldiers marching straight toward their enemy. The opposing forces would do the same. Despite the fact that cannons and rifles being fired straight at them would kill thousands, it was not until the American Revolution that this pattern was challenged. When American revolutionary soldiers fought the British, they hid behind trees, lay prone on the ground to avoid being easy targets, and fought an entirely different type of war. In this chapter, we propose a similarly radical approach to developing leadership skills. Rather than continuing the "frontal assault" approach that has been popular for so long, we propose a different way to attack the problem.

Discovering Alternative Paths for Development

Suppose that in an effort to improve your leadership effectiveness you wanted to improve your professional or technical expertise. Think about an action plan that you might formulate to accomplish the goal of improved technical/professional expertise. Write down the actions that you would take to improve. Then, thinking about your own plan, look at Table 8.1 to see how your plan compares with ones we have seen from many others facing this challenge.

Table 8.1. Sample Action Plan

One Person's Plan of Action	
Action Number	Action to Improve Technical and Professional Expertise
1	Sign up for a night class at the local university
2	Attend more professional conferences and workshops
3	Read technical and professional journals
4	Broaden network with other professionals and ask for coaching and mentoring on specific topics
5	Read latest books in the technical and professional fields
6	Get on a task force that will stretch current knowledge and expertise
7	Find some training courses that will increase depth of knowledge

Table 8.1 is a classic, linear plan. We define that as a plan that plots a straight-line development path from the current performance to a desired future state. It is a typical frontal assault. It is also extremely logical and characteristic of many people's propensity to identify a problem or challenge, put their heads down, and run straight at it with full force. This plan works especially well in circumstances where a person's performance is poor and the need for substantial improvement is clear.

In a recent conference with professionals in employee development from several different companies, we asked representatives what percentage of the action plans made by individuals were linear. Their answer was that virtually all action plans are based on a linear logic. We then asked when the linear plans worked best. Again, a consistent answer from all participants: "Linear plans work best for people who are moving from poor performance to good performance." But what about the situation where a person's performance is good and the individual is trying to move to a higher level of performance? Will the approach that helps people move from bad to good be as effective in moving from good to extraordinary?

Case Study. Jane Larson was a project leader in an exploration department of a major oil company. Her career had progressed nicely, but for the past two years she felt her career had stalled. Six months ago, she participated in a 360-degree feedback process that provided her with an assessment on a series of competencies. To her surprise, she was rated lower than the average of her colleagues on technical expertise. In this organization, the one quality that is highly valued is technical expertise. To Jane, these results were a blatant wake-up call, and so she decided to make a significant change. Even though she felt fairly current, she decided to rededicate herself and broaden her understanding of related fields. She attended a technical conference, read every journal from cover to cover, and started an independent research project with a university. To get a sense of how all this work was helping, she asked her manager to have a career discussion with her. In the discussion she described all of her efforts to hone her skills and build a broader knowledge base. Her manager was pleased with all her efforts, but then she asked the critical question: "Do you think that all this work will help others see that I have a great deal of technical knowledge and expertise?" Her manager sat back in his seat and paused to prepare his answer carefully. "Well, Jane, I don't know if any of this is ever going to make any difference until you have the guts to speak up in a meeting and share your knowledge with people. The problem isn't how much you know, it's what you do with what you know!"

Jane Larson is a good example of a linear action plan (see Figure 8.1, on the next page) not being sufficient, and sometimes not helpful at all. In reality, Jane did not need to take additional classes, read journals better, or do more research. Her problem was that she failed to share her knowledge and expertise with others. The perceptions of others were based on the behavior she demonstrated to them rather than the knowledge that she had packed in her head. In reality, others cannot tell how much she knows if she does not share the information.

Nonlinear Development Paths

Since almost all development plans are linear (because that is the prevailing logic), we looked for a technique to help people understand alternative development paths. In our approach, we took each of the 19 differentiating behaviors and analyzed the relationship between that specific behavior and the other 18, plus a number of other behaviors. When an individual showed a high level of competence on a specific behavior, we identified

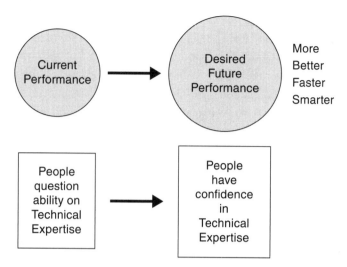

Figure 8.1. Current Approach to Change Plans

the other behaviors that were also highly rated. Then we analyzed leaders who were rated poorly on that differentiating behavior and discovered that the same companion behaviors were also rated poorly.

We call these related behaviors "competency companions." They are companions because they seem to be permanently glued together. In the spirit of Sherlock Holmes, we believe that these competency companions provide excellent clues about an alternative way to develop important leadership skills—and to improve the likelihood that you will be perceived by those about you as possessing an important, differentiating competency.

Figure 8.2 provides two examples of competency companions associated with technical expertise. Leaders perceived as having the best technical expertise were also perceived as having high competence in interpersonal skills and setting high standards of excellence. Also, those perceived as having the worst technical expertise typically had poor interpersonal skills and set lower standards of performance.

If you conclude from this analysis that having excellent interpersonal skills causes a person to have technical expertise, you are probably wrong. Just because two events consistently happen together does not prove that one causes the other. But much of science has to rely on the fact that when two phenomena are consistently linked together, you make the presumption that one of them causes the other, that each has some impact

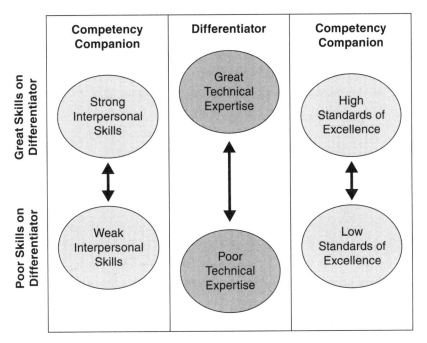

Figure 8.2. Influence of Competency Companions

on the other, or that they are both being influenced by some other common force.

In a college course on statistics, the professor was attempting to explain the purpose of statistics, particularly correlation coefficients. He chose as an example a phenomenon in nature. He said, "There is an extremely high correlation between the frequency of crickets chirping and the temperature." There was a pause. A student raised his hand and said, "Professor Peterson, are you saying that as the temperature rises, crickets chirp more frequently?" With a totally deadpan expression on his face, Professor Peterson replied, "No, I have always assumed that when crickets chirp more frequently, it causes the outdoor temperature to rise."

Most people would have an explanation for the relationship of temperature and crickets chirping, and this could easily be proved by simple experiments. However, in many situations, when two things happen together, the mechanisms that link them together are not entirely clear. All you can say is that they occur together, and you can make some educated guess about the cause-and-effect relationship that links them together.

The Link Between Interpersonal Relationships and Technical Competence

To return to our example of technical expertise and interpersonal skills being tied together, we could offer some explanations. This result is strongly supported by ground-breaking research done by Robert Kelley at Bell Labs. The research looked at the productivity of scientists. After studying hundreds of scientists, all of whom were experts in their fields, the researchers found that the engineers who were most successful (they dubbed them their "stars") were not those with the highest IQs or those who were the most knowledgeable. Kelley wrote, "Our data showed no appreciable cognitive, personal, psychological, social or environmental differences between stars and average performers."[1] What they found was that these stars performed their work differently. They developed strong networks within the organization and worked with others in a totally different manner than did the "non-stars."

To elaborate, some of the interpersonal skills identified in the Bell Labs research were behaviors such as:

- Helping colleagues solve a problem
- Helping others to complete a task
- Giving others credit for any success
- Expressing a desire to hear others' ideas
- Not imposing their ideas on others
- Being concerned with coworkers' personal needs
- Using the skills of coworkers
- Working quietly, without fanfare
- Putting the objectives of the team before their own[2]

For those who have worked in technical organizations, there is another reason why it comes as no surprise to find that there is a relationship between technical expertise and interpersonal skills. It relates to the way the "stars" communicated about technical issues.

We have observed that the most able technical people have sufficient confidence to express complex ideas in lay terms and not hide behind jargon. Insecure scientists are afraid to expose the fact that their discipline is not as precise as others are led to believe. To be perceived as being highly technically competent demands a person who can communicate effectively about their discipline to many groups.

What Happens When Interpersonal Skills and Technical Competence Are Not Connected?

Recently, one of the authors was having dinner with a friend who is currently a university president. A question was asked about what kind of interesting activities filled his day. He commented, "Well, today I had to fire a professor." Someone at the table asked, "Why? What rules did he break? Was he incompetent?" "No, he was not incompetent!" replied the president. "He was very current in his field. The problem was that no one in his department could remember a staff meeting that he attended that did not end in an argument. He was absolutely impossible to get along with and created so much friction in the department that nothing was getting done." In this case, the professor's lack of interpersonal skills made the professor's technical competence irrelevant. It ceased to matter. People no longer paid attention to his technical competence.

In another situation, we were working with the management of a chemical company research laboratory. Their work was highly specialized work and they had recruited absolutely the brightest and best scientists in the world. The productivity of the lab had come under considerable scrutiny. To understand better what some of the problems were with this group, many of the scientists were interviewed. In an interview with one of the leading scientists, the interviewer asked him to describe a typical technical review. Each of the scientists was asked to present new research studies before all the scientists for their review. The interviewer asked, "Are the technical reviews helpful?"

The scientist replied, "Not at all."

"Why?" the interviewer asked.

"Because when new scientists present their ideas for a new area of study they aren't asking for input, they are just showing off how much they know. Several times I have listened to scientists talk about research that we have already determined is never going to work. We have tried the same experiments before. They always fail. But rather than help this idiot out, we just sit back and inwardly grin because we know that they will fail. By letting them work on this research it just helps my work to look even better and gives me a lot better chance of getting a big bonus." The scientists in the lab were competing against each other for recognition, rewards, and promotions.

Here again, the lack of effective interpersonal skills seriously erodes the perceived technical competence of this laboratory. We estimate that this culture, with high scientific and low interpersonal effectiveness, was costing the company millions of dollars each year. The number could be in the billions if the comparison is made to what that group of scientists could have created, had they created a high-performance work environment.

Having strong interpersonal skills does not help people become any smarter, but it does help them to share the knowledge that they have, influence others effectively, communicate the things that they know, and build collaborative, trusting relationships with others.

The Link Between Having High Standards and Technical Competence

Similarly, having high standards of excellence does not make people smarter, but if you apply the logic of the S. Rosenberg et al. research presented in Chapter 3, a good explanation emerges. Recall that the research showed that the following adjectives were clustered together in people's minds:

- Scientific
- Persistent
- Skillful
- Imaginative
- Intelligent

We submit, then, that in most people's perceptions, the qualities of technical competence (scientific and intelligent) and high standards of excellence (persistence and skillful) are also linked together. If I see you display one, I assume you have the other.

Therefore, by championing extremely high standards for every activity, I have subtly caused others to have an elevated view of my technical competence. Certainly, on the flip side, a person with minimal technical competence would never impose lofty standards of excellence on a team or on colleagues. Similarly, the leader who remarks, "Oh, I don't care if we finish on time," or "Let's not bust our tails on this project," is not a person we assume has great technical credentials or ability.

What Are Competency Companions?

Competency companions (or behavioral buddies) are simply best friends. They tend to go everywhere together. When people are effective at one of the 19 key differentiating behaviors, they tend to do the companion behaviors equally well. Conversely, when people are ineffective at a differentiating behavior, they tend to perform the companion behaviors poorly. We discovered these competency companions by analysing data from thousands of leaders. These competency companions were not derived by intuition and logic but rather purely by analysis of large data sets. To verify these companion behaviors we utilized a variety of different data sets from with unique items. Again, we are not implying that one behavior causes the other. Later in this chapter, we provide our analysis of various reasons for why the linkage occurs.

Competency companions provide excellent clues for making significant improvements on a differentiating behavior. People need to examine their level of competence on a differentiating behavior and then review each competency companion. They can examine situations from their own experience when poor performance on a competency companion affected the perception of their ability in the differentiating behavior. The question to ask is, "If I were to improve my performance on competency companion A, would it improve my performance on the differentiating competency B, or at least would it enhance the perceptions of others regarding my ability on differentiating competency B?" Looking for situations or past experiences where two behaviors might have been linked will help people to identify a competency companion that may be the key to developing extraordinary talent on a differentiating behavior.

Mechanisms of Competency Companions

Why do competency companions leverage improvement in certain behaviors? We believe that there are a variety of reasons for the impact that is evident when both the competency and the competency companion are rated positively. We are clear that there are different mechanisms creating the impact. The following is a list of six mechanisms that we believe best explain the competency companion phenomena:

1. The competency and the competency companion fit together in people's perceptual systems. The Rosenberg research previously

referenced in Chapter 3 found that certain characteristics fit together in most people's minds. If you have attribute A, people assume you have attribute B. If they know you don't have attribute B, they question if you could possibly have attribute A. Therefore, the first explanation of why competency companions create impact is that perceptually people believe these characteristics fit together, and improving one helps create the perception that the other is more positive.

2. Competency companions facilitate the expression of another competency. Consider the linkage between interpersonal skills and technical skills. What appears to be happening is that having strong interpersonal skills facilitates the sharing of knowledge, the persuasion of others to a new position, and positive interactions in terms of solving problems. We do not believe that improving interpersonal skills makes technical knowledge grow or makes a person smarter. It is possible that because of good interpersonal skills, a person may choose to coach and mentor colleagues. This may improve actual technical ability. For the most part, however, the impact of interpersonal skills on technical ability seems to be that it facilitates the communication of technical knowledge and enhances the appreciation other people have of a person's technical skills. When Jane speaks up in meetings, others start to see how smart and capable she is, and their perception of her technical ability goes up.

3. Achieving a high level of skill in one behavior helps develop a related behavior. For example, one of the strongest competency companions for "developing other people" is being skilled and interested in developing yourself. If leaders do not have a good career plan for themselves, it is most difficult to assist their direct reports in creating career plans. If people feel stuck in their careers with no place to go, it is harder for them to be of much assistance to others. However, if leaders learn to develop their own careers, that will be an invaluable start to assisting others with the same process.

4. One competency is a building block or a core element of the other competency. One of the most interesting competency companionships that we found related to integrity. A strong companion behavior to integrity is concern and consideration for other people. Simply put, those perceived with high integrity

have a high level of concern and consideration for others, and those perceived with low integrity lacked consideration for others. Consideration for others is a vital component of the broader competency labelled "integrity." A person who has no problems taking advantage of another person lacks integrity.

5. Competency companions change the context in which we operate. We found a strong relationship between a person's ability to communicate and the extent to which a person is trusted. Typically, when people attempt to improve their ability to communicate, they focus on the message and the delivery (e.g., what they say and how they say it). This research indicates that if people trust a leader, then the leader does not need to give a world-class speech. The fact that people have a great deal of trust in the leader will cause the message to be accepted. Without trust, however, no amount of great oration can make people accept the message.

6. Developing a competency companion changes the person. Most people have had the experience of dramatically changing a skill and then finding interesting side effects. Learning to play golf well gives a person increased confidence. A regular exercise program makes a person less stressed. Focusing effort on accomplishing a stretch goal causes depression to go away. Strengthening a competency has the capacity to change a person's perspective, attitudes, and outlook on life.

Examples of Competency Companions

We have found that for each competency, there are 8 to 14 competency companions. It is beyond the scope of this book to provide an exhaustive list of every competency companion, but we provide here a few examples of the 19 differentiating competencies. We have organized these into the five elements in our leadership model. We have compiled a complete guide of competency companions. For further information on this guide and how it is used to develop leaders, contact the authors by going to www.zengerfolkman.com.

Character—the Center Pole of the Leadership Tent

Improving Integrity. When characterizing people with low integrity, we visualize a person who purposely tries to take advantage of other people.

However, many people who experience integrity problems don't always fit that mold.

Sean was a bright and very honest young man from a foreign country. He was very religious and was in his final year of school in the United States. In his home country, his family was well known. He was approached by a group of investors and offered a very good salary to go back to his home country and sell his fellow citizens on an investment opportunity. The men who approached Sean were regular churchgoers, and so he assumed that they would be able to deliver on this investment. He trusted these men, so he did not ask many questions or check out the viability of the investment. Because of the reputation of his family, Sean was very successful in signing up millions in investments. After a short time an initial payment was made to investors. That money was distributed to each investor. A short time later, Sean learned that the investment scheme had failed. He was left holding the bag.

Many other people report an experience similar to Sean's. They do not intentionally attempt to deceive other people, but in the end their integrity is compromised. They trust another person but fail to aggressively ensure that promises made by others will be kept. When we looked at the competency companions to integrity, we found that those rated high in integrity were also rated high on assertiveness. Those rated low in integrity, on the other hand, were rated low on assertiveness. Those with high integrity were very effective at stepping forward and addressing difficult issues, confronting conflict, being direct, and facing up to difficult situations.

Personal Capability—the Second Pole Lifting the Leadership Tent

Becoming a Better Problem Solver. What if a person wanted to improve in problem-solving skills? Obviously, that improvement could be in the way they are perceived, or in actually improving those skills—and hopefully both. We examined the competency companions for effective problem solving and analytical skills. We found that one of the highest correlates was initiative. People perceived as being good problem solvers and highly analytical were also perceived as taking a great deal of initiative. Those perceived as poor problem solvers were perceived as not taking initiative.

Robert Kelley describes initiative as the most important work strategy in separating the "stars" from the rest of the pack at Bell Labs. He illustrates his point by describing two new hires, both with similar credentials: 3.8 GPAs from respected universities, strong summer internships at computer companies, and lustrous recommendations from professors.

Henry holed himself up in his office as if he were writing his dissertation or studying for a bar exam. He collected volumes of technical documents to acquaint himself with the latest ideas. He began learning how to use exotic software programs he thought might be helpful in his work. He would surface only for a bathroom break or a mandatory staff meeting. "What's going to count," he remembers thinking at the time, "is whether I can prove to my coworkers how smart I am."

Lai set aside three hours each afternoon to work on her assignment. In whatever time was left of her workday, she introduced herself to coworkers and asked questions about their projects. If one of them needed a hand or faced schedule pressures, she volunteered to help. And even though Lai was new to the workplace culture, her colleagues appreciated her willingness to help them out, especially given that their problems were not hers.

Kelley continues describing Lai's actions:

- She found a colleague who could not get a software program to work, and Lai recalled a new programming tool she had picked up in an advanced course in college and offered that solution to the colleague. She offered to work on the software problem while the colleague finished the larger project.
- When new software tools needed to be installed on everyone's computers, the assumption was that everyone would use the traditional approach of installing it themselves, largely by trial and error. Lai had installed the software during her internship and thought it made more sense for one person to move up the learning curve and do it for everyone. She volunteered. It ended up taking two weeks, instead of the four days she had estimated, but she stuck it out and completed all of the installations.
- A colleague who had been scheduled for an all-night lab testing session was suddenly called away to a funeral for a family member. When the manager convened a meeting to see how this absence could be covered, there was much looking at the floor and "covering your face" behavior. As the supervisor was about to make an arbitrary assignment to some unwilling person, Lai volunteered. She later recalls, "I figured that it was most important to get accepted into the team, and what better way than to help them out."

Lai was on her way to becoming a "star" in the Bell Labs vernacular. It had little to do with being technically competent but everything to do with taking initiative. Kelley writes, "Average performers—who constitute 60 to 80 percent of the workforce—don't get it. That group is most likely to view initiative taking as activity for activity's sake, getting stuck doing someone else's work, or taking on work that is not part of their job description. Cynical average performers see it as kissing up to the boss or colleagues."

It might surprise readers to know that Henry, the loner Bell Labs hire, believed he was taking initiative. "I gathered up the latest technical information and learned about the latest software tools so that I could do a bang-up job on my assignment. Nobody told me to do any of that," he told the researchers. What Lai understood and Henry did not is that only certain actions earn the initiative label.[3]

How Do I Improve My Effectiveness in Developing Myself?

A key skill for all successful leaders is the ability to continuously improve themselves. Too often, leaders achieve some office or position and then come to believe that the learning phase of their career is over. They assume that, like graduation from school, there is a time of learning and a time of execution. Our research pointed out the importance of continuous self-improvement in order for leaders to become exceptional. Looking at those who showed great ability to practice self-development, we found a strong relationship with integrity. That is, people who were viewed as highly competent in terms of developing themselves were also viewed as being extremely honest and straightforward. At first glance, the two behaviors seem unrelated. What does self-development have to do with integrity and honesty?

Consider, however, the research done in helping people overcome alcoholism and drug addiction. One of the major hurdles in getting help for people to deal successfully with addiction is getting them to acknowledge that they have a problem. Alcoholics in the early stages are inevitably in denial. An alcoholic who showed up for addiction counseling was asked, "Why are you here?" He answered, "Because my spouse thinks I have a drinking problem." To which the counselor replied, "Go home and keep drinking. I can't help you until you think that you have a problem." In most cases of drug and alcohol addiction, it becomes evident to everyone else that the person has a problem before it becomes evident to the person himself or herself. Frequently, you hear the stories about people who have to hit rock bottom before they finally wake up and say to themselves, "I have a drinking problem." In many addiction treatment programs, people use the practice of introducing themselves by saying, "My name is John, and I am an alcoholic."

Honesty is a striking feature of the relationship between self-development and integrity. People who are good at self-development have the ability to evaluate their strengths and weaknesses honestly and to acknowledge their strengths in behavior A and that they are less effective in behavior B. Keep in mind that for some people, their problem is their lack of faith in their strengths. They discount their own abilities. People who are poor at self-development might be rationalizing their performance in less than objective ways. They tell themselves that they did a good job when they did a poor job. They ignore feedback from others. They debate the reactions of others, saying, "They are only saying that because they are out to get my job, or they are jealous of my abilities." There are levels of self-honesty. Some people come to accept the feedback others give them but still resist being perfectly honest with themselves about what they do well and problems that need to be improved. Being absolutely honest with one's self and refusing the opportunity for self-deceit is a key skill for extraordinary leaders.

How Can I Become More Innovative?

An examination of the competency companions for innovation found that innovative leaders were also good at learning from both their successes and failures. At first blush, this again seems like an unlikely combination. Most think of innovation as the ability to produce creative ideas and to get those ideas implemented. Learning, on the other hand, is the ability to absorb new information, to recognize patterns, to see cause-and-effect relationships—all ultimately culminating in new behavior.

We think it is probable that those who are not innovative have lost some ability to learn. They aren't paying attention to what is transpiring in their environment. They rationalize rather than change their behavior. Good learners carefully observe their environment, they study how things happen, and they are inquisitive about cause-and-effect relationships. A key to being innovative is increasing one's ability to learn.

Focus on Results—Another Pole Lifting the Tent

Helping Others Achieve Exceptional Results. The ability to set stretch goals is a critical skill that helps motivate people to achieve exceptional results. As one of the 19 differentiating behaviors, setting stretch goals is a behavior that is easy to talk about but harder to do. Some propose a simple path: develop what you think is a reasonable goal, then multiply by two. In the end, many leaders back off because they are uncomfortable asking others to take on a task that they themselves view as unreasonable or impossible. The first step in setting stretch goals is for you to believe in the stretch capacity of people.

We found that leaders who were effective at setting stretch goals were also effective at risk taking. It appears that leaders who are willing to challenge the status quo and take risks also have the ability to convince their work group that they can achieve an almost impossible goal. People who play it safe, carefully analyze what is possible, and take baby steps forward will never be very effective at setting stretch goals.

How Do You Get Others to Feel Responsible?

Frequently, parents struggle with children in school who forget assignments, fail to study for tests, and seem unmotivated to improve their performance. Parents often comment, "Why can't my children just be more responsible?" The implicit theory is that if people have responsible attitudes, they will act responsibly.

Recently, a daughter was struggling in school. I had a fatherly discussion with her and asked her to describe the problem. "I'm depressed," she said. "And I can't concentrate on my homework if I am depressed" was her excuse. She was obviously discouraged. In my opinion, most of her discouragement came from failing some exams in school. I challenged her to go to work and study in spite of feeling discouraged. Knowing she would probably need more than a pep talk to succeed, I arranged a tutor to meet with her several times a week. The tutor provided both knowledgeable advice and friendly support. Soon the daughter's grades started to improve. As her grades improved, her depression went away. Once her study habits had changed and she felt more confident that she could be successful, she started to act substantially more responsibly. Rather than go out with friends, she would say, "Sorry, I have homework."

Sometimes attitudes do precede actions, but more often, actions need to precede attitudes. An important differentiating competency is taking responsibility for outcomes. Oftentimes, people approach improvement by concentrating on improving their attitude. People believe that a person needs to feel more responsible before he or she can act more responsibly. One of the key competency companions to taking responsibility for outcomes is taking action toward achieving results. This research indicates that those people who are perceived as acting in a responsible manner for outcomes also are seen as taking action toward achieving results. If people begin to act, it conveys to others a great deal about their attitude. The best way to convince others that we are responsible people is by our actions.

How Do You Get More Productivity Out of Other People?

One of the most frequently used competencies is "focus on results." The underlying theme is always the same: keeping others focused on the task, aggressively pursuing assignments, driving hard to make things happen, and being totally dedicated to the accomplishment of the task. When leaders attempt to improve their focus on results, they often put a great deal of emphasis on the drive or push for results. When done to excess, such leaders become grown-up bullies who constantly prod, check, demand, and annoy others. These behaviors can be effective in the short run, but in the long run, nobody wants to work for a tyrant.

We again found an unlikely companionship. Leaders who were effective at focusing on results were also effective at giving others feedback and providing coaching. Leaders who only push people to perform better typically focus on the outcome but don't help people with the journey.

Giving people feedback is time-consuming and difficult and is frequently not done well. One employee, commenting on his lack of feedback, said, "I don't know if I am in line to be the janitor or the chairman of the board. Please give me some feedback." Why is it that most poor performers are surprised to hear that they are receiving an unsatisfactory performance review? The reason is that the majority of leaders don't like to give feedback. They send signals via their body language or facial expression, but not clear messages. They assume that employees will respond to these couched hints. Some believe that because they didn't give a reassuring smile, employees will figure out that they are doing something wrong. Sitting down with employees and providing straight, candid feedback can be time-consuming and emotionally difficult for leaders, but leaders who do this well achieve better results.

One leader had an effective approach to giving feedback. Whenever she saw a problem, she would schedule a meeting with the person and say, "Our performance review is scheduled four months from now. I want to give you a positive appraisal at that time, but if it were to happen right now I could not do that. Let me explain why, and let's figure out a way to fix it before then." She would explain her concerns about this person's performance and proceed with a joint problem-solving discussion of how to fix the issue.

Feedback on performance issues needs to be timely and in close approximation to when the problem behavior occurred. Good athletic coaches provide ample feedback. They stand on the sidelines and yell, give halftime talks, or call time-outs and give people clear, specific feedback.

Interpersonal Skills—Another Pole That Raises the Tent

Effective leadership is not grand ideas, plans, or elaborate strategies. Leadership is behavior. It is the leader's connection with people. It consists of actions that are heard, seen, and felt by colleagues in the organization.

What Could Be More Powerful Than a Good Speech?

When thinking about how a person communicates powerfully, most people concentrate on how a message is delivered. It was interesting to learn that one of the strongest competency companions for communicating powerfully is involving others. In other words, those who were viewed as powerful communicators asked people for their input, encouraged alternative approaches and new ideas from others, and made sure that others were in agreement. Leaders rated low in their ability to communicate tended to concentrate only on getting their message delivered. They gave their speech from their prepared presentation but failed to ask for input from the audience on whether they agreed and how they viewed the issue.

What Is the Key to Getting Managers to Develop Their Direct Reports?

In a recent conference of employee development experts from several different companies, we asked the question, "What is the key to getting managers to develop their direct reports?" Some of the recommended actions were:

- Teach managers how to coach others.
- Do behavioral modeling skills training on how to have a developmental discussion.
- Publish clear development pathways.
- Make the performance appraisal and improvement process more developmental and less judgmental.

- Provide people with a model to help them understand how career development works.
- Reward managers for employee development.

We then asked how many of the companies were doing most of the activities on the list. Most companies indicated that their managers had been taught, coached, provided a model, and rewarded, but that their organization needed more. Based on our research, we found that leaders who were effective at developing others practiced self-development, whereas those who were ineffective at developing others had little interest in developing themselves. We then suggested, based on this research, that one of the best ways to get managers interested in developing others was to make sure these managers had a good development plan themselves.

This was confirmed from our experience in a large food company that provided a training program for managers and individual contributors on how to create an individual development plan. In evaluating the effectiveness of the individual development plans, it was found that those managers who were interested in their own individual development were the ones most likely to facilitate the creation of effective development plans with their direct reports.

Imagine a manager who feels that she is at a dead end in her career or has no sense of what she might be doing in the future. What kind of career discussions would this leader have with her direct reports? She might be trying hard to say the right words, but inside she would say to herself, "Why should I give you career advice? If you get promoted, you will be at the same dead end that I'm in. There is no future in this company."

A good solution for making an organization more focused on people development is to make sure that managers and leaders have a clear career plan and developmental opportunities in their future. Leaders will act developmentally if they are being developed.

How Do You Build a Great Team?

Our analysis on the competency companions to teamwork revealed that having trusting relationships is strongly associated with good teamwork. Most relationships depend on trust as a basis for the relationship. Teams without trust suffer from conflicts and competition between team members. Those leaders who were trusted also had the following characteristics:

1. *Consideration for others.* A key behavior to leveraging trust is having a high level of concern for how one's behavior affects others. Often, lack of consideration is demonstrated when deadlines or problems occur in the group. It is easy to be considerate when everything is running smoothly. Balancing the need to get the job done with sensitivity for others' needs and problems demonstrates true consideration.

2. *An open, friendly style.* Trust is earned much easier when leaders are open and friendly rather than abrupt and dismissive. Those who are viewed as easy to get along with are also viewed as trustworthy. Leaders who work hard to win people over to their position rather than demanding that people accept their position also build trust.

3. *Noncompetitive.* As people go through school and finish college, they often feel they are in constant competition with others. Grading on the curve makes students view others as competitors who could hurt their grade. As new employees begin work, entry-level jobs provide the same context. Consulting firms hire hundreds of MBAs and inform them that half will be weeded out in one or two years. Only 1 in 10 will make it to partner.

   A key transition for leaders is moving from viewing others as competitors to viewing others as team members. Behaviors that kill trust include taking personal credit for the accomplishments of others or being threatened by the success of other members of the work group. Leaders show support for team members by backing them up when they make an honest mistake and accepting blame for failures of the group rather than criticizing the performance of individual team members.

4. *Others have confidence in the leader's abilities and knowledge.* Expertise builds trust. Having confidence in a leader's ability to achieve difficult goals is a key aspect of trust. In addition to being friendly and considerate, being reliable and right is a critical aspect of building trust with others.

5. *Careful listening.* It is interesting to note that there is a strong relationship between listening and trust. Some people might believe that you talk other people into trust. This finding suggests that listening is a more powerful way to build trust.

6. *Candor.* A key ingredient of trust is honesty. Being frank and honest in dealing with other people is critical to building

trusting relationships. Telling people what they want to hear in an attempt to be nice or protect them from the truth only erodes trust in relationships. Sometimes, information is confidential and cannot be shared with others. Leaders with candor can be straightforward about the fact that they cannot share specific information.

How Do You Inspire Others?

When people think about inspiring others to high performance, they often visualize giving people a locker-room-style pep talk or waving a flag while leading others into battle. What might the competency companions to "inspiring others" be? Again, we did not find the obvious.[4] As we have collected further data on leaders, our insights into inspiration have been sharpened. Leaders who were rated as highly inspirational were also rated with high scores in three categories of behaviors. First, they readily accept their role as leader. They recognize that they are a role model, like it or not. They are perceived as championing change and being out front in taking initiative. The second characteristic they possess is an awareness and comfort with emotion. They understand that human behavior is driven in large part by emotion. These leaders have also come to realize that their emotions are extremely contagious and that they can lift people to soaring new heights or depress them to dispirited lows.

The third category is six rather specific behaviors that inspiring leaders selectively use. These begin with setting stretch goals. Others include providing clarity of direction and vision, being an effective communicator, developing others, encouraging teamwork and collaboration, and encouraging innovation. It appears that inspirational leaders have faith in the people with whom they work.

They believe that others are capable of great accomplishments. They believe others will work hard, follow through on assignments, and do whatever is needed to accomplish goals. Having positive expectations of others predisposes leaders to expect more, check less, and encourage people to give their best. Having lofty expectations of others is closely related to inspiring them.

To get a more complete overview of how leaders can be more inspiring review a subsequent book we have written called, *The Inspiring Leader.*[5] For further information on our research, visit our website at www .zengerfolkman.com.

Leading Organizational Change—the Final Tent Pole

Some would argue that the main distinction between management and leadership is that leaders recognize the importance of bringing about change, while managers are more content with preserving the status quo.

Our research confirms that the major difference between the competencies required of a senior executive and those in the middle or lower tiers of the hierarchy is the cluster of behavior having to do with leading organizational change.

What Is a Powerful Way to Get Others to Change?

In our analysis of competency companions for championing change, we found that leaders who were good at creating change also were perceived as being willing to take risks and challenge the status quo. Most people can identify with a change effort where some senior leaders failed to fully support the change. It becomes much easier to get people in an organization to behave in a particular way when the leaders act as role models of the desired behavior. In fact, some change agents argue that it is virtually impossible for an organization to change its culture until the behavior of its leaders is consistent with the values of the culture. Leaders who were most effective about bringing about change were also willing to challenge those who do not fully support the change effort.

When David Kearns was CEO of Xerox, he attempted to introduce a companywide quality initiative, but two vice presidents remained carping critics of the program. Both were good performers in their roles, but Kearns constantly admonished them to get on board. If Kearns had not done anything about these two dissidents, he would have sent the message that the quality change initiative was not that important. Instead, he terminated them both and let the organization know that it was because of their lack of support of the quality initiative.

How Do I Get Others to Accept a New Strategic Course for My Organization?

Good strategists believe in logic and careful analysis. Many believe they can win almost any argument and solve any problem with enough analysis and good logic. They also typically believe that as long as a strategy is logical, others will embrace the strategy. That is how they came to embrace the strategy, so others ought to do the same.

We found an interesting relationship between strategic perspective and self-confidence. Leaders who were viewed as having excellent strategic perspective were also rated as having the ability to inspire and motivate others. The relationship here seems to be that in order to get others to believe in a new strategy and direction it takes more than just compelling logic. Self-doubt, hesitation, changing your mind, or introversion can take a well-analyzed, logical strategic plan and turn it into a dead issue. Two critical issues are relevant here in inspiring and motivating others to accept a new strategy and direction.

First, the most powerful tool that leaders have is the use of emotion. Having the ability to get others excited and passionate about a new direction is a critical skill. People need to know the logic but they also need to feel the value and power of a new strategy.

Second, leaders need to make sure that their actions are consistent with the new direction. They need to be a role model and look carefully at all their activities to ensure that their behavior is consistent with the new course of action. When a new direction emphasizes controlling costs, leaders need to take a very hard look at their personal expenditures to ensure that they are a role model.

A New Approach to Development

Our competency companion research provides a unique perspective on how leaders can change. Current approaches toward development encourage people to develop linear development plans. Linear plans can be effective especially if a person's current level of performance is poor. Most linear plans help leaders make the transition from poor to good. However, the major focus of this book is helping leaders transition from good to great. The competency companion research provides leaders with a new map on how to reach their ultimate destination. This map provides alternate routes, which, for the most part, are unintuitive.

These new routes come out of research. The statistical analysis indicated that two behaviors were highly interrelated. We then looked for the rationale of why the one behavior impacted the other. Often, when leaders try to build exceptional effectiveness on specific competencies, it becomes difficult to find an effective way to improve. When performance on a competency is good, using a linear mindset is useless because leaders already perform the competency reasonably well. However, the nonlinear approach suggests that in order to be highly effective at competency A, I also need to be highly effective at B and C.

Our experience in helping leaders develop strengths by looking through a complete set of competency companions is that, typically, leaders will find one or two of the companion behaviors in which their effectiveness is inadequate or where improving the level of performance on the companion behavior would have a dramatic positive impact on the differentiating competency. One leader commented: "The companion behaviors I needed to work on stood out like a sore thumb. It was so obvious what was holding me back." Leaders can usually arrive at their own rationale for why performing poorly on the companion behavior impacts the competency on which they are working to develop exceptional strength. The added insight provided by the competency companions is very powerful. Our analogy of the tent is useful in understanding how companion behaviors impact overall perceptions of leadership effectiveness.

Again, effective leaders have a great deal of tent in the air. The companion behaviors represent poles that are either nonexistent, short or in the wrong place. By building the effectiveness of the companion behavior, more of the tent is lifted into the air, and the overall perception of leadership effectiveness is increased. Leaders who have experienced this approach have found it to be a valuable tool in their efforts to make the transition from good managers to great leaders.

To understand more about companion behaviors and obtain more information on the competency companions, go to www.zengerfolkman .com.

Validation of the Impact of Companion Behaviors

In our original research we came up with this theory that leaders with a fatal flaw could use a linear approach to improvement but in order for leaders to build strengths they needed a different approach, (e.g., nonlinear development). In this chapter we have presented a variety of examples of companion behaviors. The question we want to address here is, "Does using companion behaviors really work?"

We discovered companion behaviors by doing research on thousands of leaders across multiple data sets. We were highly confident in our assumptions that improving a companion behavior would in turn improve a specific competency, but our initial data were based on correlations rather than experimental effects.

Having pretest and posttest data offered an opportunity for us to test the impact of companion behaviors on the improvement of specific competencies.

To study the impact of companion behaviors we looked at data from 882 leaders who had utilized the Extraordinary Leaders 360-degree assessment and workshop. Each participant created a development plan for improvement focused on one specific competency. Looking at the pretest results compared to the posttest we discovered that 157 of the leaders had made a significant improvement in their ability to inspire and motivate others. Many people believe that inspiring and motivating others is more of an inherited trait rather than a skill that can be developed. We contend that if leaders have the insights on the specific behaviors that enable inspiration, any leader can be more inspirational.

In Figure 8.3 note the significant change between the pretest and posttest results on inspiring and motivating others. Leaders were able to increase their ability to inspire and motivate others 40 percentile points. They moved from the 33rd percentile to the 73rd percentile. This is a huge shift in moving from the bottom third to above the top third.

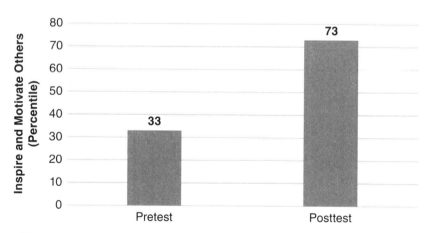

Figure 8.3.   Results from 157 Leaders on Inspires and Motivates Others

What Created This Significant Shift?

Each of the leaders in this study were provided our research on companion behaviors associated with inspiring and motiving others. We decided to look at inspiring and motivating others because this is a difficult competency to improve. Imagine you had the task to become more inspiring and motivating. What would you do? Many people are inclined to give up before they start. We found through our companion behavior research that, in fact, there were 10 companion behaviors that enabled leaders to be more inspiring. The companion behaviors were more straightforward and actionable. For example, we found that inspiring leaders were excellent communicators and they kept their team members well informed. While it appears to be difficult to be more inspiring, communicating more effectively seems easier for most people to do. Each individual leader selected just two or three of the companion behaviors that best fit their individual situation and where they had a passion to improve.

In Figure 8.4, we show the results comparing the pretest to the posttest results for the 10 companion behaviors. The companion behaviors are sorted from the one with the largest pretest/posttest shift to the smallest. All of the differences are statistically significant. The implications of this research are that by improving these companion behaviors, the competency "inspires and motivates others" also improves. Note also a statistically significant shift in every one of the companion behaviors.

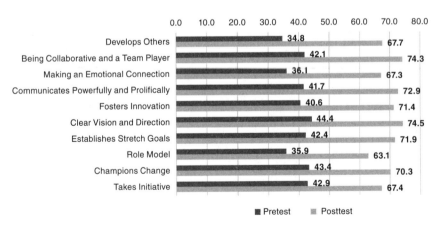

Figure 8.4. Pretest/Posttest Changes on Companion Behaviors

This research provided us with great confidence that our original research was correct. The way to build strengths is by utilizing companion behaviors that enable competencies to be improved. This is the way that leadership strengths are built.

Evidence-Based Leadership Development

This study along with all the other research presented in this book confirms the value and effectiveness of the strength-based approach and the effectiveness of companion behaviors. Leadership development programs that do not use this approach leave individuals with no clue about how to build strengths. Most leaders in those programs do nothing with their feedback because they don't know what to do to improve. Programs focused on weaknesses only help leaders to move from poor performance to good performance, but they miss out on the approach that creates the most value for both the individual and the organization. We know this approach works but we also know that leaders who using this approach see the value and are quick to identify specific actions to help them improve.

9

HOW INDIVIDUALS
DEVELOP THEMSELVES

*All over this country, in corporations and government
agencies, there are millions of executives who imagine that
their place on the organization chart has given them a body
of followers. And of course, it hasn't. It has given them
subordinates. Whether the subordinates become followers
depends on whether the executives act like leaders.*
—JOHN GARDNER

The Age-Old Questions

When the subject turns to leadership, someone inevitably asks the question, "Well, aren't leaders born that way?" A manager asks, "Can I really make myself a better leader?" Or, the young college student asks, "Do I have what it takes to become a leader?" The questions arise so frequently from savvy and well-intentioned people, we feel the need to address them yet one more time.

On the One Hand

We begin by acknowledging that there is a legitimate point of view in arguing that leaders are born that way. The revered guru of management, Peter Drucker, wrote in *The Practice of Management* that "leadership cannot be taught or learned."[1] Added to that is a long series of studies on the personality dimensions of leadership and the strong evidence that for most people, personality does not change a great deal over a person's lifetime. Other researchers have analyzed the profound influence of parents and their role in shaping the values of a child's willingness to take on responsibility, and the role that has in the child's developing leadership abilities. Those characteristics appear to change little over a lifetime.

Harrison Gough, the eminent University of California at Berkeley psychologist, has noted that the "dominance" scale of his California Psychological Inventory is a strong predictor of being selected as a leader. Other psychological tests have been used successfully to select leaders. Leadership abilities are often first exhibited in junior high school, high school, and college. Longitudinal studies of leaders in industry and the military show that key characteristics in leaders show up very early in life and remain quite fixed.

The most powerful psychometric instruments are biographical inventory tests, in which people are asked a series of questions about what they have done in their earlier lives. ("Were you the captain of any team or the president of any school group, or did you start your own business as a young child?") Because the past is the best predictor of the future, a probing analysis of people's past strongly predicts their future, and leadership patterns are often established early in life.

Add to that the evidence on leadership having some correlation with physical stature (taller people are more apt to be perceived as strong leaders) or body chemistry (higher levels of testosterone in men are correlated with leadership positions), and you can understand why the question is repeatedly asked.

On the Other Hand

Whereas there may be some predictive power of psychological tests and early childhood experience, it is clear that they fail to explain why a good number of leaders succeed. There is clearly no one factor that anyone has identified that consistently predicts who will succeed as a leader. Notable cases of "late bloomers" suggest that people with fairly undistinguished early portions of their careers turn out to be strong leaders. That could be said of both Abraham Lincoln and Harry Truman.

It is also clear that with such wide variation in organization cultures, if the right match is created, many more people could succeed in leadership. The high-tech industry, originally spawned in Silicon Valley, enabled many to succeed who would never have succeeded in traditional organizations.

In longitudinal studies of leadership, more than a third of the college graduates who were predicted not to move into higher ranks of the firm actually did so, thus proving that hard work, perseverance, and tenacity (and possibly luck) enabled these people to succeed.

Our Conclusion on This Debate

We share the conclusion with others that the right answer is between these two extremes. James Kouzes and Barry Posner wrote, "We would be intellectually dishonest if we did not say that some individuals clearly have a higher probability of succeeding at leadership than others. But this does not mean that ordinary managers cannot become extraordinary leaders."[2]

Herb Simon wrote, "A good executive is born when someone with some natural endowments (intelligence, vigor, and some capacity for interacting with his fellow men) by dint of practice, learning, and experience, develops that endowment into a mature skill."[3]

Our view mirrors those above. There is no question that some people come into the world endowed with self-confidence and a keen intellect. That is clearly an advantage. But of that group, only a small number move on to remarkable achievements as leaders. The difference appears to be hard work, thoughtful and tenacious effort, zeal for learning, and a willingness to extend beyond one's normal comfort zone.

So, a great deal of what we see great leaders doing is a result of personal effort. If you subscribe to the belief that leadership is not a person, but a series of behaviors that are displayed by a great many in an organization, then it becomes easy to argue that everyone can get better at leadership. So, our slightly compromising statements on this subject are:

- Some people start with clear advantages, but . . .
- . . . nearly all people are made better leaders from specific developmental activities.
- Leaders are a lot more "made" than they are "born."

How Individuals Improve Themselves

In the book *Results-Based Leadership*, 14 suggestions are made regarding the way people can improve their leadership outcomes or results.[4] In this book, we are focused on developing the attributes and skills of the leader. Following are 25 suggestions for ways in which leaders can improve the attributes or behaviors that are vital in producing those results. The key thing to remember is that improvement you make on any one-dimension spills over to many others. There is no such thing as working on only one leadership quality or attribute. When you improve one, you will invariably be improving several others.

1. Decide to Become a Great Leader

This is actually two decisions. First, most people do not think of "leadership" in the same terms as other roles in life. At a young age a person may aspire to become a physician, a lawyer, a molecular biologist, an astronaut, or a rock star, but chances are you have never heard of someone saying, "I want to grow up to be a leader." We think of leadership as an adjunct or frosting on some other role. Someday that may change. For people inside organizations, however, the first decision is to see that being a leader in an organization is important and worthy of your continued effort.

The second decision is to be exceptional rather than just mediocre at this role of leadership. This is the decision to go way beyond the ordinary or average and make a huge difference in the organization.

One positive element of this decision is the fact that it is not a zero-sum game. Becoming a great leader is something everyone can aspire to, and one person's effectiveness in no way detracts from others' success. In this game, everyone can win and one person's winning actually helps others to win. To become a highly effective leader requires a real dedication to that task and a willingness to act with the intensity and focus.

2. Develop and Display High Personal Character

The leader walks a difficult line between two seemingly opposing forces. First, the leader must be willing to take the role of leader. That means calling the meeting to order, pushing the agenda along, drawing some people out, and toning others down. It means saying "no" to a budget request that can't be funded. It also means having to terminate a longtime friend who is not performing effectively. Being a leader means being willing to take charge and make certain that the group performs well.

We have observed a newly appointed dean in a university who wanted to maintain close ties with former colleagues on the faculty and, in fact, did not want anything to change. So, the new dean continued to act exactly like a faculty member and talk like a faculty member (including the inevitable complaints about the university administration). In a few weeks, it became obvious that this person would not succeed in his new role, because he was unwilling to take on the requirements of the new office to which he had been appointed.

That same scenario plays out in government organizations and in industry. A leader must be willing to take that role, including all of the activities that a person occupying that role is expected to engage in or perform.

The counterforce to taking the "role" of leader is that people at lower levels in the organization resent arrogance from those in authority. They do not like the leader who conveys an attitude of superiority, condescension, or disrespect. The line between those two forces is a very fine one.

So, the counsel to all leaders is to maintain an attitude of humility. Be willing to laugh at yourself. Do not flaunt the authority you have. Humility will make you approachable. It opens the door to building relationships. The leader needs to find some mirror from which can be learned the way others perceive your character. That mirror may be a good internal mentor. It could be a trusted colleague or subordinate. It could be an effective 360-degree feedback process. Whatever it is, leaders need to have some sense about how people perceive their character. They need to know if they are trusted. Without that, it is not possible to exert strong influence on a work group.

Also, be cautious in the commitments you make, and then always deliver. Be careful not to overstate or overpromise. We are sure that some are saying, "But can people just improve their character?" "What's the best way to make changes in my fundamental personality or character?" The answers to those questions might be surprising to some. There has been a belief that the following chain exists:

$$Character \rightarrow Attitudes \rightarrow Behavior$$

The fact of the matter, however, is that people make their attitudes and ultimately their character conform to their behavior. The place to begin is with behavior. Thus, participating in powerful skill-building programs designed to improve interpersonal skills will have a decided effect on attitudes of the participants. When people learn and practice new behavior, there is a remarkable transformation of their attitudes and ultimately their character:

$$Behavior \rightarrow Attitudes \rightarrow Character$$

3. Develop New Skills: Enroll in Developmental Experiences

There are numerous developmental experiences available to most leaders. These may be available from within their organizations, paid for and sponsored by the organizations, or they may be available from a local university or college. Others may be available from various suppliers of learning and development materials. The key is for leaders to move outside their comfort zone to do something that will provide some real development. Leaders must be willing to invest in themselves, and many activities require time off from the job.

One of the authors has an acquaintance who is a legendary example of self-development. Once a year, a group gets together to meet, and the first question people ask is, "Okay, Dick, what have you done this year?" Every year Dick embarks on some new adventure into personal learning. These range from sessions with "healing shamans" to seminars on corporate reengineering. Each adds a new dimension to Dick's character and understanding. Though everyone would not choose the precise development experiences he chooses, the point is his disciplined approach to taking time every year for his own personal growth.

Attend any development program your organization provides, or those offered by local universities and private organizations. Constantly develop yourself, whether in the ability to deliver compelling presentations before a large group or the ability to write a concise memo on an important business topic. We reiterate that every new skill learned and used lifts that specific skill and numerous others along with it.

4. Find a Coach

Many organizations are hiring professional coaches to work with their key executives. They find that having someone who is capable of providing objective, constructive feedback to a leader is well worth the investment. The higher people move in the organization, the less apt they are to hear the truth about themselves from other people, so the value of coaches may increase as people move to higher levels in the organization.

It is instructive to note that world-class athletes pay for coaches to work with them. The great tennis players and golfers usually employ personal coaches. Athletes playing on the best professional teams receive constant coaching from people hired specifically to do that. In professional football, there are specific coaches for the defense, offense, and special teams. There may even be a specific quarterback coach.

Some executives have created their personal board of directors whose function is to give them feedback on the way they are managing their careers and on their current performances in their jobs.

We see the movement toward coaching as one that will continue to grow. It is driven in part by the fact that most executives are not comfortable with, or good at, providing constructive feedback to people around them. What is especially effective is the coach who calls on a regular basis and discusses the leader's success in taking some agreed-upon action steps. This process builds strong accountability and produces remarkable behavioral outcomes.

5. Identify Your Strengths

Peter Drucker argues, "Self-development is making oneself better at what one is already good at. It also means not worrying about the things one cannot be good at."[5] To accomplish this, Drucker advises:

- List your major contributions over the past two or three years.
- Specify precisely the things the organization expects from you and for which you are held accountable.
- Be clear about what you cannot do, as well as what you can do.
- Look for demanding assignments that make a difference.[6]

With characteristic wisdom and insight, Drucker gives useful advice to all leaders. Taking time to inventory the major contributions you have made in the past few years is a step that few leaders take. But what better place is there to start to understand your strengths? It also reveals where you are likely to make significant contributions in the future. Listing accomplishments also is a good barometer of your focus on results behavior. Everyone who is a leader, or aspires to serious leadership, should be able to itemize a list of contributions to the organization. If you are unable to do that, then consider seriously whether you suffer from the fatal flaw of inaction.

Repeated studies in organizations reveal that people are relatively unclear about what is expected of them, and especially what they are personally being held accountable to perform by their colleagues and bosses. We have argued strenuously that an emphasis on expanding strengths is far more valuable and productive than slogging away at trying to remedy weaknesses.

We begin by appealing to every reader's own experience. Think back to high school and college experiences. Let's assume for a moment that you were extremely adept at mathematics and anything quantitative. Your grades in algebra, trigonometry, and calculus were excellent. On the other hand, grammar and composition came hard to you. You neither enjoyed language study much nor did you do well at it. To continue, you have decided to embark on a path that would have you recognized as an excellent student. Which path should you choose? Do you work hard at becoming better at English? Or do you decide to leverage your head start in mathematics and excel in that arena?

First, where will your motivation be highest? We think your passion to excel will come in the quantitative arena. You like the fundamental activities involved. Your thought processes immediately gravitate toward quantitative analysis.

Second, where are you likely to feel some constant reward? Again, we argue that you are far more likely to continually receive positive feedback when you are engaged in quantitative activities than in anything having to do with language. It is less likely that people will praise your having gotten to "average" in grammar and composition skills.

Third, where are you apt to make the greatest amount of progress? You could make the theoretical argument that people could improve more in those areas in which they are weak. There is just a lot more room to move up. However, the ceilings are so high in every discipline that no matter how good a student you are now, there is huge room to grow.

Fourth, what is the best path by which to develop credibility? Becoming good at something creates a halo effect of overall competence. It sometimes goes to ludicrous extremes, as when a movie actress is asked for her opinions on the wisdom of building a missile defense system or a Nobel Prize winner in physics suddenly gets quoted for his or her views on the role of genetics in human intelligence. Why? Because the person is extraordinarily knowledgeable and creative in one arena, we assume those gifts spill over into other areas. Whether warranted or not, being good at one thing creates a perception that a person is good at many things, or everything.

Confidence and Competence: Why Working on Strengths Is More Likely to Build Confidence
It is impossible to overestimate the role of confidence in people developing competence. We frequently witness people who at one level would be deemed to be competent. In a safe, sanitary situation, they are able to

make an effective presentation. However, they refuse to make a presentation in front of senior managers or customers. Their lack is not of knowing what to do, or even being able to do it. Their lack is confidence to be willing to try in a more challenging circumstance.

We contend that strengths build confidence, and that this confidence spreads like yeast in a lump of bread dough and everything then rises. Hence, working on strengths will be far more likely to occur. To validate this observation, we conducted a study where we had individual leaders rate their self-confidence using a 10-item index. We then connected that assessment with evaluations from the Extraordinary Leader 360-degree assessment. We matched up 693 cases where overall leadership effectiveness was assessed by all evaluators and 623 cases where overall leadership effectiveness was rated by the manager of the person receiving the 360-degree assessment. Overall leadership effectiveness is the overall average of 49 differentiating behaviors assessing leadership effectiveness. Figure 9.1 shows the results of the study. Note there was a statistically significant improvement in perceived leadership effectiveness as leaders increased in confidence. This was true for peer and subordinate ratings, and the immediate manager's rating of the subject leader's effectiveness ($F = 4.032$, Sig. 0.003 for all evaluators; $F = 2.936$, Sig. 0.020 for manager).

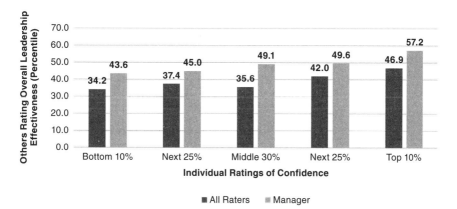

Figure 9.1. Individual's Self-ratings of Confidence Compared to Other's Ratings of Leadership Effectiveness

Data from the study seem to show that low confidence in an individual tends to drag down a their evaluations of leadership effectiveness. Leaders with high confidence were close to the overall average on leadership effectiveness.

Why Developing Strengths Will Be More Successful
Several forces are at work to make the process of working on strengths more successful than working on deficiencies:

- We have noted that people are more prone to do things they like and are good at. So, an initial willingness to even attempt a behavior is more likely with a strength than a weakness.
- The behavior will come more naturally, whereas something else may feel awkward and uncomfortable.
- Expanding strengths is far more likely to call forth the positive rewards and praise of others than remedying a deficiency.
- The application of a new skill sets into motion a number of forces that often create even further reward. For example, the leader sharpens listening skills, and learns that listening is not sufficient, but that the key is listening and doing something about it. So, the manager does listen carefully and then acts. Now, this sets into motion several other forces:

  - The leader's connection with other team members improves.
  - They take on more challenging assignments, partially stemming from the greater respect and attention being paid to them.
  - The leader's belief in the team and their focus on helping people to learn suddenly causes people to perform at a higher level.
  - They become more insistent that others improve their level of performance.
  - Customer satisfaction scores rise, as key customers experience an entirely new level of personal attentiveness from the organization's key people.

6. Identify Your Weaknesses: Find Ways to Make Them Irrelevant

This was Peter Drucker concept and philosophy. No one can do everything. Through delegation, the use of outside resources, or reallocation of work assignments, ways can be found to make weaknesses irrelevant.

The discipline of defining what things you can do and those you cannot perform (or do not like to do) is of great value. The obvious outcome is to structure your role in the organization to play to your strengths and to find ways to have others fill in the gaps.

7. Fix Fatal Flaws

If you believe you are the possessor of one (or more) of the fatal flaws identified in Chapter 7, then begin immediately to find ways to repair them. Specifically reflect on your experience:

- What lessons have you learned from your experience?
- Specifically, what did you learn from things that did not go well?
- What have you done differently as a consequence?
- What will prevent that from happening again?

8. Increase the Scope of Your Assignment

In one of the best studies of the powerful developmental experiences that leaders experience, Anna Valerio concluded that the first and most impactful experience on the job was to be given a broader scope in your current assignment. That could come via promotion but could also come as you are given broader assignments that include more functions, greater budget, or more people. The key is that the new assignment is broader and different from those previously held, and above all, an increase in responsibility.[7]

Increased scope may be granted to you from senior people in the organization, or it can be self-generated. Applying for a transfer may be one way to increase scope and breadth. The implementation of a new procedure, or the initiation of new project, can also increase scope.

This increased scope provides a good vehicle for the "Focus on Results" cluster of behaviors. To display this even further, leaders willingly accept special projects, in which working alone or with a small team, they work on an important project to a department or the corporation. From this, leaders can learn more about the total organization and achieve greater visibility.

9. Connect with Good Role Models

Through careful observation, leaders gain business acumen and hone important interpersonal skills. On occasion, the people being used as role models give voluntary coaching. They are most often willing to give counsel when asked. However, a great deal can be learned from merely watching and listening. Observe how children learn. They watch an adult eat with a spoon or fork and imitate them. They watch adults tie their shoelaces and learn by imitating the adults' actions. This concept, known as social learning theory, may be especially powerful in our younger years, but we never lose the ability to learn by watching someone else do something well. In fact, much learning is informal and not obvious to the learner. We just find ourselves adopting some of the effective behavior of another person.

Sometimes the lessons are "what not to do," but lessons are most helpful when they are good examples of the right things to do. That is why it is important to look for strong role models and to pay close attention to how they handle difficult situations.

In interviews with leaders, we nearly always are told about some senior people for whom they worked, who made an indelible impression upon them. Very often, a senior person went out of his or her way to express interest and encouragement. The senior person often took a risk and gave out challenging assignments for which, in retrospect, the person knew he or she was not totally prepared. In some cases, the senior person invited the person to visit an important client or to attend a significant industry meeting. Unmistakable in these conversations is the intense fondness felt for this senior leader who had become a role model.

10. Learn from Mistakes and Negative Experiences

We have earlier noted that one of the "fatal flaws" that causes people to have their careers hit a brick wall is the inability to learn from mistakes. The research is clear that learning from mistakes is a very productive tool for self-development. One category of negative experience may be a difficult boss. Another negative experience may be receiving some tough feedback from subordinates. For a person who is willing to learn, however, these experiences can be powerful developmental tools. A healthy attitude toward mistakes and negative experiences is crucial to growth and improved performance. Mistakes are part of the learning process, though some would argue with the following statement written by legendary basketball coach John Wooden: "The team that makes the most mistakes wins."

11. Seek Ways to Give and Receive Productive Feedback and Learn to Absorb It in an Emotionally Healthy Way

Most organizations are not good at providing feedback to anyone—regardless of level or function. For people to receive useful feedback a sincere request for it is usually required.

The learning and development process relies heavily on feedback to sustain it. There is often a huge gap between how leaders see themselves and how subordinates perceive them. The best way to close that gap is with feedback. Enormous barriers to feedback exist inside organizations. The good news is that when I am presented with disconfirming information about myself, I will more often change how I act rather than change how I see myself. That is the great power of feedback.

Subordinates are in the best position to provide feedback, and when asked for it, the process creates a more wholesome working relationship. Accept feedback as the valid perceptions of others, and first seek to understand the meaning. Assume the givers have pure, positive intent. Keep asking for feedback—it is the golden path to continual improvement.

Time and again we witness people receiving 360-degree feedback from direct reports, peers, and their boss. Often, with nothing else occurring, the individual recognizes what strengths need developing, figures out exactly what needs to be done and how to do it, and proceeds to take the appropriate steps. Our biggest contribution is often getting out of the way.

12. Learn from Work Experiences

As leaders embark on every project, it is useful to make notes of what is expected to be achieved and in what time frame. Then, the leader can periodically see how the actual results are tracking with the original expectations. That way, every activity or project becomes a learning experience. The leader can then seek to find the answer about why it is going much better than had been expected, or why it is costing more, or why it ran into roadblocks with other departments. An important part of self-development is simply finding the mechanism by which you can learn from every experience.

We turn again to an example from the world of sports. Most football games are played on the weekend, so there is the classic Monday review of the game films. Why? Coaches want the players to learn from their experience. They are fortunate to have films that record the game from several perspectives. Leaders have to create that powerful, compelling feedback process, because it is no less valuable as a way to improve performance in every arena.

13. Study the Current Reality the Organization Faces

Good development encompasses improving one's character, one's knowledge, and one's behavior. This topic focuses on knowledge. One important leadership development exercise is to step away from your organization and look at it through the eyes of a security analyst. Then look at it as if you were a competitor. Then stand away and see how it would look if you were a supplier. Then do the same thing from the perspective of a customer. Be aware of industry trends and where your organization fits into that. Stay abreast of relevant technology facing your industry.

A key quality of effective leaders is the ability to see reality without blinking. It is hard to lead an organization in the best strategic paths if you are unwilling to face the reality of where you are now. Being brutally frank with yourself, and encouraging total candor from others, is the best safeguard to keeping in touch with your organization's current reality.

14. Learn to Think Strategically

One of the frequent complaints heard from executives about their subordinates is that they are completely tactical in their thinking. They simply do not think in a strategic way. For many, strategic thinking seems a complete mystery, and they see no obvious way to acquire this esoteric ability. In fact, there are good books on strategic thinking that help people understand the basics of strategy. They give a road map to understanding your own organization's strategic choices, to understanding why organizations choose various strategic paths, and generally to becoming more comfortable in intense strategic discussions.[8]

15. Communicate with Stories

Learn to recount important messages with powerful stories that connect emotionally with those about you. Stories help reduce complexity to manageable simplicity. They are memorable. They connect with the hearer at a more powerful level. The best insight into any organization's culture comes from the collected stories that circulate among the people in the organization. So, the beginning point is to collect important stories and examples that can be used in your dialogue inside the organization. Then, practice the skill of recounting stories as the best way to convey an important message. Illustrate the major points you wish to make with appropriate examples and stories.

16. Infuse Energy into Every Situation

One of the keys of leadership is to understand that leaders bring excitement, enthusiasm, and energy to any endeavor. They ignite other people's passions to move forward. We all know people who are energy absorbers. When they are around, it is as if a giant vacuum sucks the energy from a discussion. Seldom is that person seen as a leader because leaders need to do just the opposite. They need to capture and amplify the enthusiasm of others. The best way to get that started is to inject your own enthusiasm into any discussion or activity. Watch a videotape of yourself. Listen to a recording of your participation. Are you depositing or withdrawing energy from the process or project?

17. Allocate Specific Time to People Development

A powerful tool in your own development process is to become involved in the development of people who report to you, or anyone who would benefit from your tutelage. We noted earlier that one of the keys of good leadership is the ability to obtain good results. Along with that, however, leaders also need to build the capacity within the organization to continually improve its performance and thus be able to produce long-term, sustained results.

The "law of the harvest" talks about reaping what we sow. For the organization to constantly reap high productivity and innovation from its people, there has to be "sowing." That means taking the time, putting forth the effort, and possibly spending the money required to get frontline associates trained up.

Some leaders view people development as a frill—extraneous to their real work. Amidst the punishing workload of today's business climate, finding time for people development seems impossible to them. However, taking the time to develop people is an important behavior of a leader, not only for what it does for the recipient, but equally for the impact it has on the leader. Developing others moves you from being an independent professional person, concerned only with yourself, to the role of the true leader who creates organizational capacity and builds people.

18. Weld Your Team Together

Great organizations nearly always have strong teams at the top, composed of people who genuinely like each other and who want their colleagues to succeed. A strong, cohesive team becomes a powerful development tool aiding leaders to constantly improve. Many organizations engage in team-building activities, ostensibly to improve the working relationships of the people on the team, and also to enable the group to be even more productive. What is often missed is the fact that a good team-building exercise is one of the most powerful learning experiences for the leader. First, the team has fresh, firsthand data about the leader's behavior and results. They are in the best position to provide useful feedback to the leader regarding strengths and any areas of improvement. Thus, a good team-building session is one of the most powerful and positive development activities that a leader can undertake.

19. Build Personal Dashboards to Monitor Leadership Effectiveness

Good overall measures of leadership do not usually exist in most organizations. How do you know if you are performing well? What objective measures exist that would confirm or deny that? If such measures do not exist now, then an excellent developmental activity is for you to take the initiative and develop them for yourself. These will obviously differ by organization and functional responsibility, but some measures that would be frequently used include:

- Retention data
- Customer satisfaction measures
- Productivity measures (e.g., costs to complete a given action or time to complete an activity)
- Performance against budget
- Results from organizational climate surveys

Having developed your own "dashboard" with which to monitor your leadership effectiveness, it then becomes possible to take a weekly or at least monthly reading of your effectiveness as a leader.

A visit to an Air Force base involved a meeting with a major general, the commander of the base. He was obviously proud of the management information system that had been developed and offered to demonstrate what information it could provide. The general could call up 846 measures of performance, ranging from fuel consumption to productivity measures and the number of arrests on the base in the previous eight hours. Most leaders will be content with far fewer measures, but without some information system, the leader is driving with a windshield made of opaque glass.

20. Plan and Execute a Change Initiative

A powerful developmental activity for any leader is to define a change that should appropriately be made and then undertake to make that change happen. The change could be as simple as implementing a new reporting system, a new work process, or a new organizational structure. Whatever the change, a powerful development process involves planning the change, defining the outcomes that will result from the change, implementing the change, and finally evaluating the results. The real learning and development come from comparing the final results with the predicted outcomes, and then attempting to find out what caused the differences. As Machiavelli noted, "There is nothing more difficult to carry out, nor more doubtful of success, nor more dangerous to manage, than to initiate a new order of things." Centuries later, a noted psychologist, Kurt Lewin, would observe, "If you really want to understand an organization, try making changes in it."

21. Become a Teacher/Trainer

Approximately 80 percent of all learning and development is delivered with live, classroom instruction. In a large percentage of those cases, the organization has purchased learning systems from an outside supplier, or they have developed training programs internally. Whereas the organization often has a training department, a large portion of that development is delivered by hand-picked managers selected from inside the organization. They are chosen on the basis of several criteria, and these usually include:

- Well respected by peers, subordinates, and upper management
- Perceived as a high-potential person
- Articulate and capable of making an engaging presentation
- Practices the leadership or management principles being presented in the development program

The process of being trained on how to deliver a learning and development program to people inside the organization is one that produces real growth in the instructor. Nothing cements a body of information inside someone more than teaching it. In addition to personal growth, it brings the instructor into contact with many people with whom he or she would never have had contact. It educates the instructor on the challenging issues the organization is facing and how the people are reacting to those challenges. From our vantage point of having watched many organizations select and train line managers as in-house instructors, we have seen it consistently enhance their careers and accelerate their development. Stewart Friedman led Ford Motor's Leadership Development Center. He wrote, "Every program features extensive use of teachers. Graduates of our programs serve as leader-teachers, a practice that helps participants and the instructor grow and develop new capacities for leadership. The concept of leader-teacher isn't unique, but Ford places a high emphasis on teaching. The lesson begins at the top."[9]

22. Study the High Performers and Replicate Their Behavior with Others

In every organization, there are a handful of people who have figured out how to perform a given job in the best possible manner. That is true of customer service representatives, salespeople, factory workers, supervisors, and corporate vice presidents. It will probably remain a mystery why more organizations do not identify who these people are and take the time to study what they do and how they do it. Then, armed with that information, it would seem logical to attempt to get others to perform or behave in that same way.

What more valuable process could occur than identifying someone with a job that is a close counterpart to your own and whose performance is recognized as being outstanding? Through observation and interrogation, find out what that person is doing that makes him or her so effective. Identify which elements of what that person does can be integrated into your own activities.

23. Volunteer in Your Community

The ideal leader is one who is complete. Stewart Friedman wrote, "We at Ford are pioneering a new dimension of leadership that seeks to integrate all aspects of a person's life. We call it 'total leadership.' It's different from many prior leadership models because it starts with your life as a whole: your life at work, your life at home, and your life in the community. Total leadership is about being a leader in all aspects of life."[10]

It is clear that people's work life, home life, religious activity, and community service are not as separate as they once were. The formerly sharp lines are now murky. People are striving for work–life balance, and one popular approach is to blend them rather than build walls between them. By practicing leadership skills in the other aspects of your life, leadership skills can be honed and perfected. The organization is enhanced financially and organizationally, the community is improved, the church or synagogue gets much needed talent, and the family enjoys the benefits from improved leadership.

24. Practice Articulating Your Vision for the Firm and Your Group

Leaders describe to a group their vision of the future and often assume it has been understood and internalized. Time passes and people ask questions: "Okay, what is our strategy? I don't know where we're going." The leadership lesson is that communication of complex messages must be repeated over and over. This is especially true when it concerns a topic that carries over a long period of time, and one where people will scrutinize the leader's behavior to see if it is aligned with the earlier words.

Married people or others in any lasting relationship have learned that you do not express your affection and commitment to the other person once and assume it holds until further notice. With the passage of time, things are said or done that cause the other person to question what was said earlier. And the mere passage of time dims the force and clarity of the words, so they need repeating.

That same phenomenon is at work in any organization. Yes, the leader said we value trust and openness, but look what happened to Ralph when he asked the question in the staff meeting. Or, rumors begin to swirl in the organization and they are quite contradictory of earlier messages. It is for those reasons that messages of vision, values, mission, and strategy need to be repeated over and over. How many times? Some have said that people really do not take a message seriously until the seventh time they hear it. The number is probably different for each of us, depending on the topic and what is happening in our lives. However, it is clear that the message needs frequent repeating. We advocate that you practice repeating those messages frequently to the associates with whom you work.

25. Prepare for Your Next Job: Think Ahead Regarding the Skills You Will Need

One mistake that many leaders make is not to start getting prepared for their next assignment or role. Like the chess player who sees two or three moves ahead, so are wise leaders looking into the future for the roles they will be playing, and then preparing themselves with the skills that will be needed in those new roles. Will the future require more technical expertise? More strategic thinking skills? A different kind of business acumen? Whatever those new requirements may be, it is never too early to be identifying them and taking active steps to add them to your skill set.

Conclusion

There are those who argue that all development is self-development. It has been estimated that more than 80 percent of what people learn while working in organizations has been gained on the job, casually and informally. No matter how powerful the classroom experience, it pales in comparison with the learning that comes from experience. How much people gain from their experience is nearly all up to them. Regardless of the percentage, it is clear that leaders can make huge strides by taking responsibility for their own development. They should not count on the organization to do that for them.

The 25 suggestions of things to develop your own leadership abilities were meant to convey the message that all leaders can do a great deal on their own. Do not rely on the organization to make you an even better leader. There are extensive and powerful steps you can take to move you well down the path to becoming an extraordinary leader. For further information about programs and materials designed to help leaders improve their skills, please go to our website at www.zengerfolkman.com.

PART II

THE ORGANIZATION'S ROLE IN FILLING THE LEADERSHIP PIPELINE

We now move from how individuals develop themselves to examining the role of the organization in developing its leaders. The seriousness of the need for leadership at the organization level was reported by consulting firm McKinsey and Co.:[1]

> Moreover, when upward of 500 executives were asked to rank their top three human-capital priorities, leadership development was included as both a current and a future priority. Almost two-thirds of the respondents identified leadership development as their number-one concern. Only 7 percent of senior managers polled by a UK business school think that their companies develop global leaders effectively, and around 30 percent of US companies admit that they have failed to exploit their international business opportunities fully because they lack enough leaders with the right capabilities.

Our Motivation for These Next Six Chapters

This portion of the book is driven by four consistent findings from countless surveys conducted with executives by our firm and others:

1. Senior executives consistently identify leadership development as one of their top three concerns.
2. Few senior leaders believe their organization has an adequate pipeline of leaders capable of meeting their needs for the decades to come.
3. Senior leaders are seldom content with their organization's current initiatives for developing their leaders for the future.
4. Approximately 60 percent of frontline leaders have received no formal development in leadership or management

Yet there is general agreement that the organization success is driven in large part by the effectiveness of their leadership team. Yes, technology may give the firm an edge. Operational excellence helps. Bottom line, leadership effectiveness has been shown as the single most powerful driving force for an organization's success.

We contend that organizations are not addressing the magnitude and scope of this gap. Companies fall into three groups. The first includes 60 percent of medium and large organizations. This group has done something in the past five years to develop their leaders. The second group includes another 20 percent that has never done anything in a formal way to develop their leaders, and the final group, comprising another 20 percent of firms, has not done anything within the past year.

It would be understandable to put the lion's share of attention on this second group who have never done anything, or who have done nothing in the last year. But the truth is that we are equally concerned about the first group, the 60 percent who have done something. Why? Because they are often involving a miniscule fraction of their current and potential leaders. Bottom line, both groups are contributing to the fact that organizations are generally not filling their pipeline and cause senior executives to be unhappy with their current internal initiatives.

Is This a Soluble Issue?

Yes. However, the solution is not to heave ever larger sums of money at the issue. We have seen many organizations spend huge amounts with no visible results. Others who spend much smaller amounts show evidence of real success.

We believe the following analysis will be of value to any HR professional, and especially those responsible for creating an organization's leadership development activity. These chapters provide a conceptual model for insuring that all the necessary ingredients are in place.

What if you are not an HR professional? Do the following chapters have any relevance for you? Every leader in a firm should benefit by knowing what their organization needs to be doing in order to fill their leadership pipeline:

- It provides them the rationale for the actions the organization is taking.
- It informs them of what they can do to support the company's leadership development programs.
- It enables them to help your organization fine-tune and improve its leadership development initiatives.
- It gives them the tools to be more effective in the development of their immediate subordinates.

Our experience and research shows that there are six fundamental elements of a highly productive leadership development effort. When organizations execute on these six elements they are virtually guaranteed to have great success. One important caveat, however, is that these are not alternatives from which a firm can pick and choose. Success hinges on all six being in place simultaneously.

10

TAILOR LEADERSHIP DEVELOPMENT TO THE ORGANIZATION

The only person who behaves sensibly is my tailor.
He takes new measurements every time he sees me.
—GEORGE BERNARD SHAW

One fundamental point of this chapter is that no two organizations are alike. Every organization's leadership development program needs to be tailored to fit. That doesn't mean that there won't be elements in your company's initiatives that are close to the elements in another. But one company's efforts ought not to be copied and imported to another with the expectation that what worked in Company A will work as well in Company B. "Bespoke" is a term used in Britain to describe something that was made for a particular person or for a certain occasion. While most often used to describe a tailor who crafts a suit exactly to fit an individual, we think it describes the ideal approach to designing a leadership development process for a firm.

What Is the Global Context?

Start with the big picture. What is happening in the broader environment that will influence the decisions about this specific case? The world is about to experience a dearth of effective senior leaders. Why? Several forces have combined, as if it were a perfect storm, to generate this critical situation.

1. Recent financial downturns have slowed retirements. Senior executives are staying on and creating congestion at the top.

As one observer noted, the glass ceiling has been replaced by a "gray ceiling" made up of baby boomers solidly entrenched in upper management positions.

However, at the same time, many organizations have one-half of their senior leadership teams who are immediately eligible for retirement or who will be within the next five years. The dam could burst at any time.

2. Companies have pared back investments perceived as unnecessary. In order to meet profit objectives, companies have been operating with a lean mentality. They've curtailed rotational assignments that formerly aided in development goals. Development positions such as "two in the box" have been abandoned. Overseas assignments are reduced, despite their proven value for executive development.

3. Only one-third of companies sponsor formal development programs. According to a 2011 study jointly sponsored by the American Management Association's talent management division AMA Enterprise, The Institute for Corporate Productivity, and Training magazine, the percentage of companies that report having global leadership development programs has remained stable since 2010.[1] However, only one-third of the 1,750 organizations surveyed reported that they currently have global leadership development programs.

Fifty-eight percent of companies described as high-performing reported having some form of global leadership development program, compared with 34 percent of those reported in the study as low-performing organizations.

These factors have been compounded by the accelerating pace of business. The good and bad news is that starting in 2019 and going forward, about four million executives will retire each year. The outflow valve is opening and the flood of upper management vacancies is likely to appear.

However, there are serious concerns on the part of senior executives about whether the input valve is open that prepares the generation below them to have received the necessary development to take over. Here are the conclusions of surveys of senior executives:

- Deloitte reports that 80 percent of respondents rated leadership a high priority for their organizations, but only 41 percent told us they think their organizations are ready or very ready to meet their leadership requirements.[2]

- According to the Ken Blanchard Company's annual corporate issues survey, executives said there is a skills gap and the number one initiative will be to enhance the skills of frontline and middle managers.[3]

Analyzing Your Organization

What distinguishes your organization? In Chapter 6 we identified 20 different organization cultures. We make no pretense that any one company is all one or another. Indeed, we think most organizations are combinations of several. But that is a place to start. It describes the DNA of the organization and what glues it together. Determining which ones of the 20 corporate cultures may provide useful insights that could inform your decisions about leadership development.

Additionally, it may be useful to examine the current structure. If you drew the structure, would it be an Alpine cabin—tall with a narrow base? Or is it flat with few levels? Are processes well defined?

What is the strategy of the organization? One of the most troubling criticisms of leadership development initiatives is that they are disconnected from the strategy of the firm. Like ships quietly passing each other in the night, each seems oblivious to the other. Ponder the positive outcomes of having leadership development tightly aligned with the strategy.

What data are available about the current leadership of the firm? Is it possible to review performance appraisals to see what they would present in terms of patterns and themes? Is there any 360-degree feedback data available?

What Has the Organization Been Doing?

Honor the Past

Whatever you do, it occurs in some context. We suggest you begin by talking with people who have been with the organization for a few years. What has the organization done in the past that has proven to be successful in developing leaders? Have there been any past initiatives? Taken as a group, what are the strengths of the current leadership team? Are there serious flat sides that need shoring up?

Firms have often been involved in one or more activities. This could include:

- Development programs on specific topics, such as coaching or project management
- High Potential programs for a small group of individuals who are believed to have the potential to serve in senior management positions
- Specialized programs for groups such as women or minorities, which senior management wish to better prepare for managerial roles
- Tuition reimbursement programs to encourage employees to take advantage of local college and university classes

In all likelihood, such programs should not be suddenly abandoned. They are worth reviewing to determine which have produced positive outcomes. It is always better to be perceived as building on the strong elements of the past versus jettisoning activities simply because you were not the original sponsor.

What Could (and Should) Targets Be?

For some leadership development initiatives, the goal is to get "5's" on a reaction sheet that is distributed at the end of the program. Clearly, that is not an ideal aspirational goal.

Better targets could include:

- *Improve the individual performance of the overall leadership team by some measurable amount.* One senior automotive executive challenged the leadership development function to elevate the 360-degree feedback scores by 15 percentile points within one year.
- *Motivate every leader to create for themselves a personal plan of development.* Development is more likely to occur when plans are in place and gaining attention. Set the expectation that every

leader, regardless of level or tenure, has an individual plan of development that is actively being pursued.

- *Achieve a specific business outcome.* An example might be greater employee engagement or innovation. An organization received rather low scores on overall employee engagement from an annual employee survey, which led senior executives to challenge their management team to elevate their company scores in the following year's survey by at least 10 percentile points.

- *Enlarge the number of leaders in the development pipeline required for the future.* One organization had earlier established their target population for development as the top 40 executives in the firm. Given that the firm had more than 140,000 employees, a new CEO determined that this number needed to be 4,000.

- *Significantly increase promotions from within.* Most organizations typically go outside to fill one-third of their executive positions. Consider reducing that to one-fifth. While there is value in adding outside perspectives, or filling the need for an entirely new skill set, the data clearly indicate that the failure rate of external hires is far higher than those promoted from within.

- *Change corporate culture.* The comment has been attributed to various respected experts that "corporate culture eats strategy for lunch." Yet cultures can easily lag behind, becoming stagnant or even petrified. Of the many options available to affect culture change, leadership development is one of the most effective, economical, and controllable. If culture describes "how we behave around here," one of the most direct avenues to change that is leadership development.

- *Improve employee engagement.* The quality of leadership is the most important determinant of employee engagement. Imagine the long-term effect of sending the signal that the company insists that every employee should be working for an excellent leader. Imagine the effect of practicing the policy of zero tolerance for inappropriate behavior on the part of leaders.

- *Involve all executives in the development of their colleagues.* What if everyone was expected to be interested and helpful in the development of all their colleagues—above, below, and to every side of them?

Create a Competency Model

In Chapter 3 we devoted the entire chapter to understanding the philosophy behind competency models and describing how organizations have created them in the past, along with our views of the ideal way to proceed. Here's a summary of our point of view:

> Most competency models are created by having groups of executives pool their opinions about what makes a good leader for the company. In other instances a senior executive takes it upon himself/herself to make that decision. A third method has groups of managers sort a deck of cards that has various leadership behaviors printed on each card. These results are tallied and used to arrive at a general consensus among participants.

We contend that the most effective method involves a far more empirical and scientific approach. Analyzing the behaviors of the most effective leaders in the organization leads to a far more valid understanding of the most effective leadership behavior.

A more scientific, three-step statistical approach includes the following:

1. Gather a large number of items that describe behavior, traits, and characteristics. Administer the items with a large sample of individuals across different companies, cultures and geographies. In our case we began with 2,000 descriptive behavioral statements that had been used in a variety of 360-degree or multi-rater assessments.
2. Apply a rigorous statistical technique that identifies those items that most powerfully identifies those individuals who received the highest aggregate scores on all the items, from those who received the lower scores.
3. From this group of items, select those that have the highest correlation with important business outcomes, such as employee engagement, retention, customer satisfaction, productivity, innovation and profitability.

This empirical approach to creating a competency model replaces the pooled opinions, or the opinion of a powerful leader, or the sorting of cards based on opinions versus hard evidence.

Customize the Competency Model to Fit the Organizational Culture

One of the ways to better integrate leadership development into the culture of an organization is to customize the competency model. We have a little hesitancy about bringing up this topic because internal committees so often design custom competency models that are neither helpful, predictive, nor useful for leadership development. Done right, however, it can be very helpful to customize the leadership competency model to better fit a unique culture.

1. **Names.** The names of competencies are meaningful. For example, in Europe during World War II those who worked with the Nazis were call collaborators. In some European organizations calling a competency Collaboration and Teamwork gives it a negative connotation. Some names are more familiar in organizations than others. Some organizations prefer Execution rather than Drive for Results. Carefully selecting the names of competencies can make a competency model more precisely fit a culture.

2. *Identifying unique competencies.* Having created numerous customized competency models and having reviewed competency models created by others; we know that 80 percent of the competencies selected by a variety of different organization will be the same. There is a stable set of leadership competencies that have a dramatic and measurable impact on the leadership ability of people regardless of the organization. Yet in most organizations there are some unique competencies that emerge because of the nature of the work, how the organization functions or their strong cultural attributes. It often critical that these competencies be assessed.

   Several years ago, we did a customized competency model for an organization. In creating a custom model, we like to analyze any past 360-degree feedback data they have collected. We seek for differentiating items and we also interview executives and other high potential leaders. In these interviews we heard stories related to the company's creation repeated over and over. The stories involved a group of people challenging an existing standard and taking a big risk. In our differentiation analysis we noticed some items emerging from the data that focused on courage and challenging the status quo. For that organization we created a competency we call Courage. Having that competency in the model reinforced a valued trait for that organization.

3. *Look and feel.* Have you ever walked into a home where you felt so comfortable it felt you were in your own home? On the other hand, have you ever walked into a home where it felt cold and unwelcoming? Creating a customized competency model with the right look, feel, and language makes people feel they are home. The language, look, and feel of the instrument can be a critical piece of making leadership development part of their culture.

4. *Links to company values.* Recently one of our customers analyzed if their leadership competencies and their company values were in harmony. They were trying to assess if their competencies matched up with the company values that were printed on the walls of the office building. Recently, a new value focused on valuing diversity was officially adopted. It was not measured in the current competency model. They quickly asked for an additional competency to be added that focused on valuing diversity.

5. *Aspirational competencies.* Most often competency models focus on behaviors demonstrated by outstanding leaders in the organization. Many organizations are starting to ask the question, which competencies will we need in the future? Including aspirational competencies into the competency model helps leaders learn requisite skills for the future.

Choosing the Key Business Levers and Activities on Which to Focus Development

A competency model is designed to define the important behavior required of those who manage the business in all functional areas and over the long run. In addition to competencies, there are key business levers, however, that greatly determine the success of the business in the short and long run.

An example could be a greater emphasis on seeking a certain size or type of client. It could be the decision to penetrate global markets and rely less on domestic clients. It may be the adoption and emphasis on discovering and deploying a new technology. These are not leadership competencies, but are areas that the leadership development process can identify and prepare participants to better execute. These actions are the drivers of success.

Elements of an Ideal Leadership Development Solution

There are several key elements that define a successful workplace leadership development system:

1. *A simple, non-bureaucratic approach.* The more complex the system, the more likely it will fail. If the process stakes out too broad of a scope of operation, it will fail.
2. *The pipeline is owned by the senior leadership team.* Evaluating a person's leadership talent and potential is too important to be left to any one person. No single leader should make or break someone's career. That is why the part of the pipeline that leads to senior management assignments should be owned collectively by the senior team. This provides more than one coach for every aspiring leader.
3. *Managers become significantly more involved in their subordinates' development.* Some organizations bring in outside consultants to work with their leaders and create processes by which they receive candid feedback on their performance. It often comes to light that this candid, specific performance feedback is some of the first that these key individuals have received in the past several years. At least two-thirds of the leaders we interview indicate that they want more coaching and feedback than they currently get. Managers need to be trained to offer more feedback and to do it in a positive, constructive way. The involvement of managers is one of the key ingredients in successful leadership development outcomes.
4. *A scientifically created competency model that predicts future success and aids in the development of leaders.* The performance appraisal, by definition, is usually a look in the rearview mirror and focuses primarily on past behavior, not taking into account the demands of a new job or of the future. Competencies, while they are highly correlated with a manager's ability to obtain good

results today, should also be selected for their ability to predict effective performance in the future and at higher levels.

5. *Multiple entrance points into the leadership pipeline.* One key to keeping the pipeline filled is to involve a greater number of people in the development process. Allowing people to nominate themselves to participate is one way to increase the input. Offering development to all levels in the organization, and engaging leaders in the earlier stages of their careers are other ways of ensuring an adequate input.

6. *Create a culture that values development.* Self-development cannot be the last thing on a long to-do list. It must be elevated to a higher priority and supported by all levels of management. Senior leaders need to set the example by taking development plans seriously and setting expectations that everyone will progress.

7. *Start leadership development earlier.* Behaving without the benefit of development is time-consuming and often ingrains bad habits. It is much easier to expose leaders to best practices early in their career than it is to undo bad habits learned through a "sink or swim" approach. Development is ideally a lifelong habit, driven by a set of learning skills.

8. *Continue to emphasize promotion from within.* Evidence supports the fact that promotion from within work better than recruiting from outside.

We Need to Include Science in the Art of Leadership Development

There is a great deal of nonsense that has been written about leadership. It includes meaningless statements such as, "Managers do things right; leaders do the right things." Or, "A leader is one who knows the way, goes the way, and shows the way," and goes downhill from there. The torrent of clichés and nonactionable ideas is never-ending.

If we are to really advance the practice of leadership, we believe we must adopt the fundamental premise that propelled the reform of medical practice as well. In 1972, Dr. David Eddy began a crusade to bring more science to the practice of medicine. Estimates had been made by objective observers that only 15 percent of what physicians did was based on scientific evidence. Dr. Eddy, who had been a practicing cardiologist, decided to return to school, obtain a degree in applied mathematics and statistics, and lead the charge on moving that number to a higher level.[4]

Medicine had been strongly shaped by practitioners passing on their ideas and treatments to their colleagues. Some of these ideas were sound, but a good many were not. As an example, an obstetrician believed strongly that once a woman had a child delivered by Caesarean section, she could never give birth in the traditional way. He lectured at obstetrics and gynecological seminars and taught this idea for years. There were many examples to the contrary, and there was no scientific basis to support his belief, yet the notion persisted for years.

So, what percentage of what we do as leadership development practitioners is based on good science?

In the past decades we have used multi-rater or 360-degree feedback, as a core tool in leadership development. Why? It would be easy to reply, "Because it works." But beyond that, by providing us with a stable, quantitative measuring tool, it gives us the means to measure and monitor progress. It enables us to compare various development methods and the effect they have. It gives organizations a way to measure the health of a current leadership team. It also provides a more powerful diagnostic tool to help a leader create his or her own plan for becoming a better leader. A tool like this creates a stronger incentive for change to occur.

Our opportunity in leadership development is to bring more science into what we do by creating ever better ways to measure the current state of leadership behavior, along with the change we produce. This allows us to bring science into the art of leadership development and to drive out the nonsense that will always fill the void where good science doesn't exist.

As an aside, the good news in medicine is that the statistics have significantly improved. The best estimates now put the percentage of medical practice based on rigorous science at a whopping 25 percent. (And we hope this doesn't give you too much pause as you go to your next appointment with your physician.)

Here's to continued science and continued progress as leaders of our organizations, on every front.

Conclusion

It all comes down to priorities and investments. Many companies underspend in this area, observes Josh Bersin, principal and founder of Bersin by Deloitte, the part of Deloitte Consulting focused on human-capital management. He notes that a select group of "high-impact" companies spent an average of $3,500 per person per year to develop mid-level leaders. Bersin writes: "All of our data, from this report and other research on leadership, shows that leadership development almost always comes up as the No. 1 issue and that companies that spend more on it tend to outperform those that spend less."[5]

Recently we asked a group about their experience in a leadership development program. When they described the experience they said in essence, "We stop doing our work to attend leadership development; once we are finished, we leave leadership development to do our work again." What they described were two different unconnected worlds. This lack of connection hurts the effectiveness of the leadership development experience, but it also fails to create the added benefit to their work. The more leaders and employees experience development as part of their jobs the more effective and higher impact of the development program.

11

DEFINE THE SCALE
AND SCOPE

To make an impact on an organization you have
to involve at least one-third of the leaders.
—**PETER DRUCKER**

It is important that the organization understand the target population for leadership development initiatives. It sets the parameters for who will be invited, for the budget for the activity and the overall boundaries. Expectations are also set.

Alternatives

As organizations design their initiative to develop leaders they face several key decisions. Will the initiative focus on:

1. *Top executives.* The argument in favor of that is their expanded influence and their long lasting impact.
2. *High potential candidates.* There is logic in investing in those the company believes have the greatest likelihood of ultimately filling the key leadership roles in the future. We address the special challenges of high potential programs later in this chapter.
3. *Those with faltering performance.* The argument is that the organization owes them every assistance in getting their career back on track. There is an existing investment in them.
4. *All executives and managers.* The argument in favor of this is the obvious impact it has on the overall organization, and that it enables every employee to have the opportunity to work for an excellent boss.

5. *Frontline leaders, including supervisors and team leads.* The argument in favor is that this enables leadership development to begin at an earlier age and to inculcate better leadership practices throughout the organization.

6. *Special groups or critical needs.* The argument in favor of this approach is that the organization may need a certain kind of manager. An example would be leaders prepared for global assignments. Or the organization may need greater emphasis on innovation.

7. *Individual contributors.* From the ranks of talented professionals in the organization, leaders will often emerge. The skills required of an effective leader are not significantly different from those of an individual contributor. Developing leadership skills with this group gives the organization an enormous head start.

Our Perspective

We have a point of view. We strongly support a more inclusive leadership development approach. Our arguments could be summed up as follows:

1. Every employee deserves to work for an excellent leader. Currently, employees think only half of their leaders are effective.

2. Every leader, no matter how effective, can elevate their performance, which in turn elevates the organization's performance.

3. Leadership occurs at all levels. Many people who do not have the title of manager or director are still performing important leadership functions.

4. Talented individual contributors are the pool from which future leaders will often be chosen.

5. Organizations lament the fact that their leadership pipeline is less than half-full. The only way to remedy that problem is to increase the number of individuals being prepared for leadership positions.[1]

The Need to Increase the Scope

We see far too many large organizations with thousands of managers, directors, and executives that provide formal development to fewer than

30 individuals in total each year. Many senior leaders are lulled into general comfort, believing that they have a leadership development program in place. This is despite the fact that it is clearly not reaching a significant percentage of the leadership population.

Another problem is that once leaders have been part of a leadership development effort, some assume they have been fixed and no longer need additional development. What is true in every organization is that the challenges for leaders constantly change. Direct reports change, competitors change, individual responsibilities change, and the skills leaders need to be successful change over time. Just as we know the value of regular checkups with doctors and dentists to determine our health, leaders need a regular checkup on their leadership effectiveness in order for them be at the peak of their effectiveness.

One highly esteemed business expert argued that if you were to impact the overall culture and performance of an organization you needed to reach at least one-third of the managers and preferably two-thirds. This is the single biggest deficiency we see in most organizations' overall leadership development efforts.

This is a prime example of the application of what is known as "herd immunity." A herd of cattle becomes immune to a communicable disease only when an extremely high proportion are immunized. The same applies to a human community immunization for diseases such as smallpox, measles, typhoid, and diphtheria. A recent outbreak of measles in Romania is attributed to the fact that 5 percent of the children had not been immunized. When even that few of the members of any community fail to be immunized, the non-vaccinated members of the community are again in jeopardy of contracting the disease, along with the entire next generation.

The Danger of Leaving Leaders Out

Our research confirms that leadership behavior is highly contagious. It cascades down upon the direct reports and keeps spilling down to the level below them. A senior executive who engages in inappropriate behavior contaminates their colleagues by serving as a negative role model. Bad behavior becomes the example that others follow. Worse yet, many employees are missing the opportunity to work with an excellent manager. Finally, organizational performance suffers as a result.

To illustrate this point, we did a study with more than 65,000 leaders looking at the impact of leadership effectiveness on the engagement of their subordinates. We know from other research we have conducted that the behavior of a poor leader generates low employee satisfaction. But, if a first-line supervisor in the same organization has a very ineffective leader above them, the direct reports of this supervisor are also unengaged and unsatisfied. The behavior of leaders at a higher level impacts the engagement levels two tiers below. What Figure 11.1 demonstrates is that regardless of the level of the leader in the hierarchy, the impact is consistent. If an organization has a highly effective senior leader then the direct reports of that leader are highly engaged. Believing that all you need for success in an organization is a few excellent leaders is not true.

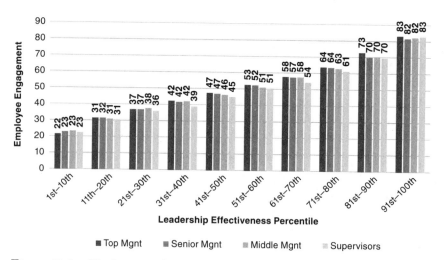

Figure 11.1. The Impact of Leadership Effectiveness at Various Management Levels on the Engagement of Their Subordinates

Every leader at every level lifts others up or pushes them down. Excellent organizations need excellent leaders at all levels and positions.

When Should Organizations Start Leadership Development?

How early in a person's career should the organization start to offer development? We believe most organizations are starting too late. We analyzed data for several client organizations and were startled that they were involving more leaders 60 years of age and older than those who were younger than 30 years old. They were surprised and sought to rectify that obvious mistake.

The average age of participants in the hundreds of leadership development programs that our firm supports is 42 years. If the average supervisor is appointed to that role in their late 20s, it suggests that most supervisors function for nearly a decade before receiving any formal training in leadership and management.

Our conclusion is that this is a missed opportunity to help more leaders have successful careers, to provide better overall management to the employees of the firm, and to help the organization achieve even higher levels of success.

Benefits of Investing in Younger Leaders

One of the authors was talking recently with the executive responsible for leadership development in a prominent Silicon Valley software firm that has been a long-term client. This organization had done a remarkable job of identifying their top talent and providing ongoing development experiences to this high potential group, in addition to their work with their most senior-level executives.

"So," I asked this executive, "if you were doing all this again, what would you do differently?" Without hesitation the answer was, "We'd begin this earlier in people's careers." Since that conversation we have given considerable thought to this statement. Why don't we start earlier in people's careers? Would this make a difference? Would dollars spent on the development of younger leaders in the firm have an even higher payoff? What about the risks?

In an article for *Harvard Business Review*, "We Wait Too Long to Train Our Leaders,"[2] we discussed the importance of leadership training earlier in a person's career. We analyzed data on roughly 17,000 leaders for whom we had precise data regarding their age at the time they participated in their company's leadership development process. It was no surprise to discover that the average age of all participants was 42. Half of all the participants were in a 13-year age band between 36 and 49. Less than 5 percent of all participants were younger than 27 years old, and only 10 percent were younger than age 30.

Think of the advantage of beginning formal leadership development at an earlier age, rather than waiting for nearly a decade of leadership experience before this valuable development work can begin. Prior research has shown that less than 10 percent of leaders, left to their own devices, will have any personal plan of development without the encouragement of a formalized process their company sponsors. Ponder the impact of leaders who make an additional nine years of contribution to their companies at a higher level of effectiveness.

Here are some conclusions:

1. *Leadership principles are more easily learned at a younger age.* Most readers can identify with the advantages of learning a skill at a younger versus an older age. If you go to a tennis club and watch the younger players who have had excellent instruction at a young age, and then visit a typical public court and watch young people playing who have had no instruction, the differences are obvious. If we want expert leaders, why not begin to find those interested in becoming effective leaders and help them accelerate their progress? The research on expert performance in any discipline, whether it be music, golf, or chess, confirms that experts are:

   * created by beginning at an early age, they
   * have an adult who guided them, and
   * practice 10,000 hours in contrast to the majority who might practice 2,000 hours.

2. *Generations Y and Z are capable of leading.* There is a high demand for more talented leaders in organizations. Rather than pirating from other firms, wouldn't it make greater sense to utilize the talented people within the company? Most organizations have significant numbers of leaders who will be retiring in the next 5 to 10 years. Our research with Gen X'ers, Gen Y'ers, and Millennials shows that these younger employees are every bit as focused on producing good results focused as their elders, and that they are more open to both seeking and acting on feedback from colleagues. Here are the data:

   * One of the stereotypes we have about the youngest generation is that they are more focused on themselves and less focused on company objectives. After analyzing the data on these different groups, we learned that the Gen Y group had the highest scores when it came to driving for results.

- Gen Y is sometimes stereotyped as being self-centered. Yet on the leadership competence of Collaboration and Teamwork, they were at the 60th percentile, while the percentile scores were lower for each older generation.
- Probably to no one's surprise, the Gen Y group received the highest scores on Innovation.
- The final surprise was the extremely high scores of the Gen Y group on the dimension of Practicing Self-Development. Here they were at the 64th percentile while baby boomers were at the 52nd percentile. This contradicts the image of complacent know-it-alls that is held by some.

Are there risks in a program like this? Naysayers will argue that the individual may move on and the investment will be lost. That is correct. However, the organization will still reap the gains from the improved performance of this person during the time they're employed. The likelihood of talented people leaving diminishes when they feel they are continually developing and improving.

Using repeated 360-degree feedback measures, we have found compelling evidence that the majority of leaders who participate in development programs are getting higher scores on essentially every leadership competency they measure. In most cases the changes are statistically significant, confirming they were not just chance occurrences. The payoff has been palpable and highly reassuring. If upper management, is not already highly supportive of development efforts, now there is hard evidence that confirms the value of their investment.

Challenges of "High Potential" Programs

Identifying high potential employees is a high priority for many companies. These individuals are the ones you assume to be capable of moving to senior positions in the organization. Organizations count on them to grow and ultimately make the most important strategic decisions. In sum, they are the best and brightest, most capable, and highly motivated. So naturally, the company will groom them for positions of responsibility and power.

But what if companies are unclear about what they are seeking? Are these people all potential C-Suite executives? Or are they better aligned for one or two levels beyond their current role? But what if the organization is using the wrong yardstick to measure potential? Or worse still, what if you identify the wrong people?

We analyzed data from three large, highly respected organizations. Our analysis showed the following:

1. **More than 40 percent of individuals in high potential programs may not belong there.** We determined this by collecting information on 1,964 employees from three organizations who had identified these individuals as their high potential picks. We measured their leadership capability using a 360-degree feedback assessment that consists of feedback from their immediate managers, peers, direct reports, and, in some cases, former colleagues or employees who had worked with them from two levels below them. On average, each leader had been given feedback from 13 assessors.

   Rather than being in the top 5 percent, we found that 12 percent of these individuals were in the bottom quartile and 42 percent were below average on their scores of overall leadership effectiveness. That is a long way from the top 5 percent to which they supposedly belong.

2. These individuals appeared to have been chosen primarily for current performance instead of long-term potential. In fact, we found three common characteristics these individuals possessed across all three organizations:

   • *Technical/professional expertise.* Having deep knowledge and expertise goes a long way in terms of getting a person noticed and valued. When you are one of the few people with specific understanding and experience in an area, you are valuable to the organization.

   • *Takes initiative and delivers results.* When a person can be counted on to achieve objectives and deliver results, they are viewed positively by senior leaders. When we asked more than 85,000 managers what was most important for their direct reports to be successful, their number one choice was "Drive for Results."

   • *Consistently honored commitments.* When these people say, "It will be done," you have strong assurance that indeed it will be done. This creates trust and a willingness to look beyond other skills that are not as excellent.

3. It is true that the best predictor of the future is the past. But what past performance should count? Clearly it is best if the performance is recent rather than decades ago. Past performance in a similar role should count more than performance in a totally different position. Should the number of promotions received be given greater weight than other measures of performance?

4. The skills that were consistently missing in the misplaced high potential employee were a lack of a strategic perspective and the inability to inspire and motivate others. Strategic perspective is the biggest difference between leaders at the highest levels in organizations and those in mid-management. The ability to inspire and motivate others is a close second. These two factors must be present for a person to succeed in a position two or more levels above their current role. One obvious concern is that organizations may easily be lulled into assuming that they have a full pipeline of future leaders, when in reality, it may have only a fraction of the future talent required.

Looking at this from the individual's perspective, another concern is that individuals who have been told (or figured out) they are part of the company's high potential program may become complacent and assume that their likelihood of being promoted is high, when it actually isn't. In fact, they may be steered in a less than optimum career direction when they were extremely effective individual contributors.

In summary, companies need to consider a broad set of attributes in the individuals they identify as future leaders. Those identified as high potential need to be intellectually curious, be voracious learners, possess the requisite technical knowledge and skills, aspire to move to higher positions, and be comfortable with responsibility and power. If they lack these qualities, they are probably not equipped for a more senior leadership role (although they may be highly valuable in individual contributor roles).

For those who are currently in a high potential program and really do not belong there, all is not necessarily lost. If these individuals aspire to more senior positions in the organization, many of the leadership skills they need can be acquired. However, it is vital to help these leaders understand the urgent need for skill development and acquiring new mindsets.

We are genuinely concerned about the number of individuals currently in the high potential programs of their organizations who don't really belong there. Our biggest concerns are that organizations may be investing their leadership development resources unwisely, while missing other candidates who have greater potential. Those with poor leadership skills can be developed, but it requires that they and their organization face up to their deficiency. Accurate assessment can help organizations and high potential candidates to understand their current capabilities and to recognize that the traits that get high potentials invited onto the roster do not necessarily equate to the skills it takes to get them on the varsity squad.

Conclusion

Organizations thirst for excellent leaders. This thirst is not satisfied by a small number of people at the apex of the organization. It is also not satisfied by the existence of several stars sprinkled in the midst of the organization. It is seldom satisfied by a group of elite "high potential" leaders who have been singled out from all the rest. It is also not met by a remedial program designed for those leaders who are faltering. Filling the leadership pipeline requires the involvement of a substantial percentage of the leaders of the firm.

12

ENSURE EXECUTIVE SUPPORT

*The greatest gift of leadership is a boss
who wants you to be successful.*
—JON TAFFER

Ensure Senior Manager Support

One of the authors, early in his career, worked in an organization that had not engaged in any leadership development in the past. As he began introducing this to the firm, he said to the CEO, "We need your support for this new initiative." The CEO was quick to reply, "You've got my support." Over time, however, it became apparent that the two had quite different understandings of what support meant. To the author who was heading up these initiatives, "support" meant:

- Financial support
- Attending initial development sessions to welcome participants and provide personal endorsement of the importance of these efforts
- Meeting with the CEO's immediate subordinates to ensure their active participation
- Actively participating in sessions as a role model for others
- Making leadership development an item on leadership team agendas
- And much more . . .

To the CEO "support" meant:

- Verbally telling others of his personal support of the initiative if asked

Being objective, however, the author realizes he was completely at fault for the misunderstanding. This was all new to the CEO. The problem was the HR vice president's failure to communicate a clear picture of what support truly meant and the specific actions the CEO needed to take.

Everyone who has worked in an organization knows that people pay attention to the actions of their boss. Yes, their words have some effect, but their actions send the loudest and clearest signal.

Research confirms that when executives serve as faculty for leadership development programs, it makes a difference. Spending an evening with participants, informally answering questions, and being actively involved in the give-and-take of serious discussions all make a difference. When a senior executive attends every development session and attests to the applicability of what an instructor is teaching, that makes a difference. When managers relate to their subordinates what they personally learned from attending a development session and how they are applying it in their job, it makes an enormous difference in the outcomes.

The issue of executive support for leadership development solutions is far more complex than often acknowledged. Unfortunately, all too often, we hear generalizations ("We don't have executive support for this") without due consideration of the variables that must be taken into account. What are these variables, and what clear strategies do learning professionals need to determine whether the required degree of executive support for a leadership development initiative is present?

When considering executive support, three variables are in play:

- The degree of influence of each executive member
- The purpose of the leadership development initiative
- The nature of the support given

Executive Organizational Influence

The word "executive" is used to describe several individuals, each with differing degrees of influence within the organization. Some have more and others have less influence. Some have more influence on a specific topic or issue, while others have less.

Organizational influence in general is derived from power. The more that an executive controls resources, makes strategic decisions, promotes or terminates key people, and forms important alliances the more power that person has. The degree to which an executive exhibits admired qualities and the more coworkers defer to their ideas and directives, the more power and influence they possess. An executive's place in the corporate organization chart bestows upon him or her "position power" or "role power." A CEO generally has more authority, and thus influence, than the other members of the executive team. Titles such as executive vice president or senior vice president confer greater power than vice president. The amount of power and influence given by titles and positions is also driven by the culture of the organization and often the industry. Banks are notorious for having multiple vice presidents and the weight or muscle of the title in many organizations has become eroded.

Above and beyond power, influence can stem from the use of effective influence tactics such as ingratiation, threats, reason and logic, and coalition building.[1] In addition, research also suggests that influence stems from personal characteristics, and specifically, the fit between the person and his or her organization. Extraverts tend to have more influence in a team-oriented organization, whereas conscientious introverts attain more influence in an organization in which individuals work alone on technical tasks.[2]

This suggests that the formal authority of various executives is not sufficient to determine their degree of influence within the organization. Even if two individuals have the same level of power, they might differ in their levels of influence if one uses more effective influence tactics than the other or has a personality that is better matched with the culture of the organization.

For example, a CEO may have the greatest organizational authority, yet a chief operating officer may wield the most day-to-day influence. Organizational influence may be present around the executive table, but it is often the up-and-coming young leaders who are seen as future successors who will have the most influence within the organization. Some around the executive table may have a lesser influence, particularly if they are heading for retirement.

The degree of organizational influence an executive holds determines the type of support that is required for a leadership development initiative from each executive. While the nature of the leadership development training initiative is also a factor, it is safe to assume that more overt support is needed from those with significant organizational influence. Conversely, less support is required from those with lesser degrees of organizational influence.

Purpose of the Leadership Development Solution

Leadership development undertakings vary in purpose. Some solutions are strategic in nature, but such initiatives tend to be full-scale, organization-wide solutions focused on behavioral change and are best regarded as organizational change initiatives. Conversely, leadership training focused more on education and knowledge acquisition is unlikely to change the very essence of the organization and thus can be considered more tactical in nature.

In terms of executive support, the more influential the solution, the more support required. Leadership development that can in any way be considered strategic or transformational, requires significant executive support. In this regard, it is no different from other strategic undertakings such as an acquisition, new marketing initiative, or launch of a new product. It would be difficult to envision these strategic initiatives taking place without full executive support. Leadership development focused on organizational transformation should be no different.

The Nature of Executive Support

The final factor to be considered is the nature of support. All too often, it is viewed as an absolute—you either have it or you do not. In reality, executive support comes in many shapes and sizes, from being active participants in the learning or organizational sponsors, to simply permitting the initiative to take place and not sabotaging it.

When faced with a leadership solution, an executive may assume any one of a number of attitudes. He may be opposed, neutral, attentive, engaged, or responsible.

Opposed

When an executive is opposed, he concludes that a learning initiative is unnecessary, either culturally or from an expense point of view. While he may not openly verbalize his opposition, he may actively sabotage the program by preventing his people from participating in it, criticizing it, or discouraging new behaviors and ideas promoted in it, or withholding funds in some way. When dealing with a resistant executive, it is critical to get buy-in for at least some element of the initiative. The good news with the resistant executive is at least there is passion, which has the potential to be redirected. Although it will be a tough battle, it can be done.

Neutral

The most troublesome executive is the one that is neutral. Unfortunately, this is quite common within organizations. In this case, a senior executive may believe that the accountability for people and organizational development does not lie within her scope of responsibilities and instead abdicates everything to human resources, the organizational development group, or external consultants.

While this may free up those functions to do whatever they want (as long as it is in keeping with budget), the chance of any initiative gaining traction within the organization is slim at best because the initiative is seen "only" as an human resources program and is conceptually shelved as irrelevant to strategy.

Furthermore, it is likely that participants, especially senior managers, will conclude that the executives don't care about development. This typically makes it hard for anyone to take development seriously, and in ways that make it effective. It is certainly possible to do skill-building and knowledge acquisition without any executive interest. But in our experience, it is foolhardy to believe that initiatives framed against a disinterested executive will have any major organizational consequences unless that executive has very limited influence within the organization.

Attentive

The first level of positive support is being attentive. In this case, executives see the possible benefits of a well-designed learning or change initiative and thus are likely to support it in one or more ways. For example, they may be present for launch and closure, they might ensure that their people are sufficiently freed up to spend time on their learning, and they may support any changes in behavior they see. While clearly such behaviors are more effective than those exhibited by an opposed or neutral executive, all too often executives convince themselves that simply being interested in the program qualifies as sufficient support.

In these cases, executives typically underestimate the impact of their actions. Interest with neither involvement nor accountability is a long way from what is required to create meaningful organizational change. Participants will "read" meaning into the lack of involvement from an executive and conclude that the initiative is not a strategic imperative. Equally, a lack of accountability around the initiative can mean that it is not tied to specific organizational strategies.

Engaged

When executives become engaged, they step inside the initiative not only as a supporter but as an active participant. In this case, an executive will temporarily drop her role and stand side by side with other organizational members as a participant in learning. The modeling of learning that takes place creates a powerful statement for all employees and demonstrates that learning is important and something that is valued by the organization. It is not just a reward or gift; it is something worthwhile for everyone in the organization, regardless of rank. Obviously, managing executive participation in an initiative requires careful planning to keep traditional hierarchical patterns out of the environment, but the payoff can be powerful.

Responsible

The highest level of support is one in which an executive takes responsibility for the impact and success of the training solution. By taking accountability for learning strategies, an executive publicly acknowledges the initiative as a tool for organizational change. This executive frequently and publicly pays close attention to the program and in so doing sends a loud message to participants that it is an important initiative. While, just as the interested executive, they may attend launches and graduations, their tone is different and the questions they ask portray a greater intensity. They are focused on outcomes, impact, and results and continually stay in touch with how the program is unfolding. The accountable executive also makes sure the initiative is integrated into other parts of the organizational system and does not see this as a simple training program.

The ultimate expression of responsibility is one that can lead to the most significant organizational impact. It is when the executive is totally invested in the initiative—emotionally, personally, and organizationally. The responsible executive combines the very best of the attentive and engaged executive. By taking responsibility for learning strategies, executives see the learning as a tool for organizational change.

By being an active participant and investing in their own development, executives publicly acknowledge they have a responsibility in the organizational transformation and it is not simply up to others to implement the strategic change. To create "invested" executives for learning, it is important that learning professionals not only involve executives in strategic organizational and people development, but also ask them both to make such initiatives part of strategic planning and invest time and commitment into their own development. This level of support can create amazing results and is exactly what is required for a high-impact organizational change solution.

Case Study

John was an excellent CEO. He agreed that all the executives in his organization would participate in a leadership development experience. The experience involved 360-degree assessment along with one and a half days to training. Prior to the training event, John participated in a webinar to kick off the assessments and the training program. He did a great job of asking everyone to give the training event their full attention. He also indicated that he wanted to see the action plans for all his direct reports and would encourage them to do this same thing for their direct reports. John was told up-front that he would need to complete 10 assessments on his direct reports. He agreed and did them all in one weekend. We were very impressed with his involvement and commitment. Once all of the 360-degree assessments had been collected, we analyzed the data and had a short meeting with John to brief him on the results.

One of the first slides that we showed to John was the overall leadership effectiveness of his senior team their direct report managers. We compared their results to our global norms, and as a group they came in at the 42nd percentile. John was visibly shocked. He said, "I thought I had a very competent team. I imagined them being in the top quartile of leaders." We commented that several of the leaders rose to that level, but the majority of the leaders were below average. He then said, "This changes everything, I really have some work to do." John had been following the advice we had given him to initiate and kick off the program but he imagined that the results would be very positive and not require much involvement on his part. Once John had a valid measure of the level of effectiveness of his leaders, he became truly accountable.

Conclusion

Any learning initiative is fundamentally a change initiative. Many leadership development efforts are treated as "training," and training is often not seen as organizational change. A lack of strong senior support usually self-fulfills this prophecy. However, for leadership development to "stick," all of the ingredients of managing and leading a successful organizational change must be present.

John Kotter reminds us that a coalition must be built to support change.[3] Our observation based on years of working with organizations on leadership development is that the nature of the coalition supporting development can vary depending on the executive "players" but also the nature of the desired outcome of the development.

Fundamentally, however, a leadership development effort aimed at changing the way people lead in an organization must be supported visibly from those senior leaders that are viewed as touchstones for leadership within the organization. Without this support, the development aim will almost certainly fall flat—how could it not? If the actual influential leaders in an organization do not support a new way of talking and thinking about leadership, we cannot expect a change in the culture until the players themselves shift—in effect, leave.

A strong leadership development initiative needs to be as carefully planned as any change initiative and the appropriate coalition of support needs to be sought. As our model illustrates, "support" can come in many forms and crucially must be matched to the actual and symbolic power senior leaders have within the organization.

Today, the notion of purposefully developing the company's executive talent pool and cultivating the future leadership cadre is almost universally embraced. Most CEOs accept the logic of tying their executive and leadership development programs to the long-term strategic goals of their companies. Yet, even though they get it in theory, many CEOs do not embrace this concept in practice. How do we know? It quickly becomes evident when examining where leadership development as a function typically falls within an organization.[4]

One of an organization's most sustainable sources of competitive advantage is its leadership talent, yet leadership development often falls layers down within most organizations. It is frequently buried under a human resources vice president who, in many cases, does not have the ear of the CEO and may not be trained in the leadership development side of the human capital space. HR professionals and leadership development professionals are fundamentally different in their focus as well as their background and training:

- HR professionals' jobs often lean toward the legal and compliance side of the house in that they cover recruiting, hiring, performance evaluations, reorganizations, diversity issues, grievances, benefits, employee compensation, state and federal policy compliance, disciplinary actions, layoffs, and firings.

- Executive and leadership development professionals are corporate educators. Their areas of expertise span both management and leadership development. They conduct needs assessments for the entire organization as well as its divisions and business units to evaluate current skills against business objectives, and then develop programs to close gaps. They ensure smooth delivery of and continuous improvements to each program, while maintaining consistency of key learnings. They need to work closely with senior management teams across the enterprise to identify and anticipate learning needs of all employees, from the frontline to the senior-level leaders, to ensure that the right people are ready when the company needs talent to step up into key roles. They must define prioritized annual objectives and provide leaders with the coaching and guidance needed to cultivate success. They must also enable change management efforts and organizational planning at the highest level to position the company for ongoing future growth.

Shareholders are consistently demanding higher returns, and we know that an organization's executive and leadership talent are its greatest and most sustainable sources of competitive advantage. Then why do executives still cite lack of bench strength in their future leadership group as the primary concern on their ability to deliver key results? Why is it that most leaders failing in this area do so due to leadership issues, not skill-related issues? Our trends research shows that this has been the same story for more than a decade. So why haven't we conquered these problems? Is it that we don't know how or are we unwilling to make changes in order to rectify the situation?

A strong case can be made to separate the HR and leadership development functions completely within any given organization, with HR reporting to the general counsel due to the litigious nature of the job functions, and have leadership development report to the CEO. Why? Because the CEO ultimately owns leadership. He/she is the chief leader of the company, the person ultimately accountable for ensuring that the company has a clear sense of purpose and vision, is appropriately aligned at all levels, and delivers results. Employees must know where the organization is headed and be trained and prepared to take it there.

If the CEO owns leadership development, then the person over that function should be near the CEO on the organization chart. He or she would ideally have a seat at the senior leadership table to be able to hear the daily struggles of the business, and then recommend the best methods to educate and train the workforce to tackle problems and achieve desired goals. He or she can learn about new lines of business, new projects, and/or products in the pipeline firsthand and then ensure that the talent pool is packed full of prepared leaders to support any critical new functions. The CEO, then, becomes a champion for leadership development by utilizing the function to achieve real and practical business results. The days of floating corporate education with no real tie to the performance of an organization are over. It's time for a change, which ultimately starts and ends with the CEO.

13

USE POWERFUL
LEARNING METHODS

Tell me and I forget, teach me and I
remember, involve me and I learn.
—BENJAMIN FRANKLIN

In the world of medicine, there is principle that a disease or injury should be treated with the least heroic treatment method that will successfully cure it. What is also understood but not always stated, however, is that it does little good to treat something with medicines or procedures that are incapable of curing it. The safety and efficacy of treatments are the two greatest concerns monitored by the Food and Drug Administration. Pharmaceutical companies should not sell products that fail to do what they purport to do.

We have often mused about the idea of some regulatory body testing the various activities that are conducted in the name of leadership development. These range from assembling Tinkertoys to outdoor rope courses. Large amounts of money are being spent and the little research that has been conducted show many to be ineffective.

If it is to be successful, leadership development must use learning methods that have the power to make behavioral change. Historically that was not the case. Many of us recall the days when leadership development was largely an academic exercise, built exclusively on the practices of traditional university instruction. Development programs consisted of lectures, reading assignments, and interactions with the professor. Successful leadership development doesn't work if there is only information transfer. There may be many new insights, but they must be put into action. Our methods would ideally change behavior for keeps.

What Does Not Work?

There are a variety of activities with which we are all familiar that fail to meet this behavioral change test. They include:

- *Lectures*—Research shows that a minimal amount heard in a lecture registers on the human brain and is put in memory. Worse yet, 75 to 80 percent of the content that is learned is quickly forgotten.
- *Articles*—Most adults encounter dozens, if not hundreds, of articles per week. There is seldom any behavioral change resulting from reading an article.
- *Films*—A good film can serve as an excellent example of correct behavior. But even the most engaging TED Talk seldom results in new actions or behavior on the part of the viewer.
- *Books*—Books are powerful vehicles to bring knowledge, facts, and ideas. Unfortunately, they also do not often lead to implementation, action, or new behavior.

What Works

There are some generally accepted and widely used workhorses of leadership development. They have been proven to impact a leader's behavior. They are widely applauded by the participants. The most frequently used ones include:

1. *Multi-rater feedback or 360-degree process.* Far beyond only giving people greater self-awareness, this process provides heightened motivation and the tools for individual leaders to better manage their personal development. At the organizational level, it provides aggregate data about groups of leaders and informs those responsible for leadership development about those areas in which development would be most productive.

2. *Individual development plans.* Complex and important activities invariably work better when there is a plan for their execution. Our data show that fewer than 5 percent of leaders, left to their own devices, create a personal plan of development for themselves. The development plans that do stand out are

those that encourage a leader to create a personalized development plan to which they are personally committed. This is an important step in them becoming a better leader.

3. *Coaching.* There is a wealth of evidence confirming that combining any development activity with a coaching engagement is extremely powerful and improves the final outcome. The coach helps the person being coached to explore alternatives, jointly monitors their progress, and provides useful suggestions for further action. The coach holds the participant accountable for implementing what he or she has learned.

4. *Simulations.* Well-constructed simulations replicate the way a company or a market functions. Participants are able to make a series of decisions in minutes and hours that replicate months and years of an organization's operations. Great learning occurs from discovering the consequences of decisions, the necessity of a clear operating strategy, how decisions affect each other, and what constitutes effective execution.

5. *Skill-building through practice or rehearsal.* Skills can be learned. They are a complex set of behaviors that combine to accomplish a worthwhile task. Coaching, for example, is a valuable skill for every leader to possess. It is best learned when participants see positive examples of it being done well. Learning a simple conceptual framework is vital, but the key to acquiring a new skill such as coaching is practicing the behavior and receiving feedback on how effectively it is being used.

6. *Using a current position to experiment or apply a new skill.* Building relationships, for example, is an important skill. Virtually every position a person may hold in a business affords valuable opportunities to utilize and enhance this skill of building relationships. Most jobs are the ideal classroom and laboratory in which to learn and practice leadership behavior.

7. *Senior executive involvement.* Interaction with senior executives is a proven way for leaders to learn valuable lessons. Hopefully, executives serve as excellent role models. They illuminate the practical implications of what participants learn. Recounting their own leadership journey (along with the mistakes they made) can be highly informative, motivating, and reassuring for participants.

8. *Immediate manager interaction.* The immediate manager of every participant can play a powerful role in that leader's development. Immediate managers can provide valuable coaching and are a source of valuable feedback because of their unique vantage point. They have strong influence over the leader's career. Most important is the influence an immediate manager can have on following up on a direct report's action plan. Doing this increases the accountability of the direct report to make changes.

9. *Action learning projects.* Inviting participants to tackle a timely and important challenge the company faces provides excellent opportunities for learning. Having a team of leaders diagnose a company problem or opportunity, create practical solutions, and then take responsibility for implementing those decisions is simultaneously a valuable learning activity and a great benefit to the organization. Many organizations have a facilitator work with an ad hoc team to increase the likelihood that both the task is accomplished and that maximum learning takes place in the process.

10. *Nonlinear development.* Chapter 8 described the theory and research behind this unique developmental approach. When people are already quite good at something, their development pathway may be greatly enhanced by looking at the companion behaviors that go hand in hand with a leadership competency. Rather than always running headlong into an area for personal improvement, there are side doors that are also available. (Those familiar with billiards or pool know that there are times when the only way to hit the correct ball involves a bank shot.)

What These Learning Methods Have in Common

Why are these the most useful methods used in leadership development? What do they have in common?

1. *They are built upon a common mindset.* They assume that people can grow, improve, and change. They are grounded in a positive view of human potential.

2. *The North Star for each of them is behavior change.* They are more than content that provides people with greater awareness or flashes of insight. They do not stop at providing more information. They are grounded upon the idea of action and implementation.

3. *They are highly involving and fun.* Participants cannot be passive while doing them.

4. *They emphasize the identification and building of strengths.* While weaknesses are not ignored, identifying faults and shortcomings is not the primary focus of the development activity.

5. *They are forward leaning rather than focused on recounting past actions and behavior.* Their clear purpose is to improve the future behavior of the leaders involved.

6. *They are tailored and personalized.* They do not rely solely on general principles, ideas, or practices that blanket everyone uniformly. The data in a 360-degree feedback instrument are totally personalized for the individual. The participant normally selects those who provide feedback. The development plan participants create is unique to them. While a general topic, such as coaching, may be learned, the learning experience becomes specific and personal for them.

7. *Responsibility is transferred to the participant.* The person ultimately responsible for the individual's learning is not the manager, human resources, the facilitator, the company, nor other participants. All participants are ultimately responsible for their own learning. At the same time, participants in the same firm should be especially motivated to help their colleagues grow and develop. As our colleague Marshall Goldsmith says and has written, leadership is definitely a team sport. Participants benefit from helping each other.

8. *They invite immediate application.* The assumption behind these methods is that the learning can in most cases be immediately applied. The participant need not wait days, weeks, or months before using this new behavior.

9. *They are aspirational.* The goal is never to "just get by" or become average. The goal is to behave like the best.

10. *They help the learner to be accountable for making progress.* Most every leader would like to change and improve, but some lack

the discipline necessary to change while others get distracted by shiny objects. Finding ways to create accountability makes a huge difference between those who change and those who try.

The Importance of Choosing Powerful Methods

If we are to really advance the practice of leadership, we must adopt the fundamental premise that propelled the reform of medical practice. We have mentioned earlier the work of Dr. David Eddy in leading the charge toward evidence-based medicine. In 1972, Dr. Eddy began a crusade to bring more science to the practice of medicine. He had awakened one morning and recalls telling his wife that he had concluded that about 15 percent of what physicians and surgeons did had any scientific evidence to support it. Adults were undergoing annual chest x-rays to detect tuberculosis, and he suspected that the harm being done far outweighed the infrequent detection of a disease. Hospitals were putting silver nitrate drops in newborn infant's eyes, yet there was no evidence that this did any good. As it turned out, both processes were doing harm. Operations to insert tubes in children's eardrums to drain fluid behind the ear drum were doing more damage than good and leaving children with hearing loss.

The problem was that individual practitioners were using methods that they thought worked, and they saw some patients improve afterward. This convinced them that their methods were of value. But practitioners were seeing only a few cases. The epidemiologist and researcher were necessary to see the big picture. Only then could it be determined what was having benefit and what was not.[1]

So what percentage of what we do as leadership development practitioners is based on good science?

As the authors reflect on the various stages of their own careers, it is clear to us there are some activities that seemed right at the time, but in hindsight were not ideally effective. One author, for example, spent many years immersed in sensitivity training and the "T-Group" movement. The university he attended had been at the center of its development. Yes, there were notable successes. It was an exciting process. But after a number of years, when research analyzed the actual business outcomes, it was clear the overall results were not as positive as other methods.

At about this time he became aware of a very different approach to development, this time based on solid research. The business outcomes were consistent and the process was much more efficient than what he had seen in the past. That technique, behavior modeling, has now become the most highly accepted methodology for helping leaders acquire new skills.

The lesson is to continually adopt methodologies that have better research to support them, and abandon those that are not working as well. But to accomplish this we need to apply a rigorous, research orientation to leadership development.

Medicine, while having made great progress, still struggles to get practitioners to abandon its less effective procedures or treatments. Sometimes this means avoiding a new drug or procedure because the old ones actually produce better results. In other cases, it means giving up old ways that worked on occasion (many times people get better without any treatment or despite what you've done) in place of something that is clearly better.

Ideally, we should refine our tendency to continually seek for something new and instead seek purely for the techniques that work the best. Better means they may be more efficient. Or they may produce more behavioral change. They may be more appealing to leaders and easier for them to implement. These should become the litmus tests we apply as we select the various methodologies to use.

Our opportunity in leadership development is to bring more science into what we do by creating ever better ways to measure the current state of leadership behavior, along with the change we produce. This allows us to bring science into the art of leadership development and to drive out the nonsense that will always fill the void where good science doesn't exist.

Conclusion

Medicine has greatly benefitted from the strong and pervasive movement to evidence-based medicine. It finds its way into conversations you hear in clinics and hospitals. It has clearly elevated the practice of medicine, which was one of the more scientifically rigorous professions in existence.

Think of the progress that could accompany a similar movement within the leadership development profession. With estimates ranging from $150 to $350 billion being spent annually on this activity worldwide, it is hard to estimate the dollars that could be saved. More important, because leadership development is such a high-leverage activity, consider the added gains that could elevate the performance of organizations and the careers of individuals. Leadership effectiveness is the single most important determinant of organizational performance and long-term survival.

14

EMBED LEADERSHIP DEVELOPMENT INTO THE CULTURE

*The stronger the culture, the less corporate process
a company needs. When the culture is strong you
can trust everyone to do the right thing.*
—BRIAN CHESKY, COFOUNDER AND CEO OF AIRBNB

One criticism directed at many leadership development programs has been that they were disconnected from the day-to-day operations of the company. It is as if they are two ships passing in the night. Not only must the leadership development initiative link with the strategy of the organization, it needs to be in complete harmony with the day-to-day operating procedures and behaviors of the firm.

We propose three major ways in which the leadership development initiative can be better integrated with the culture of the organization:

1. Embed the leadership development concepts and nomenclature into other human resources systems.
2. Assist participants to inject leadership development content into their current position and daily activities.
3. Thoroughly involve the immediate manager of the participant in the development process.

I. Integrate the Concepts and Nomenclature Used in the Leadership Development Initiative into All HR Systems

In Chapter 3 we described at length the importance of a competency model that defines the behavior that is expected of leaders in the organization. It is common for senior leadership teams to spend a significant amount of time in hammering out these competencies. However, ironically, in many organizations, these competencies are used only for the leadership development initiatives and do not find their way into other HR systems. We strongly advocate the complete alignment of the content of leadership development with all other HR systems, such as:

- Recruitment
- Selection
- Onboarding
- Performance management
- Promotion
- Compensation

We have seen the consequences of organizations populating the other HR systems with the same terminology and competencies of their leadership development program. It is easy to predict the consequence of this action. There is now greater consistency and alignment between all the systems. Everyone becomes familiar with the behaviors that are emphasized.

Now the recruitment process emphasizes the same behaviors that have been identified for development. Hiring managers are using these concepts when they decide which candidate to bring on board. Behavioral interviewing questions can be structured that align with the competency model. These same behaviors are described and emphasized in the onboarding process for all new hires. All performance management systems are built on the same skeleton structure as the leadership development initiatives. Performance discussions and coaching interactions are structured to follow the same competencies being taught in every leadership development initiative. When promotion decisions are made, they are carefully linked to the competency model used in the leadership development programs. Compensation decisions are geared to reward individuals who consistently adhere to the principles that are now common to all HR systems.

II. Integrate Leadership Development Content into the Participant's Daily Work

The everyday activities of virtually every position afford the opportunity to experiment and use new ideas and behavior. Some of those are described in the following sections.

1. Expand Knowledge

The concepts gained in a leadership development program can provide useful guidance in terms of the additional learning and knowledge the participant pursues as part of his or her job. For example, one of the competencies included in many organizations' competency model has to do with technical knowledge. Pursuing further information about your firm's products and services is now aligned. Most competency models also include strategic thinking, and this is fulfilled in a current position by seeking information regarding the organization's current strategy, how the overall market functions, and the long-term decisions with which senior executives are wrestling. In addition, competency models almost always include skills having to do with human interactions—collaboration, teamwork, and building strong relationships.

2. Build New Relationships

Nearly everybody in an organization is afforded the opportunity to learn to build stronger and more extensive relationships. These can be with other departments as well as with members of an immediate team. It can involve building relationships with staff support groups that provide assistance, as well as with other organizational cousins whose work connects with your own.

Most positions also provide the opportunity of building relationships with outside individuals and groups. These can be customers, trade associations, academic institutions, and suppliers.

3. Initiate Special Interest Groups

Being inside an organization provides the opportunity to spearhead the creation of special groups. If an employee's personal development plan calls for gaining more expertise in strategic planning, a group could be formed that was specifically interested in that topic. In a large organization, the head of strategic planning or corporate development could be invited as a special guest speaker. As another example, many organizations have a women's group created to address the specific challenges and opportunities that women face.

4. Develop New Habits for Planning and Reflection

Every position offers the opportunity to apply better planning habits and to reflect on a workday. If better planning of a day's activities is a developmental goal, virtually every job is a good place to practice that skill. If the development target is to become better at assessing personal productivity and observing ways in which it could be magnified, that can occur in virtually every position. If a development target is to streamline work processes and improve the overall efficiency of the systems in an arena, you have the perfect laboratory or classroom for that.

5. Create New Feedback Mechanisms

At the heart of virtually all leadership development programs is a strong component of feedback. A leader's performance is greatly enhanced when there is an abundant stream of constructive feedback. Our research shows that while all kinds of feedback can be helpful, people benefit most from reaffirming, positive messages. Next most helpful are the corrective or redirecting feedback that suggest new behaviors that could be initiated, better ways of executing certain tasks, and actions that should be stopped. Leaders can learn new and effective ways of gaining such feedback.

The key step, whether you are a subordinate or the boss, is simply to ask—feedback is more likely to be provided when you sincerely ask others for it. One successful technique is simply asking an individual for "one suggestion for how I could do [name something] better." That question (or something like it) sends the message that you are not simply fishing for compliments, but that you genuinely want constructive suggestions.

If your organization makes available a multi-rater (or 360-degree) feedback process, by all means volunteer to take part. As mentioned earlier, it is the most effective mechanism for receiving honest feedback from one's colleagues and can be a life-changing experience if people pay attention to the results.

Managers can solicit feedback at the conclusion of every meeting, seeking ideas for how future meetings can be even more effective. There is a wide variety of mechanisms that can be instituted whatever your position in the organization.

6. Experiment with New Management Practices

Your current position offers the opportunity to experiment. You can try various formats for staff and team meetings. You can implement what the military has called "after action reviews" that involve meeting at the conclusion of a project and conducting a postmortem on the outcomes. The usual questions are:

1. What did we intend to happen?
2. What really happened?
3. What made the difference?
4. What should we do differently next time?

This simple exercise is not meant to find fault or point fingers. It works best when people have symbolically "taken off their stripes" and can discuss the event as a group of equals coming together. It is important to identify the good things that transpired so that they can be repeated.

III. Better Involve the Immediate Manager

One of the boxes on most performance appraisal forms is a summary of the individual's plans for development during the ensuing year. Such plans are usually sketchy. They most often include some outside or internally sponsored course or programs the individual can attend. But there is often a shortage of detailed planning, and such plans typically give way to the pressures of the job as the year unfolds.

As a result, the percentage of such plans that get completed is rather small. Yet most would agree that one key to improving your career and meeting long-term aspirations is to constantly strive to improve your knowledge and skills. That applies to the professional staff of the firm, and it equally applies to the cadre of managers in the firm.

Is it possible to improve the likelihood that such plans are actually implemented? How could we elevate both the quantity and quality of such plans moving from paper into actual performance? Our first recommendation is to involve your manager in your personal development. Note that we didn't say, "Inform you manager." The message is to truly involve your immediate boss in your development.

Why Managerial Involvement?

Figure 14.1 provides some insights into the importance of managerial involvement.

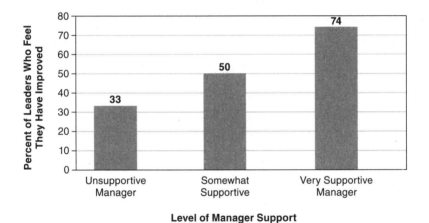

Figure 14.1. Impact of Perceived Managerial Support on Perceived Development

These data come from a study of 61 financial managers, who were asked to describe the level of support they had received from their current manager in their own development process. They were also asked to evaluate the degree to which they thought they had improved in their leadership skills. This is not a large study and is based on the perceptions of the individuals involved. Nevertheless, note the dramatic relationship between the amount of progress these leaders felt they had made and the level of support they received from their manager.

What the Manager Needs to Know and Do

In order for managers to help in their subordinates' development, they need some information. Here are a few of the things we think they should learn from every subordinate:

1. What are this person's career goals and ambitions?
2. What do they think they need from management to further their career?
3. What do they plan to do in order to further their career ambitions?

Then there are some things the manager needs to do:

1. Schedule time for periodic coaching conversations.
2. Allocate part of the time to discussions of this person's career.
3. Identify and create time for them to attend formal development sessions through the year.
4. Plan and schedule follow-up conversations after each development program to review how new knowledge and skills are being applied.

How to Get the Manager Involved

It could be argued that the development of direct reports is part of every manager's job and that the manager should take the initiative to make it happen. While that is nice in theory, those who have worked in large organizations know this is frequently the exception, not the rule.

Why doesn't it happen? The reasons range from the time crunch leaders live with, to the fact that some managers don't exactly know how to do it. Others aren't sure how it will be received by their employees. Some may confess or complain that no one did it for them. In some cases, immediate pressures win out in the competition for what's top-of-mind.

In a conversation with a group of managers, we asked them about the level of managerial involvement they had received in the time since attending a development session some 10 months earlier. On a scale of 1 to 10 (with 10 being high involvement), the average was between a 2 and 3. We asked if we should intervene and let the next level of managers above them know that they had collectively not followed through as they should. Virtually to a person, the group said, "No." In different words, the same message was expressed: "We didn't invite them to get involved." "We're largely responsible for their lack of involvement."

Since then, every comparable group we've talked with, following an original leadership development experience, has confirmed their belief that their leaders would be far more involved if only they were invited and knew they were wanted and needed.

When the manager gets involved, everyone wins. The likelihood of the individual following through on their development plan increases substantially. The skill level of the direct report improves. The manager is more likely to fulfill a major responsibility they know they have. The organization benefits from improved performance and from having a better-developed pool of talent. If you want to jump-start your development, take immediate steps to get your manager involved. Everyone wins in the process.

When Is It Better to Receive Than to Give?

We were all taught while we were young that it is better to give than to receive. After all, giving has great benefits for both the recipient and the giver. There's one exception, however, and that has to do with the exchange of feedback between bosses and those who report to them. In this case, it's usually better to receive.

First, let's acknowledge there are enormous benefits when bosses provide feedback to colleagues. Why? Because people want to know how they're doing. Most want to continually get better, and feedback is a great way to facilitate this progress. Such feedback could be exclusively positive reinforcement, or it could be a mix of praise along with suggestions for improvement. .

For example, the manager could say: "Great presentation, Jim. Good information and really clear graphs of what's been happening. Next time, could I suggest that you give a few examples—tell some stories. That's what convinces this senior team as much as the data."

Or it could be more difficult feedback that is intended to correct their behavior that detracts from their performance. "Greg, are you open to hearing some information about how people are reacting to some of your recent emails on cost containment?"

"Yes. What have you heard?"

"Well, people think you are focused on some inconsequential items, like delivery costs and packaging materials, and that you put the customer's interests way below saving a few pennies on the delivery of an order. Now, I know we need to keep some balance, but I've looked over your emails and listened to what others are feeling. I believe they are correct. You've put too much emphasis on the small stuff."

That's direct feedback, and for most of us it is the hardest to give. And let's face it, the great majority of managers shy away from giving such feedback. Such messages are uncomfortable at best, and downright painful at worst. The arguments in favor of doing it are not only that it leads to better performance, but that it also greatly increases the level of employee engagement.

We have some new research that shows that there is an even better way to increase employee engagement. Surprisingly, the secret is for the manager to ask for feedback. The impact of asking is even more powerful than giving it. Based on a study we conducted, here's what happens to the employee engagement percentile scores in different conditions of the manager asking for and giving feedback:

- 29th percentile: Manager neither asks nor gives feedback
- 34th percentile: Manager doesn't ask but gives feedback
- 48th percentile: Manager asks but doesn't give feedback
- 74th percentile: Manager both asks for and gives feedback

Good things come from asking for feedback. Seeking other's opinions has a host of benefits. It conveys respect. It reduces barriers between the levels. The manager learns valuable information that comes in no other way. Empirically, it also reduces employees' intention to leave and go elsewhere by 10 percentage points.

Clearly the ideal is for managers to both give and get, but if you have to choose one or the other, our data suggest that it is better to receive than to give.

Conclusion

The process of integrating leadership development into the culture of the organization is a topic fully deserving heightened attention. Those in the leadership development profession have focused much of their attention on the content, followed by the delivery methods of gaining knowledge and changing behavior. An afterthought, it seems, was the issue of how these ideas and practices would be imbedded into the warp and woof of the organization. A metaphor may be the preparation of a savory meal, with healthy ingredients including wonderful tastes and outstanding appearance and preparation.

If the ultimate purpose of eating, however, is to gain effective nutrition, the meal is only as good as how much of it is actually digested into the organs and systems of the person who eats it. How much of a leadership development initiative is digested into the systems of the organization? That is the ultimate question and the real measure of success.

15

SUSTAIN AND
FOLLOW-THROUGH

*It's not that I'm so smart. It's just that
I stay with problems longer.*
—ALBERT EINSTEIN

"One and done" is by far the most frequent criticism we hear about leadership development initiatives. The comment is seldom mean-spirited. Rather, it is said quite matter-of-factly. "It was a wonderful time being with my colleagues. I learned a lot. I came back to my job and put the binder up on my shelf. I went back to 'things as usual.'"

Why Is This Such a Major Issue?

Organizations have put nearly all their attention and effort on the training event itself. Far less attention has been paid to what happens following the event. Time for attending the learning event is blocked out on our calendars. This program or class successfully protects the participants from the pressures of their jobs. When that is over, however, added work is waiting for them. There is pressure to catch up. In the meantime the learning experiences begin to fade, the newly acquired insights and behaviors are not practiced and become increasingly rusty. The goals to apply the new learnings are often forgotten.

When individuals reach a managerial level they increasingly feel accountable for a number of things. There are specific deliverables or outcomes that they are to produce. The behavior of their subordinates is expected to always be at an acceptable level. When it comes to participation in a learning event, it is clear that the participant is expected to arrive on time, be attentive, and actively participate. What is seldom understood is the degree to which the participant will be held accountable for the actual implementation of what is learned. The participant's manager seldom identifies what is expected. Increasingly, the manager may operate from a different location and can't see the degree to which the participant's behavior has been changed. Most managers could make a list of their major job responsibilities, but few would include "follow up and apply the new skills I learned in a development program."

The leader's implementation receives no attention. Failure to attend a development event would undoubtedly be noticed, but failure to apply what was learned would seldom be noticed. This is often because there are no follow-up systems in place to provide visibility to the participant's manager or to those responsible for learning and development. Further, no mechanisms exist to remind us to practice a new behavior.

The Need for Ongoing Sustainment

The father of modern change theory is Kurt Lewin, who in 1940 introduced the notion that change occurs in three steps. It begins with unfreezing, moves to change or transition, and concludes with refreezing. While he began with a focus on group behavior his concepts are equally applicable to individuals. He wrote:

> A change towards a higher level of group performance is frequently short-lived, after a "shot in the arm," group life soon returns to the previous level. This indicates that it does not suffice to define the objective of planned change in group performance as the reaching of a different level. Permanency of the new level, or permanency for a desired period, should be included in the objective.[1]

It does little good to instill new behaviors or teach new concepts that are then put on the shelf and buried. Sustainment is all about keeping the new behavior alive and continuously implemented.

The most stinging (and unfortunately accurate) criticism leveled at leadership development, in our opinion, is that no one has solved the problem of sustainment. A slightly more optimistic view was reported in an American Workforce study conducted by Root Inc. in 2015. They noted that only 18 percent of managers thought they had been successful at sustainment. Worse yet, 67 percent did not have a strong belief that sustainment was even possible.[2]

A great deal of research has been done on how to improve the traditional educational process. We know that following most educational experiences, people will forget 50 percent of what they learned within the one day and 90 percent after 30 days. We know that breaking learning apart into smaller chunks increases the likelihood of retaining what you have learned. Spaced learning always excels over massed learning. Research shows that recall and testing improve the retention of learning. Repetition also aids in the retention of information.

But leadership development is a different problem. It is not only about acquiring new ideas and concepts. It is about fundamentally learning new behavior and keeping that behavior in place. Knowledge acquisition can take place. Concepts can be thoroughly understood, and despite that, there can be no behavior change whatsoever.

We propose dividing the learning and development process into three phases. We quickly acknowledge that the lines between them are unclear and a bit fuzzy, but segmenting them allows for a useful analysis.

Phase 1

This phase encompasses all of the activities that take place prior to someone attending any kind of a developmental session. It includes all of the prereading of articles or books, any surveys or assessments that need to be completed (including a 360-degree feedback process), and any conversations that need to be held in preparation for the session, such as what the boss expects the participant to gain from the development process.

This process is the beginning of the "unfreezing" stage of change.

Phase 2

This phase describes the learning event, or series of events. This could be a training class, workshop, e-learning course, or self-study program. Such events may be two hours in length or in rare cases it could be weeks long. These often involve participants being brought together in the same room, but they may be participating via videoconferencing technology or using some other forms of distance learning. This phase usually involves an instructor or facilitator conducting it. However, it may also be a self-instructional experience.

This phase is the continuation of unfreezing and usually includes much of the "change-transition" portion of the change process.

Phase 3

This phase describes all of the subsequent activities that follow the more formal learning event. It includes all of the activities that are designed to provide better ways to remember what was learned, to assist in its implementation, and to make the new behavior a permanent part of the leader's repertoire.

This phase of the learning and development process is the "refreezing" component. The hope is to lock in the changes. There are some metals that can be heated and given a new shape, but when allowed to cool, they immediately return to their original form. Unfortunately, human behavior is very much like that. Without sustainment activities, the combination of the established work environment, the coworkers, and the force of old habits bring about a return to previous behavior.

Each Phase's Contribution to the Final Outcome

There is good evidence to suggest that roughly one-fourth of the final outcome from a learning event comes from phase 1. Another one-fourth comes from the activities during phase 2. The remaining half of the learning outcomes will result from what the individual does in Phase 3, after the learning event is completed. What takes place during the final phase makes a big difference between learning just for learning's sake and learning that makes a significant difference on the job.

How These Phases Are Currently Funded

We are not aware of any rigorous studies that accurately report on how organizations allocate their funds for each of these three phases. However, after conferring with many of our colleagues, we have learned that most estimate the following:

- Phase 1: Receives at most 10 percent of the funding (It is behind the scenes.)
- Phase 2: Receives 85 percent (It is the most visible and tends to be attractive and more fun.)
- Phase 3: Receives at most 5 percent (That may be because it is more obscure.)

Those estimates are reinforced by the oft-cited 1988 study by L. M. Saari, T. R. Johnson, S. D. McLaughlin, and D. M. Zimmerle, "A Survey of Management Training and Education Practices in U.S. Companies,"[3] that concluded any form of follow-up was rare.

What is the contribution of each phase on the ultimate outcome of the learning and development process? Marshall Goldsmith and Howard Morgan conducted a study on the impact of phase 3 on the final results of several leadership development programs. They wrote:

> Follow-up refers to efforts that leaders make to solicit continuing and updated ideas for improvement from their coworkers. In the two companies that compared "followed up" with "did not follow up," participants who followed up were viewed by their colleagues as far more effective than the leaders who did not.
>
> In the companies that measured the degree of follow-up, leaders who had "frequent" or "periodic/consistent" interaction with coworkers were reliably seen as having improved their effectiveness far more than leaders who had "little" or "no" interaction with coworkers.[4]

In Figure 15.1 (see next page), "perceived change" refers to the respondents' perception of their coworker's change in leadership effectiveness; for example, a rating of "+3" would indicate that the coworker was seen as becoming a much more effective leader; a rating of "0" would indicate no change in leadership effectiveness.

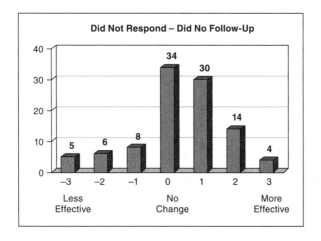

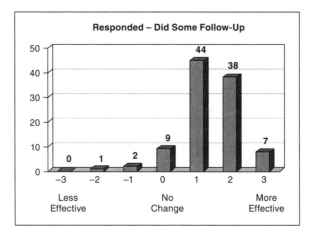

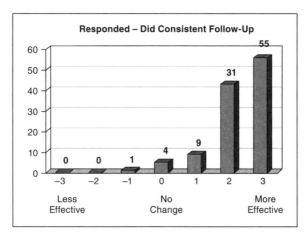

Figure 15.1. Impact of Follow-Up on Perceptions of Leaders' Improvement

Effective Sustainment Activities

Following are examples of sustainment activities:

1. Coaching on specific behaviors selected by the participant
2. Review of the business impact of a behavior
3. New but related content to the skill being focused on
4. Pulse surveys: short surveys asking a small number of key questions about targeted behavior
5. Repeat 360-degree feedback surveys
6. Coaching sessions
7. Articles
8. Videos
9. Manager feedback
10. Group discussions on effective implementation techniques being used by others
11. Blogs available on the Web
12. Podcasts and webinars

One element that encourages sustainment activities is the measurement of outcomes. The use of repeated 360-degree feedback sends a clear signal that the organization expects change to occur and wants to give participants accurate information about the degree to which they are personally accomplishing that.

Outcomes

We would like to report that everyone who participates in leadership development initiatives becomes a more effective leader. Unfortunately, we cannot say that. However, we can attest to three outcomes:

1. Based on repeated 360-degree feedback assessments, the majority of participants make a statistically significant improvement on one or more competencies.
2. Following the recommendations presented in this and previous chapters dramatically raises the percentage of those who improve.
3. Leaders who have some serious behavioral deficiency (a behavior scoring in the lowest 10 percent of all leaders assessed) can

dramatically improve. We identified 1,469 who were focused on fixing their fatal flaws. In an 18-month period they went from the 18th percentile to the 46th percentile. Starting at a low point gives even further room for growth. This is important because 29 percent of leaders we assess have one or more serious weaknesses that drag down how they are perceived by their working colleagues.

Example of Thorough Sustainment Process

In an ideal implementation, several elements would ideally be in place for sustainment to effectively occur. Here are a number of elements listed in chronological order:

1. *Message from the senior executives to participants and their manager* about a new emphasis on better follow-up and accountability for implementing all development programs. The message could say that critics invariably lament that developmental programs lack sufficient follow-up, and this organization has decided to work on fixing that. Top management's endorsement is given as the backdrop for this new effort. This message could come from the CEO, the CHRO, the head of Learning and Development, or the executive of a group.

2. *Instructions for the managers* who have participants in any developmental activity. It would define the manager's role in developing their people. This could be in the form of:

   - A brief instructor-led session
   - Self-instructional module
   - Video
   - Article

   The big change is that the manager will now be receiving periodic information about how well a subordinate is implementing the new behavior he or she has learned. This developmental step for the manager will explain how the system will work, and what the manager's role is. They will be given specific guidance about how to provide follow-on coaching to those who are effectively following through, and to those who are not. They are encouraged to have discussions in advance with any subordinate attending a development session to provide their endorsement and set expectations. Anticipated outcomes should be spelled out. Reviews of what participants gained and how they are implementing it should be scheduled.

(Optional) Some organizations put teeth in this by mandating that if a participant is enrolled in a development program, the manager must first complete the above instructional step.

3. *The participant attends the development session.* As part of that session, the participants create a brief development plan, indicating the specific actions planning they will take.

4. *The organization implements a simple, quick monitoring system with the participants.* The feedback process will take participants less than two minutes once per month.

There are two options for this monitoring system:

1. *Email Option*

- A monthly email is sent to each participant asking five questions (see below).
- Participants are informed that aggregated response data, not their personal responses, will be shown to senior leaders.
- The leadership and development staff will also have access to the data.
- To protect confidentiality, immediate managers will get data only if they have three or more participants involved.

The five questions for the email are:

i. Is this a worthwhile behavior for you to implement?
   Yes = 1   No = 2

ii. In the past month how much effort have you put forth to develop this strength?
   1 = none   2 = some   3 = great deal

iii. How much progress do you think you've made?
   1 = none   2 = some   3 = great deal

iv. In the past month, how much involvement and support has your manager given to you on your development?
   1 = none   2 = some   3 = great deal

v. *Optional:* Briefly describe a specific action you took in this past month. (One sentence.)

The system can respond with messages of encouragement, more information, and timely tips. These will be lighthearted, pleasant, and informative. (They will not be guilt-inducing.) Depending on the answers given, the message would be:

i. (If person has progressed) a message of commendation.
ii. (If person has regressed or stayed same) a message of encouragement. (These messages could come from senior management, outside experts, or colleagues.)

2. Cell Phone Option

- Call is automated. If the call goes to voicemail, it can be returned and the participant replies to four questions:

   i. Are you still focused on improving this skill or changing this behavior?
      Yes = 1   No = 2

   ii. On a three-point scale, indicate the level of effort and time you've put forth.
      1 = none   2 = some   3 = great deal

   iii. Assess your progress:

          1 = none   2 = some   3=great deal

   iv. How much involvement and support has your manager given you?

          1 = none   2 = some   3 = great deal

   v. Optional: The participant records a one sentence summary of their progress. The request is that they give one example of what they did that produced positive results from their perspective.

The system can respond with messages of encouragement, more information, and timely tips. These will be lighthearted, pleasant and informative. (They will not be guilt-inducing.) Depending on the answers given, the message would be:

   i. (If person has progressed) a message of commendation.
   ii. (If regressed or stayed same), message of encouragement. (These messages could come from senior management, outside experts, or colleagues.)
   iii. A curated "content" message containing specific suggestions regarding the skill or competency on which they are working.

5. ***Learning and development staff monitor the data*** and contact those who are actively following up. The message is a reinforcing, complimentary one. The staff also contact those who are not following-through on their development commitments. They offer some suggestions, specific tips, and other guidance.

    They relay aggregated data to senior leaders and to immediate managers, based on the agreements in that organization.

6. ***Immediate managers receive a monthly report*** of the follow-through of those who report to them.

7. *Pulse surveys are made available to participants* to monitor how their subordinates are responding to the manager's changed behavior. This information is made available to the participant, and aggregate data are made available to senior management.

8. *Senior executives report on implementation of learning and development* as they communicate to the organization. This means reporting quarterly or at least twice a year on the metrics of both effort and outcomes.

9. *The company provides follow-on materials to each participant.* This is pushed out to them on a regular basis. The participant is given a link to a web page where they can then receive suggestions for developing their selected strength.

TOPICS OF SPECIAL INTEREST

Chapter 16 describes research that we have done regarding the unique opportunity that organizations have to reach into a mostly untapped reservoir of talent. Our research was among the first to discuss the seeming contradiction that women are underrepresented at the senior levels of management, while at the same time performing at or slightly above the level of their male counterparts. That fact is true at virtually every level in the organization, and in nearly all the functional areas of a company.

The third part of this book deals with three topics of special interest. The second, Chapter 17, describes the challenges and solutions for measuring leadership improvement. The third, Chapter 18, discusses the fact that leadership is seldom a solo activity, but most often occurs in teams and small groups. What are the special challenges found in leadership teams?

16

WOMEN IN LEADERSHIP

If more women are in leadership roles, we'll
stop assuming they shouldn't be.
—SHERYL SANDBERG

You need to hire a senior leader to replace a retiring executive. After weeks of interviews by multiple team members the decision has come down to two candidates—a man and a woman. They seem equally matched on experience, expertise, and recommendations from former colleagues. The question in your mind is, "Is there any research that would give an edge to one candidate over another?" Based on analysis of more than 60,000 leaders across the globe, our advice would be, bet on the woman. Not every female leader is better than male leaders, but on average, female leaders are rated as being statistically significantly more effective on 80 percent of the leadership competencies we measure. Men end up being rated better at 13 percent, and the rest are a toss-up.

In 2012 we published our first article in the *Harvard Business Review* comparing the leadership effectiveness of male versus female leaders. It's one of their most highly quoted and referenced pieces of research. Since then we have published more than 20 additional articles in which we identified differences between the performance of men and women.

There are a great number of claims, theories, and speculations about the differences between males and females. We have data on more than 60,000 leaders that enable us to compare the leadership effectiveness of men versus women. The data come from hundreds of the most successful organizations, both public and private, in the world. This data set was generated from the Extraordinary Leader 360-degree feedback assessment with ratings from managers, peers, direct reports, and others. On average every leader had 13 different assessors evaluating their performance. Because the assessments gather data from the management ranks which have a higher population of males, 64 percent of the leaders assessed were men and 36 percent were women.

The fact that women are underrepresented in the upper levels of organizations is common knowledge. Figure 16.1 shows the percentage of males versus females in our population of leaders who were assessed. This graph vividly demonstrates the fact that women are less likely to be promoted into the top ranks of leadership, with 74 percent of top leaders being male and 26 percent female. At the individual contributor level there is a higher percent of women than men. These statistics describe only those participating in development programs, not the actual populations in organizations. However, the actual population numbers are highly consistent with the graph below.

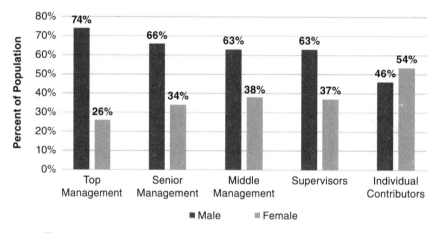

Figure 16.1. Percentage of Male and Female Leaders by Position

In 2016 Mercer produced a "When Women Thrive" report surveying 583 organizations and 3.2 million employees. They found that women were 33 percent of managers, 26 percent of senior managers, and 20 percent reaching the level of executive.[1]

Who Are Better Leaders, Men or Women?

Our assessment creates an overall measure of leadership effectiveness, consisting of the mean average of 49 individual behaviors. We know from hundreds of previous studies that this overall leadership effectiveness measure is highly predictive of key business outcomes, such as employee engagement, customer satisfaction, employee turnover, sales, profit, and discretionary effort (see Chapter 2). High scores on this measure are highly correlated with better results from leaders. Comparing the results from 40,187 males to 22,603 females in Figure 16.2, we found that the females were statistically significantly more effective (t-value = 13.65, Sig. 0.000). This is not to suggest that in absolute terms there are giant differences between the two groups.

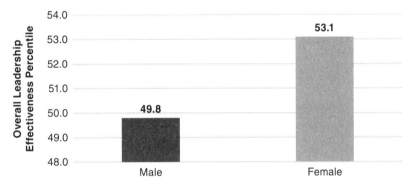

Figure 16.2. Overall Leadership Effectiveness of Men Compared to Women

Who Sees the Biggest Differences Between Males and Females?

Which rater group perceived the largest difference between male and female leaders? In all the rater groups (e.g., manager, peer, direct report, others [customers or suppliers], and self), there were statistically significant differences between the two genders. As you study Figure 16.3(see next page), note that the biggest perceived differences in overall leadership come from managers. Other studies we have conducted suggest that the manager ratings are the most accurate perception of true performance.* The next most accurate group is made up of peers. Peers tend to be a highly critical group when they give feedback to other peers. The third group to see the gender difference is the direct reports. In many ways they have the most frequent and direct experience with the manager. The other raters show

---

* We have used the total of all ratings, excluding the self rating, as the most valid measure of overall leadership effectiveness.

the smallest difference, though still statistically significant. The self-rating (individuals rating their own leadership effectiveness) demonstrate a fascinating trend because males rate themselves more highly than females rate themselves. Simply put, females are more critical of their own effectiveness.

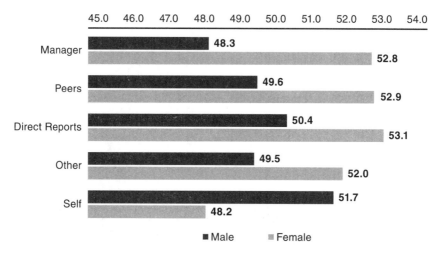

Figure 16.3. Overall Leadership Effectiveness of Males and Females by Rater Group

Are There Differences Between Males and Females by Level?

Analyzing the results by different levels of management shows that females are rated as being statistically more positive in top management, senior management, middle management, and individual contributor positions, but not as supervisors.

In the transition from individual contributor to supervisors, the males had significantly better scores than the females on technical expertise, strategic perspective, innovation, and solving problems. The females were significantly better only at taking initiative. Perhaps in this transition period the males were better prepared for a supervisor role while the females needed time to learn and develop.

However, note in Table 16.1 that when the time came for promotion into middle management, the females were significantly more effective than the males. That continued to be the case when promotion to top management positions occurred.

Table 16.1. Overall Leadership Effectiveness of Males and Females by Position

	Male	Female	t-value	Sig. (2-tailed)
Top Management	48.4	52.6	−6.01	0.00
Senior Management	46.0	51.1	−11.22	0.00
Middle Management	48.3	52.8	−11.00	0.00
Supervisors	59.4	58.5	1.69	0.09
Individual Contributors	45.4	48.6	−3.32	0.00

Are Females More Nurturing?

On personality tests women typically rate themselves as being warmer, more sensitive, and friendlier, whereas men rate themselves as more assertive, extroverted, and gregarious. There is a common stereotype that female leaders are more effective at these "nurturing" competencies. Nurturing competencies would be building relationships, developing others, and collaboration and teamwork. Following the same stereotype logic for men, they would be more extroverted and assertive, scoring higher on competencies such as taking initiative, driving for results, championing change. The problem with this is that these personality tests are self-perceptions and as was demonstrated in Table 16.1, often our self-perceptions are very different from the perceptions of others.

We measured leaders on a variety of different leadership competencies and indexes. Comparing men to women we found women were rated higher on 16 of the 19 competencies and indexes. Table 16.2 (see next page) shows a list of all the competencies and indexes sorted by t-value, which is an indication of the difference between the two groups. Note that some of the competencies at the top of this list are the more extroverted competencies such as Taking Initiative, Drive for Results, Inspires and Motivates Others, and Bold Leadership. Women were also better at the nurturing competencies such as Develops Others and Build Relationships on the top of the table.

It is interesting that men tend to be rated more positively on two competencies, Develops Strategic Perspective and Technical or Professional Expertise. During the decade that we have been gathering and analyzing this data the findings remain very consistent year to year.

Table 16.2   Perceived Effectiveness of Males and Females on 19 Competencies

	Male	Female	t-value	Sig. (2-tailed)
Takes Initiative	48.2	55.6	−30.90	0.00
Resilience	49.3	54.7	−22.68	0.00
Practices Self-Development	49.6	54.8	−21.59	0.00
Drives for Results	48.8	53.9	−21.23	0.00
Displays High Integrity and Honesty	49.1	54.0	−20.45	0.00
Develops Others	49.8	54.1	−17.85	0.00
Inspires and Motivates Others	49.7	53.9	−17.42	0.00
Bold Leadership	49.8	53.2	−13.92	0.00
Builds Relationships	49.9	53.2	−13.86	0.00
Champions Change	49.8	53.1	−13.69	0.00
Establishes Stretch Goals	49.7	52.6	−12.29	0.00
Collaboration and Teamwork	50.2	52.6	−9.95	0.00
Connects to the Outside World	50.3	51.6	−5.37	0.00
Communicates Powerfully & Prolifically	50.7	51.8	−4.82	0.00
Solves Problems and Analyzes Issues	50.4	51.5	−4.46	0.00
Leadership Speed	50.5	51.5	−4.31	0.00
Innovates	51.0	51.4	−1.84	0.07
Technical or Professional Expertise	51.1	50.1	4.26	0.00
Develops Strategic Perspective	51.4	50.1	5.19	0.00

What conclusions can we draw from the data? If women on average are more effective than men, why does the percentage of female leaders diminish as we go up the levels of management? It is possible that blatant discrimination is a potential explanation. Another important question is, "What are women doing that cause them to be perceived as more effective?" Is this an inherited characteristic or is this something learned later in life? As we have discussed this in forums and presentations, we often hear women say comments such as:

- "In order for a woman to succeed, they need to be better and work harder."
- "I cannot make a mistake! If I make a mistake my career is over."
- "I feel that I constantly need to prove my value to others."

Many women do not feel that their current position is safe, and they cannot rest on their laurels. They believe that they will need to stand out significantly from their peers to get to the next level and they are driven to take initiative, be open to feedback, and resilient to difficulties or setbacks.

Many men do not feel that same kind of pressure. They feel their efforts will be noticed and they have the ability to stand out from their peers. They know what they need to do to get to the next level and don't have a strong need for feedback from others.

Trends for Men and Women over Time

Figure 16.4 shows overall leadership effectiveness results for 40,091 men and 22,471 women. As can be seen in the graph, there is a downward trend in overall leadership effectiveness as people age.

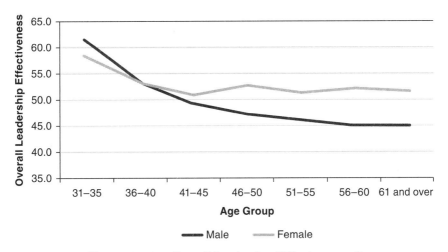

Figure 16.4. Overall Leadership Effectiveness of Male and Female Leaders by Age Groups

Part of the reason for this is that many of the younger leaders in our database are high potential leaders selected for leadership development at an earlier age. What is very noticeable in the chart is that the trend lines for men and women shift at 40 years old. Women remain above the 50th percentile while men continue to decline to the 45th percentile. After age 60 there is a 7 percentile point gap between the overall effectiveness of men and women.

Why Women Excel Post-40?

We were very curious about what causes this gap. Why do men decline in their effectiveness as they age, and women maintain their effectiveness? Looking at a variety of different factors we identified the one that seemed to help us answer the question the best. We looked at two behaviors—asking others for feedback and then taking action when feedback has been given. Figure 16.5 shows the trend for both men and women. Early on in a career people are generally good at asking others for feedback on their performance and taking positive action to change based on that feedback. Notice an equal decline for both men and women until age 40 at which point women continue to be above average and men slide down to the 40th percentile.

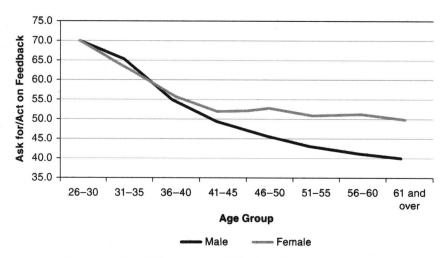

Figure 16.5. Effectiveness of Male and Female Leaders on Asking for/Acting on Feedback by Age Groups

As you consider the attitudes that many women have about the need to do more and be better, it makes sense that they are more open to feedback and tend to ask for feedback more often. We do not feel that this difference is a genetic difference between men and women but more the environment they are in, societal norms and the conditions that they face. Those who feel they need to do more and be better, tend to ask for feedback whether they are male of female. Those who are highly confident that they will succeed and who never worry about needing to change don't ask for feedback. Our data show clearly that those who are better at asking for and acting on feedback regardless of whether they are male or female, tend to be rated as more effective leaders at any age.

The Impact of Confidence

When we had done our first study we thought that confidence had an impact on the effectiveness of a leader. Leaders with little confidence would be motivated to check in with others and desire feedback on their performance. Once a reasonable level of confidence was achieved, leaders would be more likely to be bold, push back, and take initiative. Several years ago, we created a self-assessment that included a measure of confidence. We have been able to generate a global data set of 7,837 assessments. The gap in confidence between males and females at a young age is surprisingly large, as shown in Figure 16.6. While it's discouraging that young women lack confidence, it is not surprising that young men have an average level of confidence without much experience.

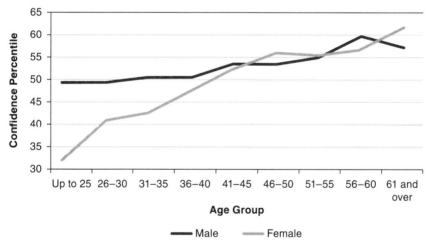

Figure 16.6. Confidence of Male and Female Leaders by Age Groups

What is fascinating in Figure 16.6 is once again how the two lines converge at 40. We are not sure what happens at 40 years of age for women, but the trajectory of the confidence line continues up as both men and women age.

Suggestions for Organizations

What can organizations and their leaders do with these findings? Here are our thoughts:

- All of our clients are concerned about talent. There is a strong concern in most organization that they lack the talent they will need in the future. Every organization needs to be aware of the fact that many women have exceptional skills and can play a significant role in an organization success.
- In a recent assessment where we measured managers' skills at valuing diversity and inclusion, we found that 17 percent of the managers got a failing rating from their direct reports. These data came from a progressive organization with a very positive culture. What organizations need to realize is that in today's culture having leaders with biases is unacceptable. The biggest part of the problem here is that those failing leaders were completely unaware that they had a problem.
- In the United States, since 1970, 26 percent of the growth in gross domestic product has been directly attributable to having more women in the workforce. Hiring women has clearly been beneficial, but the benefits don't stop with a mere headcount. Companies are in need of strong individuals in key leadership positions. Women are a huge and largely untapped resource that is often not recognized. Vik Malhotra, a senior partner at McKinsey & Co., has said, "For women, the corporate talent pipeline is leaky and blocked."[2]
- A study done at MIT showed that teams with mixed gender are more productive and creative. In fact, the economists found that simply moving from an all-male or all-female office to one that was evenly split could possibly increase revenue by 41 percent. How? Their research found that "greater social diversity implies a greater spread of experience, which could add to the collective knowledge of a group of office workers and make the unit perform more effectively."[3]

Again, our point is not to say that one gender is better than the other. Rather, both are effective and with the rising shortage of senior leaders, both are needed. For example, Kevin Kelly, CEO of Heidrick &

Struggles, found that "40 percent of executives hired at the senior level are pushed out, fail or quit within 18 months."[4] Organizations can greatly benefit from putting more emphasis on identifying women in their ranks, and working to develop them for senior roles they can succeed in.

In all, our findings should be clear: Companies need the diversity and benefits women leaders provide. Every company can benefit from placing much greater emphasis on getting more women in its leadership ranks.

17

MEASURE IMPROVEMENT

*Measurement is the first step that leads to control and
eventually to improvement. If you can't measure something,
you can't understand it. If you can't understand it, you can't
control it. If you can't control it, you can't improve it.*
—H. JAMES HARRINGTON

Why Assess Your Leadership Effectiveness?

There are two fundamental reasons why an individual ought to participate
in a 360-degree assessment. The first is to provide that individual with
an accurate evaluation of his or her leadership effectiveness. Our research
has found that the person who is least accurate at predicting personal
effectiveness is that person. Other assessors are approximately twice as
accurate as the person themselves. (We use the total score of all evaluators
combined as the benchmark.) Ironically, the highest performing people
tend to underrate themselves. The less effective leaders tend to overrate
themselves. Managers, peers, direct reports, and others are fairly consistent and more accurate in their assessments. The only way a person can get
an accurate read on whether he or she is the world's best or worst leader is
by using a predictive 360-degree assessment that includes feedback from
others.

The second reason why people should assess their leadership effectiveness is that once they have an accurate evaluation of their current
effectiveness, they are more likely to improve. Receiving feedback from a
number of colleagues greatly increases the motivation to improve as well
as providing helpful information to make that happen.

We fear that too many organizations focus too much on the first
reason (evaluation) and not enough on the second (improvement). Communicating that the assessment is simply the first step in helping an
individual to improve is essential. The most helpful view is that this

assessment is not permanent but rather a picture of one point in time. The assessment can and should change over time.

Another interesting and important point to note is that scores can improve or decline. Asking others for feedback can raise expectations that change might occur. Those who do nothing with their feedback can violate that expectation. The result, then, is that occasionally the follow-up assessment is more negative than the original one.

Analysis of Pre- vs. Post-Assessments from 6,029 Leaders

The best way to determine if a leader has improved is to collect pretest 360-degree data and then compare these results with a posttest reassessment using the same survey items after 18 to 24 months. In a perfect world the same evaluators would be used in both assessments. While some of the leaders were able to do this, the reality of organizations is that people quit, get promoted, or move. In many cases there is some difference in the evaluators between the pre- and posttest. While some people would argue that this invalidates the research, others would point to the fact that having new evaluators provides leaders with a significant challenge. It would be much easier for the same evaluators to see improvement or a lack of improvement but having different evaluators actually makes the demonstration of improvement more challenging.

There are many ways to look at improvement when evaluating the data. Leaders involved in this research were challenged to improve one of the competencies measured. Comparing the pretest results to the posttest on each of the competencies, we found that 6,029 leaders (or 85 percent) were able to show a significant improvement on one or more of the competencies. That is an impressive figure, but it only requires effort on one of the leadership competencies.

A more difficult test of improvement would be to look at the overall leadership effectiveness rating, which is the summary of all competencies in the assessment. An improvement in overall leadership effectiveness would represent a much bigger challenge. The implications of an improvement in their overall leadership effectiveness is that evaluators see an overall marked improvement in a leader. Looking at this criterion we found that 51 percent of the leaders (4,974) made a significant overall change in their leadership effectiveness.

To measure the amount of change it was necessary to divide the those who made a significant change into two groups. One group had what we have referred to as a fatal flaw. A fatal flaw is a behavior that has a negative impact on how a leader is perceived. It generally detracts from overall leadership effectiveness in a significant manner. We found that this happens when any competency was assessed by raters to be in the bottom 10th percentile, compared to our global norms. Those with one or more fatal flaws as a group scored at the 18th percentile in their pretest results on their overall leadership effectiveness. Leaders with fatal flaws were encouraged to focus on fixing the flaw. In other words, they were encouraged to focus on fixing their weakness. Twenty-nine percent of the total group of leaders had one or more fatal flaws. This is very close to the 30 percent of leaders with fatal flaws we find in our global database of more than 100,000 leaders. The second group was composed of those with no fatal flaws. For this larger group we encourage leaders to build on their strengths.

We discovered that 61 percent of the leaders with fatal flaws (1,469) made a significant positive change. Figure 17.1 shows the results from this study. On average leaders with fatal flaws moved from the 18th percentile to the 46th percentile on their overall leadership effectiveness. One might describe this as moving from a very poor effectiveness rating to a slightly below average effectiveness rating.

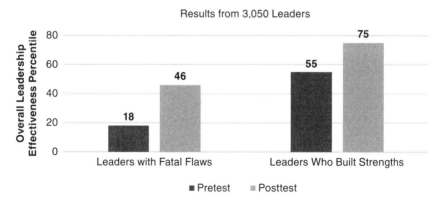

Figure 17.1. Improvement in Overall Leadership Effectiveness Comparing Those Overcoming Flaws vs. Developing Strengths

Looking at those leaders without fatal flaws, we found that 1,589, or 46 percent, were able to make a significant positive change. Leaders without fatal flaw were rated at the 55th percentile in their pretest results but moved to the 75th percentile in their posttest. One might describe this as moving from slightly above average to the top quartile.

As can be noted from Figure 17.1, this is a significant improvement in overall leadership effectiveness for both groups. Looking at the pretest and posttest differences note that leaders with fatal flaws had a 28 percentile point gain while those building strengths had only a 20 percentile point gain. It looks like from the data that those leaders focused on fixing weaknesses made more progress that those focused on building their strengths. While the gain is larger for those fixing fatal flaws, we would submit that it is much easier to move from poor to good than to move from good to great.

The other issue to keep in mind is that leaders with fatal flaws had a dominant issue that needed fixing while leaders with no fatal flaws did not have any significant negative issues to address. These data provide additional evidence that leaders can build strengths and that building strengths had a positive impact on a leader's effectiveness.

Keep in mind that this is the average improvement, which means some individuals improved more, some less but all those individuals in the group made significant improvements. These improvements represent substantial shifts in how these leaders are perceived by their managers, peers, direct reports, and others. For those who are pessimistic about leadership development in general and a leader's ability to significantly improve, these data provide assurance that it is in fact possible for poor leaders to become good and good leaders to become great. It is also evident that it is more than just a rare few leaders that were able to change but the majority of leaders evaluated.

In the first chapters of this book we have shown a variety of studies proving that better leaders generate better results. To measure the impact of improved leadership effectiveness in this study, we also measured the level of employee engagement of direct reports of each leader. Engagement has been shown to have significant correlations to additional organizational outcomes such as productivity, quality, lower turnover, and profit. Figure 17.2 shows the employee engagement scores for the same 3,050 leaders. Once again note that for those leaders with fatal flaws, engagement went from the 34th percentile in the pretest to the 50th percentile in the posttest. For those leaders with no fatal flaws, engagement moved from the 52nd percentile in the pretest to the 62nd percentile in the posttest. These are both significant and meaningful improvements in engagement.

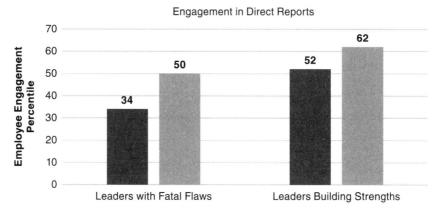

Figure 17.2. Improvement in Employee Engagement Comparing Those Overcoming Flaws vs. Developing Strengths

Differences by Position

Were top managers able to improve more than supervisors or individual contributors? Is it more difficult for a senior leader to demonstrate improvement than someone at a lower level in the organization? When we broke the data out by position, we found that leaders at all levels showed significant improvement. Figure 17.3 (see next page) shows improvement results for those with fatal flaws. Every group made a significant gain, but supervisors did show the most improvement.

For leaders who were building strengths we saw once again a consistent level of improvement by level. The data in Figure 17.4 (see next page) confirm that the strength-building approach works at all levels of the organization. Once again supervisors showed the most substantial improvement.

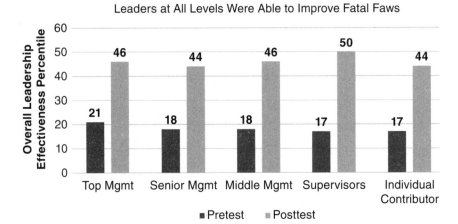

Figure 17.3. Overall Leadership Effectiveness Gains for Leaders with Fatal Flaws, by Organizational Level

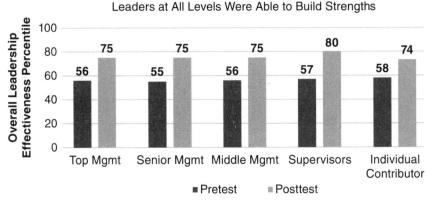

Figure 17.4. Overall Gains for Leaders Building Strengths by Organizational Level

Which Competencies Show the Greatest Improvement?

Looking at the data on the 51 percent of leaders who improved, we were curious if there was improvement in all the individual competencies and if some competencies showed more improvement than others. Looking at the results we calculated a t-test to examine the difference between the pretest and posttest mean percentile scores. The t-value is a good indicator of the biggest differences. In Table 17.1 all the results in the list are sorted by t-value. Note that while all the differences are substantial there were some competencies that showed more improvement than others. The biggest pretest/posttest difference came in communicating powerfully. In our view this is the easiest competency to demonstrate improvement. Just by increasing the frequency of communication between direct reports, colleagues, and the manager an individual can show noticeable improvement.

Table 17.1.

	Pretest	Posttest	t-value	Sig. (2-tailed)
Communicates Powerfully	42.1	63.6	−58.94	0.00
Develops Strategic Perspective	43.3	64.7	−57.61	0.00
Collaboration and Teamwork	41.4	63.1	−55.87	0.00
Inspires and Motivates Others	42.3	61.5	−54.61	0.00
Solves Problems and Analyzes Issues	43.3	63.3	−54.61	0.00
Champions Change	43.5	63.1	−54.08	0.00
Establishes Stretch Goals	43.4	63.5	−53.91	0.00
Develops Others	41.7	61.9	−52.71	0.00
Builds Relationships	41.5	61.6	−52.60	0.00
Connects to the Outside World	44.2	63.6	−52.57	0.00
Practices Self-Development	41.8	62.4	−52.25	0.00
Technical/Professional Expertise	43.0	62.0	−50.98	0.00
Displays High Integrity and Honesty	42.5	60.6	−49.68	0.00
Takes Initiative	44.3	62.0	−48.87	0.00
Innovates	43.0	62.1	−48.75	0.00
Drives for Results	45.6	62.5	−43.13	0.00

It is interesting that the smallest improvement—yet still showing a substantial shift—was driving for results. We suspect that for many leaders this was an important area of focus before the pretest and so showing a significant change was more difficult.

Organizational Differences

Looking at the data we were able to isolate improvement results from 48 different organizations. The organization with the lowest percentage of leaders who improved had only 14 percent, while the organization with the highest had 100 percent. The standard deviation on the percentage of leaders who improved was 16.8. The large standard deviation indicates that there is a substantial impact that comes from how each organization setup, administered, followed up, and encouraged participants. The message here is simply that while leadership development seems a bit like an individual sport (e.g., people are on their own to make improvements), it's really a team sport (e.g., the organization support has a great deal of influence over how much improvement will occur). In the last half of this book we have focused on the organization's role in assisting with improvement and its impact cannot be overemphasized.

Growth Mindset

Stanford professor Carol Dweck's research on learning mindsets[1] indicated that individuals have a "growth" or "fixed" mindset. A growth mindset is focused on improving, learning, and effort; while the fixed mindset assumes that our abilities are based more on inborn talents and traits and unlikely to change.

These two mindsets in turn produce predictable behavior. People with a growth mindset seek out challenging situations and welcome feedback, including criticism. On the other hand, people express a fixed mindset by striving to prove themselves to others. They avoid feedback and criticism, and usually select tasks at which they can look good and succeed.

Obviously, the results of this study show that it is possible for leaders to grow and improve. Organizations should seek people with an improving mindset because they are open to feedback and seek to continually improve. Their productivity and contributions can and will increase over time.

18

DEVELOP LEADERSHIP TEAMS

No matter how brilliant your mind or strategy, if you're
playing a solo game, you'll always lose out to a team.
—REID HOFFMAN

After studying leadership for more than four decades, we have learned that leaders have significantly more influence on both organizational outcomes and on other people in the organization than we ever thought possible. Leaders not only influence the outcomes of their immediate team and their direct reports, but their influence spreads down and across the organization. In 2016 we published research in the *Harvard Business Review* titled, "The Trickle-Down Effect of Good (and Bad) Leadership."[1] This chapter reviews what we found.

Emotions and Behavior Are Contagious

UC San Diego's James Fowler and Harvard's Nicholas Christakis conducted fascinating research that demonstrated that happiness is contagious. They looked at social networks, such as a friend of a friend of a friend. What they found is that if you had a friend who was happy, the probability that you will be happier goes up by 25 percent. In another study they found that if you have friends who are overweight, you are more likely to also be overweight. If you succeed in quitting smoking, your friends are also more likely to quit. Is divorce contagious? Rose McDermott of Brown University found that if you have a close friend who is divorced, you are 33 percent more likely to also be divorced.

After reading this research on "social contagion," we wondered if leaders had a similar impact on those they worked with. In this book we have already demonstrated in Chapter 2 the effect leaders have on the engagement of employees, along with other outcomes such as employee turnover, sales volume, customer satisfaction, safety, and productivity. Our question was, Would the behavior of a leader significantly impact others in the organization?

To research that question we matched up data from 265 high-level managers with their mid-level direct reports, who were also managers. All of the managers in this study participated in the Extraordinary Leader 360-degree assessment. On average they were assessed by 17 raters (manager, peers, direct reports, and others). Our questions were:

- Would working for an excellent leader influence their direct reports to be more effective?
- Would working for an ineffective leader have a negative influence?

Our assumption was that if the high-level manager had no influence, then the mid-level manager would score near the 50th percentile.

Figure 18.1 shows the results of the study. High-level managers were divided into five groups based on their overall leadership effectiveness. High-level managers in the bottom 10 percent, based on their perceived effectiveness, were paired with their direct report mid-level managers whose average leadership effectiveness was at the 29th percentile. The effect of working for a poor leader was that the mid-level manager's effectiveness was 21 percentile points below average. Note that when the high-level managers were in the top 10 percent, the effectiveness of their

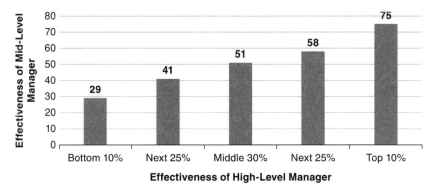

Figure 18.1. Impact of High-Level Managers Effectiveness on Mid-Level Managers

direct report mid-level managers was at the 75th percentile. Working for highly effective senior managers is correlated with the mid-level managers' ratings moving up 25 percentile points above average.

Why? Our conclusion from this study is that poor leaders, for a variety of reasons, pull down the effectiveness of those who work for them.

- It is possible that they select less effective subordinates to start with.
- Subordinate managers over time mimic their bosses' bad behavior.
- The senior leaders' ineffective behavior creates a negative climate that in turn lowers motivation and performance.

And the effect of great leaders is exactly the opposite. They boost the effectiveness of their direct reports.

- The more effective managers seek them out and want to work with them.
- They select higher caliber subordinates.
- Subordinate managers learn excellent leadership behavior by having a strong role model.
- The effective leader creates a positive working environment that elevates motivation and performance.

We also became interested in the impact of leaders on employee engagement and how far down the organization would be impacted by good and bad leadership. For those same leaders we looked at the overall leadership effectiveness of the high-level leaders. In Chapter 2 we demonstrate that poor leaders tend to have unengaged and dissatisfied employees while the best leaders have highly engaged employees.

In Figure 18.2 (see next page) we once again split the high-level managers into five groups based on their leadership effectiveness. The bars represent the level of employee engagement for the direct reports of the high-level leaders and the direct reports of the mid-level leaders. It's clear from these data that the impact of a leader's effectiveness extends beyond their own direct reports.

In Figured 18.3 (see next page) we have displayed how high-level leaders impact mid-level leaders, which impacts their direct reports, which affects a number of critical organizational outcomes.

These data demonstrated that our leaders' skills are as contagious as our happiness. After doing these studies we asked ourselves how much we

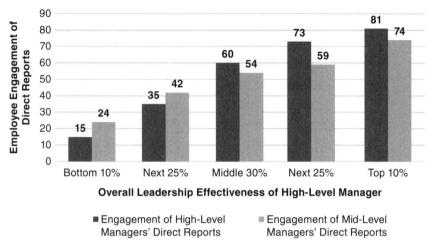

Figure 18.2. Employee Engagement of High- and Mid-Level Managers

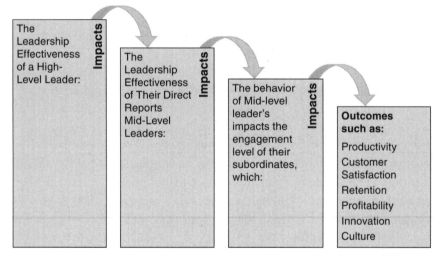

Figure 18.3. Trickle-Down Effect of Good (and Bad) Leadership

are influenced by our peers. Often, we spend less time with peers and they have less control over our interaction and performance but are their leadership skills also contagious? To answer that question, we compiled a data set of 25,248 peers. We matched up one peer (primary) with another peer (secondary). We divided the primary peers into five groups based on their overall leadership effectiveness. We then analyzed the overall leadership effectiveness for the secondary peers. Figure 18.4 shows the results. While the effect is not quite as strong as that for the managers, it is still highly significant. If you work with a highly effective, very competent group of peers, it is highly likely you will be a more effective leader. That is the upside potential but there is also a downside. Working with a less competent and effective group of peers drags down a person's effectiveness.

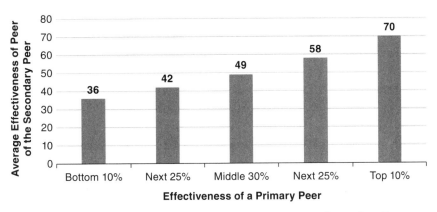

Figure 18.4. Impact of Primary Peer Effectiveness on Secondary Peers

If you have ever had a teenager start to hang out with some questionable friends, no doubt you recommended that they change their friends. We are all significantly influenced by those with whom we associate. The warning for everyone is, if you work with a group you don't want to be like, find a new group.

Implications

It is very clear from these studies that we are all significantly influenced by our managers and peers and others who work with us. As you consider the impact of these studies, think about how we typically approach leadership development. Have we thought about leadership development as more of an individual sport or a team sport? Our experience has taught us that the majority of times organizations treat leadership development like an individual sport. Most organizations take individuals out of their team to attend training. In many situations we like to create training events with groups of strangers. The benefit of this approach is people may be more comfortable practicing new behaviors with a stranger group and it may promote networking. The downside is that the people who have the most influence over an individual's leadership behaviors are absent. Since the team has so much influence over an individual's behavior, shouldn't the team go through leadership development together?

Team Leadership Development

One of the advantages of a development experience is that we can generate a team profile. If you ask a group of leaders to rate their own effectiveness, they will generally be quite optimistic. You may hear things like "very good" or "clearly above average." We had a recent experience where we met with 11 leaders who were in charge of the sales for a pharma organization. When we asked this team how effective they were, the senior leader of the team said, "This is one of the most effective teams in the company." I then showed them their results from the 360-degree assessments. To their surprise, the group average was at the 45th percentile. Thirty-six percent of their leaders were scoring above average, but 64 percent were below average; pulling the overall score down. When we displayed that graph the senior leader said, "Now you have our attention."

Next, we asked, "What is the level of engagement for this group?" Once again, everyone said, "very good," "everyone loves working here." Of the 11 managers, the engagement average for their 75 direct reports was once again at the 45th percentile. We then showed Figure 18.5 for the 11 leaders in the room. We split the leaders into two groups, those below average on overall leadership effectiveness and those above average. The above average group had engagement scores at the 60th percentile while the below average group were at the 41st percentile. What the group understood at this point was that there was an excellent correlation between their leadership effectiveness and the engagement level of their direct reports. And, because it was their data this conclusion was easily accepted.

This team had a few highly effective managers, some average managers, and a few managers who needed improvement. We next showed the leaders their results on each of the 19 differentiating competencies. We had both rating on effectiveness and importance. The scatter plot in Figure 18.6. (see next page) provided some useful insights.

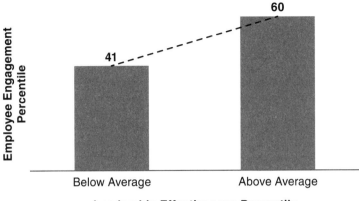

Figure 18.5. Engagement Comparing Leaders Who's Effectiveness is Above and Below Average

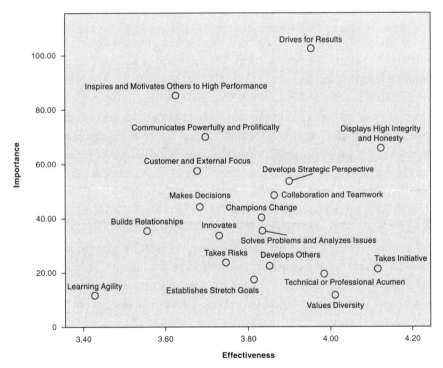

Figure 18.6. Scatter Plots of Leaders Effectiveness and Importance Ratings

Team Strengths

1. Displays Integrity and Honesty
2. Takes Initiative
3. Drives for Results

High Importance

1. Drive for Results
2. Inspires and Motivates Others
3. Communicates Powerfully

Areas of High Importance but Less Effective

1. Inspires and Motivates Others
2. Communicates Powerfully

The team identified two high importance, lower effectiveness areas as team development issues. They then created a plan for improvement with all team members.

As each individual team member shared the competencies they had selected to work on, other team members who had strengths in these competencies volunteered to provide coaching and mentoring. By working together and supporting each other in their development, more progress can be achieved but also the accountability of each team member to work on their development increased significantly.

Several years ago, one of the authors attended an education conference in Amsterdam. A speaker at the conference showed data on how schools in Finland had significantly better results than schools in the United States. He then gave an example of what happens in Finland that made their schools better. The example was of a grade school teacher who was underperforming. In the United States when a teacher in the school is underperforming, very frequently the other teachers and the parents worked hard to get that teacher fired. In Finland when a grade school teacher is underperforming, the other teachers in the school provide support, assistance, and development to the underperforming teacher. The Finnish people believe that they only way they can survive is to work together and support each other. The temporarily poor-performing teacher in Finland often becomes one of the better teachers in the school.

While the poorly performing teacher is learning to improve, the other teachers in the school assist with his or her teaching to ensure all the students get an excellent education.

Recommendation

There can be great benefit from measuring and developing leadership within teams and organizations. By measuring the leadership within a team, each team can understand their level of performance as well as their contribution to the team's need for leadership. Most teams assume they are much better leaders than they objectively are, just like most automobile drivers assume they are above average. Helping teams to understand their current level of performance is a strong incentive for improvement. Our research on trickle down and contagion have taught us how much our skills are influenced by others. Uniting a team in building their leadership skills creates a positive environment in which extraordinary leaders can more easily be grown.

Appendix

RESEARCH
METHODOLOGY

Assessing the Relationship Between Leadership Effectiveness and Employee Commitment (Figure 2.1)

We administered 360-degree assessments to 1,450,813 employees from a variety of different organizations (public, private, government) that cut across a broad set of business sectors. The survey contained both a 49-item leadership effectiveness measure based on the Extraordinary Leader 16 differentiating competencies and a five-item employee satisfaction/commitment index. The two indexes were highly correlated. A Pearson correlation coefficient between the two indexes was calculated at 0.57 (PC 0.000). The relationship between the two variables indicated that 32 percent of the variance in employee commitment could be accounted for by perceptions of managerial effectiveness. Typically, the correlations are substantially higher in individual organizations. For example, two organizations in the sample have correlations of 0.75 and 0.71 in which case the percent of variance would be 56 percent to 50 percent, respectively. To produce the graph in Figure 2.1, individual responses from each leader were aggregated by leader. The study included results from 90,252 leaders. The leadership effectiveness index was divided into 20 groups based on the distribution of the data. The groups ranged in size from 4,511 to 4,537 leaders. All employees were direct reports to the leader. The graph shows the raw mean score on the employee commitment index for each of the 20 groups.

Evaluating the Relationship Between Leadership Effectiveness and Profitability (Figure 2.3)

A total of 1,672 assessments were distributed to employees, who assessed managers in 35 regions of a mortgage bank. Managers had an average of nine assessments done on them by their boss, peers, and direct reports. The 360-degree assessment was custom-designed to measure specific competencies thought to differentiate high- and low-performing managers. The assessment survey had 65 items. A leadership effectiveness index composed of 15 survey items was correlated with the net profit for each region. The Pearson correlation between the leadership effectiveness index and net profit was 0.40 (PC 0.000). The leadership effectiveness index was then divided into three categories based on the distribution of the index.

The three categories were: bottom 10 percent, middle 80 percent, and top 10 percent. Figure 2.3 shows the strong impact of poor and extraordinary leadership.

Impact on Sales Figure (Figure 2.4)

A total of 1,534 assessments were distributed to employees, who assessed managers in 96 individual stores. Managers had an average of 16 assessments done on them by their managers, peers, direct reports, and internal clients. The 360-degree assessment was custom-designed to measure specific competencies thought to differentiate high- and low-performing managers. The assessment survey had 16 items. The Pearson correlation between the leadership effectiveness index and percentage growth in accumulated sales versus prior year was 0.22 (PC 0.031).

The five categories of the overall leadership effectiveness index were: bottom 10 percent, 11th–35th, 36th–65th 66th–89th, and top 10 percent. Figure 2.4 shows the strong impact of poor and extraordinary leadership on growth in sales versus prior year. In addition to growth in sales turnover in each store was also measured.

Evaluating the Relationship Between Leadership Effectiveness and Turnover (Figure 2.5)

An insurance company administered a survey to work groups in which leadership effectiveness was assessed. Eighty-nine groups matched up aggregated survey results with annual turnover data. The leadership effectiveness measured was composed of 10 survey items assessing the effectiveness of the work group manager. The Pearson correlation between the leadership effectiveness index and turnover was 0.29 (PC 0.007). The negative correlation was created because the higher (more positive) the leadership effectiveness measure, the lower the turnover. The leadership effectiveness measure was divided into three categories (bottom 30 percent, middle 60 percent, and top 10 percent) to create Figure 2.5. The cut points on the categories were chosen because of the consistency of turnover within each of the groupings.

Evaluating the Relationship Between Leadership Effectiveness and Intention to Leave (Figure 2.6)

The same data set that was used to create Figure 2.1 was also used to measure intention to leave. This was the combined results from hundreds of different organizations. A total of 90,252 leaders were assessed on their leadership effectiveness, and their direct reports were asked to indicate the extent to which they considered leaving their jobs and going to another organization. The percentages represent the percent of employees who responded in a neutral or negative way to the item. Intention to leave is an excellent predictor of actual turnover with about 50 percent of the employees who think about quitting actually turning over. The leadership effectiveness index was divided into 20 groups based on the distribution of the data.

Evaluating the Relationship Between Leadership Effectiveness and Customer Satisfaction (Figure 2.7)

A high-tech communications company conducted a companywide employee survey and the same year collected 360-degree survey results from 612 managers. The 360-degree survey results were merged with the employee survey data. The 360-degree survey was customized with 50 items designed to measure overall leadership effectiveness. The aggregate of the 360-degree survey items formed the leadership effectiveness index. The employee survey was aggregated and merged with the aggregate 360-degree results. The data set also contained additional demographics. The employee survey contained a series of items measuring customer satisfaction. Percentile scores were calculated on the customer and intention to stay measures for the 612 managers. Percentile scores for the leadership effectiveness index were calculated and then divided into the bottom 20 percent, the middle 60 percent, and the top 20 percent.

Replications of Findings

Since publishing the original version of this book, we have been engaged with hundreds of organizations in replicating the relationship between leadership effectiveness and critical organizational outcomes. After conducting all of these studies, it has become clear that there is consistency in the findings. We have never studied an organization where there was not a strong relationship between leadership effectiveness and employee satisfaction/commitment. The studies on intention to quit and percentage of highly committed employees are also very consistent. In spite of telling our clients about the number of replications of the research, they are always more fascinated by seeing the replication of their own data. In most organizations, leaders still ask the question, "Is that true in our organization?" When leaders see how their own data show that great leaders create substantially higher levels of employee satisfaction and commitment, they begin to be more serious and dedicated in their efforts to become extraordinary leaders.

We frequently get questions about differences between U.S. and international leaders. As we have used the Extraordinary Leader approach around the world, we have found a large number of similarities between leaders in different cultures. The graph in Figure A.1 shows results from four different countries. The results were generated from the following:

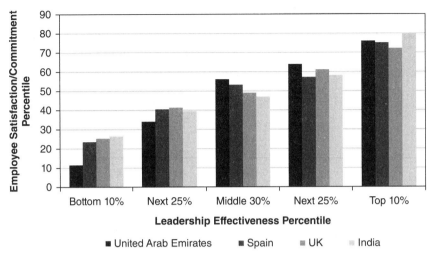

Figure A.1. Employee Satisfaction by Country

- 81 leaders from a government organization in the United Arab Emirates
- 361 leaders from a variety of different organizations in Spain
- 727 leaders from a variety of different organizations in the United Kingdom
- 44 leaders from a financial services company in India

Leadership effectiveness was measured by a 49-item index assessing the Extraordinary Leader 16 differentiating competencies. Employee satisfaction/ commitment were measured by a five-item index. It is clear from Figure A.1 that the relationship between leadership effectiveness and employee satisfaction/commitment in these four different countries is very similar to the findings from North America.

Nineteen Competencies That Best Differentiate High- and Low-Performing Leaders (Chapter 4)

To accomplish the original analysis, thirty-two 360-degree feedback data sets were analyzed, containing results from more than 100 different companies. Table A.1 provides a listing of the different data sets used in the analysis.

Table A.1. Composition of 32 Data Sets Used in the Key Differentiator Analysis

Data Set No.	No. of Assessments Completed	No. of Leaders Assessed	No. of Survey Items	Organization(s) Description
1	2,872	290	64	Research and Development
2	10,691	762	36	Bank/Investment
3	4,178	639	45	Generic Survey—Many Different Organizations
4	1,346	19	66	Chemicals
5	3,782	486	18	Food Processing
6	6,365	687	54	Food Sales
7	9,395	925	47	Foods
8	137	17	86	Manufacturing
9	2,670	349	48	Foods
10	21,786	3,022	60	High Technology
11	2,573	357	61	High Technology
12	1,502	147	52	Information Processing
13	3,512	259	84	Publishing
14	19,671	2,030	61	Generic Survey—Many Different Organizations
15	7,290	943	60	Oil—Upstream
16	1,221	180	53	High-Technology Manufacturing
17	2,648	276	91	High-Technology Development
18	2,177	262	73	High Technology
19	11,048	1,123	88	High-Technology Development
20	12,060	1,175	79	High-Technology Sales/Service
21	1,183	165	51	Automotive
22	9,323	901	50	Foods
23	1,831	210	99	Foods
24	2,001	194	50	Restaurant
25	7,155	1,009	66	Research and Development
26	14,630	2,125	70	Generic Survey—Many Different
27	62,919	6,716	73	Generic Survey—Many Different Organizations
28	2,300	146	52	Forest Products
29	2,174	196	60	Paper
30	4,083	338	54	Banking
31	1,297	130	55	Mortgage Bank
32	1,303	126	50	Insurance
Total	237,123	26,314	1,956	

The original analysis was completed using results from 237,123 survey responses on 26,314 leaders. Each of the different data sets represented different customized 360-degree surveys. A total of 1,956 360-degree items were used. Very few of the items were repeated in the different surveys. This provided an extraordinarily rich data set of competencies and items from a variety of different organizations.

Extensive analysis was done on each data set. First, data sets were compiled into aggregated format by computing an overall average of all responses (e.g., boss, peers, direct reports, others), with the self-response excluded. This was done for each leader in the data set. Next, an overall score was computed by averaging all 360-degree items into an overall index. We next determined from the overall score the top 10 percent of highest-scoring leaders and the bottom 10 percent of lowest-scoring leaders. Using these two groups, an independent t-test was performed on each item. The t-values from the t-test were then sorted for all survey items. The 10 to 15 items with the largest differences were then selected from each data analysis and put into a combined set of key differentiating items. Once all of the analysis was completed, the combined list was again sorted, selecting only those with the highest t-values. Each item was then put on a 3-inch by 5-inch card. The cards were sorted into groups separately by both authors, and after several iterations the items were grouped into 16 different clusters. Because the survey items crossed more than 32 different data sets, we were not able to perform a factor analysis on the overall results. But we did perform a factor analysis on individual data sets, which helped in creating the appropriate clusters.

In 2017 we decided to replicate our original research with new data collected during the past 15 years. Since doing our original research we had been collecting 360-degree data using both our standard Extraordinary Leader, Extraordinary Performance, and Extraordinary Coach assessments and custom assessments from hundreds of different organizations. In addition, we partnered with 25 international distributors across the globe, which provided us with additional international data. Our purpose in replicating our original research was to understand if our original 16 differentiating competencies were still as relevant in today's business environment and to identify if there were any additional differentiating competencies. In our new study we assembled 1,596,938 assessments on 121,138 leaders. Table A.2 shows a listing of the 44 different data sets that were analyzed.

Table A.2. Composition of 44 Data Sets Used in the 2017 Key Differentiator Analysis

Data Set No.	No. of Assessments Completed	No. of Leaders Assessed	No. of Survey Items	Organization(s) Description
1	27,961	2,081	64	Telecommunications (Managers)
2	7,182	603	59	Telecommunications (Individual Contributors)
3	6,579	407	20	Pharma (Individual Contributors)
4	14,296	809	56	Pharma (Managers)
5	2.503	147	60	Insurance
6	5,012	339	54	Manufacturing
7	43,585	4,077	56	Oil (Manager)
8	7,461	660	82	Oil (Manager)
9	8,691	712	81	Oil (Individual Contributor)
10	6,301	330	82	Oil (Manager)
11	1,462	186	56	Professional Services
12	2,120	164	73	Professional Services
13	8,626	570	58	Entertainment and media
14	1,622	762	16	Retail
15	34.358	2,490	43	Food
16	5,070	390	25	Food
17	8,063	195	47	Food
18	2,237	762	47	Food
19	1,358	135	72	Construction Materials
20	3,417	225	72	Real Estate
21	1,065	94	52	Real Estate
22	2,110	139	47	Religious Organization
23	2,216	121	51	Publishing/Technology
24	1,402	87	46	Health Care (Executive)
25	6,829	550	46	Health Care (Manager)
26	1,326	91	64	Bank
27	2,256	245	80	Entertainment
28	1,615	136	62	Food
29	41,771	3,664	54	Generic Survey—Many Different Organizations
30	3,520	226	89	Research and Development
31	9,288	854	55	Telecommunications
32	1,217,363	87,684	54	Generic Survey—Many Different Organizations

Table A.2. Composition of 44 Data Sets Used in the 2017
Key Differentiator Analysis, *continued*

Data Set No.	No. of Assessments Completed	No. of Leaders Assessed	No. of Survey Items	Organization(s) Description
33	73,375	5,987	54	Generic Survey—Many Different Organizations
34	1,783	108	63	Technology
35	1,296	99	77	Manufacturing/Refining
36	2,519	433	66	Financial Services/Investment
37	832	71	98	Financial Services
38	2,414	170	97	Pharma
39	28,087	1,960	64	Technology (Manager)
40	3,339	223	65	Technology (Executive)
41	2,657	236	65	Technology (Individual Contributor)
42	13,091	982	47	Technology (Manager)
43	4,994	336	71	Technology
44	10,710	598	61	Investment

In the years since we first identified the 16 differentiating competencies much has changed. The challenges businesses face today are very different from those faced in 2002. To help us understand if the 16 differentiating competencies were as relevant and critical today as they were in the past, we replicated the original study with more recent data. While many of our clients utilized our standard Extraordinary Leader 360-degree assessment, almost half of our clients utilize a customized competency model. The customized competency models often include many of our standard competencies but add new competencies to the mix. The intent of our research was to validate the original 16 competencies, as well as determine if any new competencies have emerged.

In doing this research we now had significantly more data. We looked at 1,596,938 assessments of 121,138 leaders. We had 44 different unique data sets with more than 2,000 items. We used the same procedure to analyze the data identifying which items were most differentiating.

Findings from the Updated Research

What we discovered was as follows:

1. The 16 differentiating competencies that we discovered in 2002 are still differentiating well today. It became apparent to us that in our original research what we had uncovered were some fundamental aspects of leadership that don't change over time.
2. As we looked through the data, we discovered that there were some new differentiating competencies that had become more critical over the years:

   a. *Values diversity.* Valuing differences in others by gender, race, age, or background has increased in its importance over the years. In most organizations across the globe this is a significant issue and leaders who fail to value diversity will not be successful.

   b. *Makes decisions.* Leaders have more information available to them than ever before, but the mass of data has caused many leaders to be afraid to make timely decisions. To survive, organizations need to disrupt themselves before their competitors disrupt them. Leaders need to be decisive and move forward quickly.

   c. *Takes risks.* The number of new companies in the Fortune 500 is changing rapidly. Organization that play it safe will fail. Leaders need to push boundaries but do so in an ethical way.

3. As we looked at several of the differentiating competencies, we could see some evolution in terms of what needed to be measured. We broadened two of the existing competencies into the following:

   a. *Practices self-development.* Through the years we have noticed that this competency was consistently rated as the least important competency—yet it was strongly associated with increases in leadership effectiveness. We also noticed that in addition to our existing items a new element was becoming very important: agility, or the ability of a person to adapt quickly to changes and new situations. Organization were changing quickly, and leaders needed to keep pace. We added an addition behavioral item to our 360-degree assessment and changed the name of this competency to **Leaning Agility**.

b. *Connects the group to the outside world.* A significant trend in the past five years has been a shift from customer satisfaction to customer experience. In essence, many companies believe that if they can provide customers with a significant experience when they use or purchase their product it will guarantee them customer loyalty. In our original version of the survey we had one item focused on the customer. Given this trend we added an addition behavioral item and changed the title of the competency to **Customer and External Focus**.

Impact of Profound Strengths on Overall Leadership Effectiveness (Chapter 6)

In Chapter 6, a study was presented assessing the impact of profound strengths on overall leadership effectiveness. Figure A.2 (see next page) presents an updated study. The data from the study came from the aggregated results of 85,093 leaders with eight or more evaluators from a variety of different organizations. The 360-degree assessment was based on the Extraordinary Leader 360-degree assessment and the 16 differentiating competencies. To conduct the study, we calculated percentile scores on each of the 16 differentiating competencies. We determined that a profound strength was a competency at the 90th percentile or higher. We also calculated percentile scores on the overall leadership effectiveness index, which is the overall average of 49 items assessing leadership effectiveness. Note that the results on this broader study are very close to the results listed in Chapter 6.

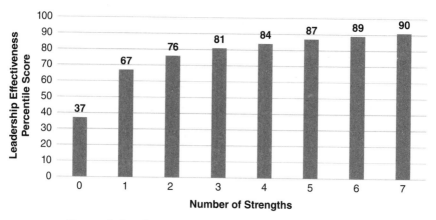

Figure A.2. Impact of Strengths at the 90th Percentile

After the publication of the first edition of *The Extraordinary Leader*, there was some criticism regarding this study. The criticism centered on the fact that the overall leadership effectiveness index and each of the individual competencies used to determine strengths were part of the same measure. That being said, it is no surprise that with the addition of strengths, the overall effectiveness percentile score increased. What impressed us in the research was not that the scores went up but rather the substantial increase that came from just a few strengths.

To show the impact of strengths, we did an additional study with 1,040 leaders. In this study, we examined some additional independent measures that showed the impact of strengths. The 360-degree assessment data was collected from managers, peers, and direct reports. Leaders were assessed on 16 dimensions. Leaders with strengths (e.g., a competency at the 90th percentile) were identified. The total results (e.g., average of manager, peers, and direct reports) were assembled. This data set also included a series of ratings by direct reports on employee satisfaction. One item assessed the overall effectiveness of each manager (e.g., "Overall, I feel my immediate supervisor/manager is doing a good job"). This item was not one of the 360 items used to calculate the leadership effectiveness index. Leaders with strengths were compared with the leadership effectiveness index (the average of all 360 items), an independent rating of managerial effectiveness (the item, "Overall I feel that my manager is doing a good job") and an employee satisfaction index (12 items assessing satisfaction with the company, job, direction of the organization, etc.). Results of this study are presented in Figure A.3.

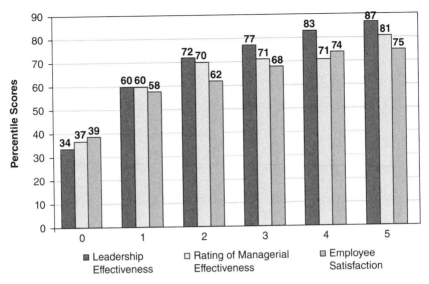

Figure A.3. Impact of Strengths on Three Different Outcomes

Note that Figure A.3 shows in the first column the overall leadership effectiveness data. It should not be surprising that these results are very similar to the results found in our original research because this part of the study was done in the same way. The second column (Rating of Managerial Effectiveness) presents results from the independent rating of overall leadership effectiveness. This displays the results from the one item assessing the overall effectiveness of a manager as seen by his or her direct reports. Though not as comprehensive as the leadership effectiveness index, it provides an overall evaluation of the manager by direct reports. Note that the results track very consistently with those in column one (although slightly lower at 3 to 5 strengths). The third column represents a measure of employee satisfaction. This 12-item index also follows a consistent trend. The insights from our original research were that "The key to developing great leadership is to build strengths." We noted that building strengths created a substantial positive impact on overall leadership effectiveness. This later research provides even more evidence for that claim.

NOTES

Chapter 1

1. Bennis, Warren G., *Why Leaders Can't Lead: The Unconscious Conspiracy Continues*, Jossey-Bass, San Francisco, CA, 1989, p. 143
2. Yukl, Gary, *Leadership in Organizations*, Prentice Hall, Englewood Cliffs, NJ, 1994.
3. Dalton Gene, and Paul Thompson, *Novations: Strategies for Career Management*, Scott Foresman, Glenview, IL, 1986.
4 Katzenbach, Jon, *Peak Performance*, Harvard Business School Press, Boston, 2000.
5. Weick, Karl E., *The Social Psychology of Organizing*, McGraw-Hill, New York, 1979.
6. Polanyi, Michael, *Personal Knowledge: Towards a Post-Critical Philosophy*, University of Chicago Press, Chicago, 1958, p. 53.
7 Ulrich, Dave, Jack Zenger, and Norm Smallwood, *Results-Based Leadership*, Harvard Business School Press, Boston, 1999.

Chapter 2

1. Rucci, Anthony J., Steven P. Kim, and Richard T. Quinn, "The Employee-Customer-Profit Chain at Sears," *Harvard Business Review*, January–February 1998, pp. 82–98.
2. Johnson, Carla, "Recruitment: Capturing Turnover Costs," *HR Magazine*, July 2000, Vol. 45, No. 7, pp. 107–119.
3. Senn, Larry E., and John R. Childress, *The Secrets of Reshaping Culture*, The Leadership Press, 1999.

4. Collins, Jim, "Level 5 Leadership: The Triumph of Humility and Fierce Resolve," *Harvard Business Review*, January 2001, pp. 67–76.
5. Kelly, Walt, creator of Pogo, 1917–1973.
6. "If It Was Good Enough for Jack Welch . . . ," *Business Week*, October 15, 2001, Online.
7. Ericsson, Anders K., and Neil Charness, "Expert Performance, Its Structure and Acquisition," *American Psychologist*, 1994, Vol. 49, No. 8, pp. 725–747.

Chapter 3

1. Gardner, John W., *On Leadership*, Free Press, New York, 1990.
2. Spencer, Lyle M., *Competence at Work*, Wiley, New York, 1993.
3. Dalton, Maxine, "Are Competency Models a Waste?" *Training and Development*, October 1997, pp. 46–49.
4. Ibid.
5. Asch, S. E., "Forming Impressions of Personality," *Journal of Abnormal and Social Psychology*, Vol. 41, 1946, pp. 258–290.
6. Kelly, H. H., "The Warm-Cold Variable in First Impressions of Persons," *Journal of Personality*, Vol. 18, 1950, pp. 431–439.
7. Rosenberg, S., C. Nelson, and P. S. Vivekananthan, "A Multidimensional Approach to the Structure of Personality Impressions," *Journal of Personality and Social Psychology*, Vol. 9, 1968, pp. 283–294.
8. Ibid.
9. Dorsey, David, "Andy Pearson Finds Love," *Fast Company*, Vol. 49, August 2001, pp. 78–82.
10. Bronowski, Jacob, *The Ascent of Man*, Little, Brown, Boston, 1974, pp. 115–116.

Chapter 4

1. Ulrich, Dave, Jack Zenger, and Norm Smallwood, *Results-Based Leadership*, Harvard Business School Press, Boston, 1999.
2. McClelland, David, "Achievement Motivation Can Be Developed," *Harvard Business Review*, Vol. 43, 1965, p. 178.

Chapter 5

1. Seligman, Martin, *Authentic Happiness*, Free Press, New York, 2002, p. 13.
2. Cameron, Kim, *Positive Leadership*, Berrett-Koehler, San Francisco, pp. 52–53.
3. Kaplan, Robert and Robert Kaiser, "Stop Overdoing Your Strengths, *Harvard Business Review*, Feb. 2009, pp. 36–41.
4. Festinger, L. A., *The Theory of Cognitive Dissonance*, Stanford University Press, Stanford, CA, 1957.

Chapter 6

1. Zenger, John H., Joseph Folkman, and Scott Edinger, *The Inspiring Leader: Unlocking the Secrets of How Extraordinary Leaders Motivate*, McGraw-Hill, New York, 2009.
2. Sandholtz, Kurt, "Achieving Your Career Best," *National Business Employment Weekly*, July 11–17, 1999.
3. Dalton, Gene, and Paul Thompson, *Novations: Strategies for Career Management*, Scott, Foresman, Glenview, IL, 1986.
4. Sandholtz, July 11–17, 1999.
5. Dalton and Thompson, pp. 218–236.
6. Ibid.

Chapter 7

1. Galford, Robert, and Anne Seibold Drapeau, *The Trusted Leader*, Free Press, New York, 2002.
2. Zenger, John, Joseph Folkman, and Scott Edinger, *The Inspiring Leader*, McGraw-Hill, New York, 2009.
3. McCall, M. W., Jr., and M. M. Lombardo, "Off the Track: Why and How Successful Executives Get Derailed," Tech Report No. 21, Center for Creative Leadership, Greensboro, NC, 1983.
4. Higgins, E. Tory, "Regulatory Focus Theory: Implications for the Study of Emotions at Work," *Organizational Behavior and Human Decision Processes, Special Issue: Affect at Work*, Vol. 86, September 2001, pp. 35–66.
5. Dweck, Carol S., and Ellen L. Leggett, "A Social-Cognitive Approach to Motivation and Personality," *Psychological Review*, Vol. 95, No. 2, 1988, pp. 256–273.
6. Dweck, Carol S., *Self-Theories: Their Role in Motivation, Personality, and Development*, Psychology Press, Philadelphia, 1999.

Chapter 8

1. Kelley, Robert E., *How to Be a Star at Work*, Times Business, New York, 1998, pp. 43–44.
2. Kelley, Robert E., and Janet Caplan, "How Bell Labs Creates Star Performers," *Harvard Business Review*, Vol. 71, July–August 1993, pp. 128–139.
3. Kelley, *How to Be a Star at Work*, pp. 43–44.
4. Krames, Jeffrey, *The Jack Welch Lexicon of Leadership*, McGraw-Hill, New York, 2002, p. 123.
5. Zenger, John, Joseph Folkman, and Scott Edinger, *The Inspiring Leader*, McGraw-Hill, New York, 2009.

Chapter 9

1. Drucker, Peter F., *The Practice of Management*, Harper & Row, New York, 1954.
2. Kouzes, James M., and Barry Z. Posner, "On Becoming a Leader" in *Growth Strategies*, American Management Association, New York, NY, September 1987.
3. Simon, H. A., *The Science of Management Decisions*, Prentice Hall, Englewood Cliffs, NJ, 1977.
4. Ulrich, Dave, Jack Zenger, and Norm Smallwood, *Results-Based Leadership*, Harvard Business School Press, Boston, 1999, pp. 169–180.
5. Flaherty, John E., *Peter Drucker: Shaping the Managerial Mind*, Jossey-Bass, San Francisco, 1999, p. 335.
6. Ibid., pp. 336–337.
7. Valerio, Anna M., "A Study of the Developmental Experiences of Managers," in *Measures of Leadership* (Kenneth E. and Miriam B. Clark, eds.), Leadership Library of America, West Orange, NJ, 1990, pp. 521–533.
8. Perry, Lee Tom, Randall G. Stott, and W. Norman Smallwood, *Real-Time Strategy: Improvising Team-Based Planning for a Fast-Changing World*, Wiley, New York, 1993.
9. Friedman, Stewart, "Leadership DNA: The Ford Motor Story," *T&D Journal*, March 2001, p. 25.
10. Ibid., p. 27.

Part II

1. Gurdjian, Pierre, Thomas Halbeisen, and Kevin Lane, "Why leadership-development programs fail," *McKinsey Quarterly*, 2014.

Chapter 10

1. AMA Enterprise, "Developing Successful Corporate Leaders: The Second Annual Study of Challenges and Opportunities 2011," sponsored by The Institute for Corporate Productivity (i4cp), *Training* magazine, and AMA Enterprise. Survey participants included AMA members, i4cp's global survey panel, and *Training* magazine subscribers.
2. Deloitte, "Human Capital Trends," 2014.
3. Ken Blanchard Annual Corporate Issues Survey, available from KenBlanchard.com
4. Eddy, David M., "The Origins of Evidence-Based Medicine: A Personal Perspective," *Virtual Mentor* 13(1):55-60.
5. Volini, Erica, Jeff Schwartz, Indranil Roy, Maren Hauptmann, Yves Van Durme, Brad Denny, and Josh Bersin, "Leadership for the 21st Century: The Intersection of the Traditional and the New," 2019 Global Human Capital Trends, Deloitte, *Insights*.

Chapter 11

1. Gentry, W. A., "Managerial Derailment: What It Is and How Leaders Can Avoid It." In E. Biech (Ed.), *ASTD Leadership Handbook*, Alexandria, VA, ASTD Press, 2010, pp. 311–324.
2. Zenger, Jack, "We Wait Too Long to Train Our Leaders," *Harvard Business Review*, December 17, 2012.

Chapter 13

1. Carey, John, "Medical Guesswork," *Bloomberg Businessweek*, May 2006, pp. 75-80.

Chapter 12

1. Kipnis, David, Stuart M. Schmidt, and Ian Wilkinson, "Intraorganizational Influence Tactics: Explorations in Getting One's Way," *Journal of Applied Psychology* 65(4):440-452.
2. Anderson, C., S. E. Spataro, and F. J. Flynn, "Personality and Organizational Culture as Determinants of Influence," *Journal of Applied Psychology* 93(3):702-710.
3. Kotter, John P., "Leading Change: Why Transformation Efforts Fail," *Harvard Business Review*, March-April 1995, pp. 59-67.
4. Executive Development Associates, "Trends in Leadership Development," 2019.

Chapter 15

1. Lewin, Kurt, "Frontiers in Group Dynamics: Concept, Method and Reality in Social Science; Social Equilibria and Social Change," *Human Relations*, 1947, Vol. 1, 1, pp. 5-41.
2. "America's Workforce: A Revealing Study of Corporate America's Most Neglected Employee," available from Root Inc., 2015.
3. Saari, L. M., T. R. Johnson, S. D. McLaughlin, and D. M. Zimmerle, "A Survey of Management Training and Education Practices in U.S. Companies," *Personnel Psychology* 41(4):731-743.
4. Goldsmith, Michael, and Howard Morgan, "Leadership Is a Contact Sport: The 'Follow-Up Factor' in Management Development," *Organizations and People*, Fall 2004, Issue 36, pp.71-79.

Chapter 16

1. Mercer, "When Women Thrive" global report, 2016.
2. Maholtra, Vik, "Women in the Economy," speech, quoted in the *Wall Street Journal*, April 11, 2011.

3. Malone, Thomas, MIT Center for Collective Intelligence, reported in "Intelligent Organizations, Management and Leadership" blog, posted March 22, 2017.

4. Kelly, Kevin (CEO, Heidrick & Struggles) discussing the firm's internal study of 20,000 searches in an interview with Brooke Masters for "Rise of a Headhunter," *Financial Times*, March 30, 2009.

Chapter 17

1. Dweck, Carol, *Mindset: The New Psychology of Success*, Random House Publishing Group, New York, 2006.

Chapter 18

1. Zenger, Jack, and Joseph Folkman, "The Trickle Down Effect of Good (and Bad) Leadership," *Harvard Business Review*, Jan 10, 2016.

INDEX

Page numbers followed by *f* refer to figures.

Accountability:
  for implementation of new
    skills, 252
  in leadership teams, 292
  of participants, in development
    programs, 237–238
Achievement, need for, 86–87
Action learning projects, 236
Adhocracy organizations, 125
Age:
  and confidence, 273
  of target population for
    leadership development, 25,
    216–219
  and women leaders, 271–273
Agilent Technologies, 37
Alternative development paths,
    23, 149–175
  for Character, 159–160

and competency companions,
    157–159
discovering, 149–151
evidence-based leadership
    development, 175
for Focus on Results,
    163–166
high standards and technical
    competence, 156
impact of companion
    behaviors, 172–175
interpersonal relationships
    and technical competence,
    154–156
for Interpersonal Skills,
    166–169
for Leading Organizational
    Change, 170–171
new approaches to, 171–172

nonlinear development paths,
151–153
for Personal Capability,
160–163
American Management
Association, 202
Apathy, 139
Arrogance, 137–138
Articles, in leadership
development, 234
Asch, Solomon, 62, 64
Aspiration level:
increased by development
programs, 237
increased by success, 68
Assessments, 28, 277–284
analysis following, 91–92
analysis of pre- vs. post-
assessments, 278–281
designing useful, 69–70
differences in, by position, 281,
282f
and growth mindset, 284
improvement in, 282–283
of individual competencies,
68–70
lack of standard, 8
organizational differences in,
283–284
presentation and reading of, 43,
44f
purpose of, 277–278
in self-development, 192–193
of women leaders, 267–268
Assignments, broader, 187
Athletes, coaching of, 182
Attentive position, to learning
initiative, 227

Attitudes:
changing, with behavioral
changes, 86, 164–165
and personal character, 181

Baby boomers, 8
Bad leaders:
and good, 31
halo effect for, 105
Balance, among strengths, 103
Barnhouse, Ruth Tiffany, 127
Behavior(s):
changing attitudes and, 86,
164–165, 237
as contagious, 285–289
effect of poor, 215–216
and personal character, 181
replicating high performers',
194
sustaining change in, 253
Bell Labs, 154, 160–162
Bennis, Warren, 4, 74
Bersin, Josh, 211–212
Bersin by Deloitte, 211–212
Bespoke, 201
Books, in leadership development,
234
Bottom line, impact of leaders on,
41
Broader assignments, 187
Bronowski, Jacob, 68, 71
Building positive relationships
(competency), 81, 104
Bureaucratic organizations, 122
Burns, J. M., 3
Business knowledge, 77
Business levers and activities,
208–209

California Psychological Inventory, 178
Cameron, Kim, 94
Candor, 168–169
Candor organizations, 121
Career stages, 6–7
Celebration organizations, 122
Cell phone monitoring system, 260–261
Champions change (competency), 82, 170
Change:
　championed by leaders, 82, 83–84
　directing, 84
　implementation of, 19
　involving others in, 84
　resistance to, 136–138
　in self-development, 193
Change theory, 252
Change-transition phase, of change, 252, 254
Character, 74–76
　as competency, 77
　competency companions for, 159–160
　defining, 74
　and Focus on Results, 86–87
　and Interpersonal Skills, 85–86
　and Leading Organizational Change, 88
　self-development of, 180–181
　in tent model, 15
Charness, Neil, 46, 47
Chesky, Brian, 241
Child abuse, 49
Christakis, Nicholas, 285
Churchill, Winston, 7

Clan/club organizations, 122
Coaches:
　encouragement to practice from, 47
　and Focus on Results, 165–166
　in leadership development, 235
　in leadership teams, 292
　managers as, 247
　performance feedback given by, 94–97
　for self-development, 182–183
Cognitive dissonance, 106
Collaboration, lack of, 133–134
Collaboration and teamwork (competency), 81
Combinations, of competencies, 21–22, 88–89
Commitment:
　as contagious, 40–41
　honoring of, 220–221
Communicating powerfully and prolifically (competency), 81, 166
Communication:
　and leadership, 28–29
　with stories, 190–191
　of technical competence, 158
　and trust, 159
Companion behaviors, 172–175 (See also Competency companions)
Competence at Work (Spencer), 57
Competencies, 18–19, 53–70
　assessment of individual, 68–70
　assessments of improvements in, 282–283
　complexity of, 55
　in CPO model, 113–120

Competencies, *continued*
and discovering strengths, 112
faulty assumptions about, 55–58
gender differences in ratings of, 269–271
importance of different, 58
as linked, 20, 57, 62–68
models for, 55–61
organizational culture and prized, 120–125
Competency companions, 23, 152–153, 157–159
Competency model:
for organizational leadership development, 206–208
used in hiring practices, 242
Competency movement, 53–55, 59–60
Competition, 133–134, 155–156, 168
Complacency, 139
Complexity, of competencies, 55
Confidence:
and competence, 184–185
increased by success, 67
in leader's abilities, 168
and women leaders, 273
Consideration of others:
and integrity, 158–159
and trust, 168
Contagious behavior:
commitment as, 40–41
and emotions, 169, 285–289
of leaders, 286–287
and leadership effectiveness, 26–27
Cost, of leadership development, 41, 254–255

Covey, Stephen, 74
CPO model, 113–115, 118–120
Credibility, 133
Cross training, 67
Customer and external focus (competency), 83
Customer emphasis organizations, 124
Customer satisfaction:
and employee engagement, 35
impact of leaders on, 38–39
Cutadean, Ron, 113

Dalton, Gene, 112, 114, 126
Dalton, Maxine, 60
Dashboards, 192–193
De Pree, Max, 74
Decision making (competency), 79
Dell Computer, 8–9
Deloitte, 202–203, 211–212
Development of others (competency), 81
lack of, 138
as outcome of development training, 205
and self-development, 158, 167
in self-development, 191–192
teaching managers to engage in, 166–167
Developmental experiences, 182
Develops strategic perspective (competency), 82
Direction, lack of, 132–133
Discipline, 46
Dissonance, 106
Diversity, valuing, 81–82, 274
Doyle, Sir Arthur Conan, 4–5

Dr. Watson, 5
Drapeau, Anne, 133
Drucker, Peter, 59, 177, 183, 186, 213
Dweck, Carol, 145–146, 284

Eddy, David, 210, 238
Effective learning methods, 234–236
Einstein, Albert, 251
Eisenhower, Dwight D., 20
Email monitoring system, 259–260
Embedded leadership development, 27, 241–250
  in HR systems, 242–243
  management's involvement as, 245–249
  in participant's daily work, 243–245
Emotional intelligence, 139
Emotions:
  as contagious, 169, 285–289
  as tool for championing change, 171
Employee engagement:
  assessments of, 280–281
  and feedback from managers, 249
  impact of leaders on, 32–33
  increasing, 205
  and leadership effectiveness, 290
Employees:
  high potential, 213, 219–222
  impact of leaders on commitment of, 40–41
  as targets of leadership development program, 214

Energy and enthusiasm:
  lack of, 131–132
  of leaders, 191
Entrance points, in leadership development, 210
Entrepreneurial spirit approach, 10
Ericsson, Anders, 46, 47
Error avoidance organizations, 123–124
Evidence-based leadership development, 175, 210–211
Evolution, of competencies, 58
Excellent execution organizations, 123
Executive support, 223–232
  case study of, 229
  and leading organizational change, 170
  nature of, 226–229
  and organizational influence of executives, 224–225
  and purpose of leadership development solution, 226
  senior management support, 223–224
Executives:
  leadership owned by, 231–232
  organizational influence of, 224–225
  as targets of leadership development program, 213

Fair organizations, 121–122
Fatal flaws, 127–148
  acceptance of mediocre performance, 132

Fatal flaws, *continued*
  assessments of, pre- and post-
      development, 279–280
  commonalities in, 139–140
  consequences of, 130
  detection of, 140
  failure as role model, 134
  fixing, 23, 140–148, 187
  as focus of performance
      feedback, 96
  frequency of, 130
  lack of collaboration, 133–134
  lack of development of others,
      138
  lack of innovation, 136–138
  lack of inspiration, 131–132
  lack of Interpersonal Skills,
      135–136
  lack of self-development,
      134–135
  lack of vision, 132–133
  loss of trust, 133
  most common, 130–131
  multiple, 131
  of people with prevention
      orientation, 144–147
  profile of, 128–130
Feedback:
  asking for and acting upon, 77,
      272–273
  from employees, 137
  in fixing of fatal flaws,
      142–143
  and Focus on Results, 165–166
  giving appropriate, 146–147
  global, 1
  in leadership development,
      234

  new mechanisms for, 244–245
  for people with prevention
      orientation, 144
  productive, 189
  provided by managers,
      248–249
  regarding flaws, 140
  in research about leadership,
      12–13
  and sustainment of leadership
      development, 257
  in sustainment process, 262
  as tool for improvement,
      277–278
Festinger, L. A., 106
Films, in leadership development,
      234
Finland, teachers in, 292–293
Focus on Results, 78–80
  and broadening scope of
      assignments, 187
  and Character, 86–87
  competency companions for,
      163–166
  and Interpersonal Skills, 87–89
  and Leading Organizational
      Change, 88
  and Personal Capability, 87
  in tent model, 15
Follow-up, to leadership
      development, 255, 256*f*
Ford Motor, 194
Fortune, 68
Fowler, James, 285
Franklin, Benjamin, 233
Friedman, Stewart, 194, 195
Friendliness, 168
Fun organizations, 122

Funding, of leadership
    development, 41, 254–255
Future, preparation for, 61, 196

Galford, Robert, 133
Gardner, John, 3, 53, 55, 177
General business knowledge, 77
Generation X, 8, 218
Generation Y, 8, 218–219
Generation Z, 8, 218
Genteel organizations, 120–121
Gestalt, 66
Gilbert, Thomas, 59
Giuliani, Rudolph, 7, 75–76
Goldsmith, Marshall, 255
Good leaders:
    and bad, 31
    challenging, to improve, 41–48
    great vs., 31–33
Gough, Harrison, 178
Great leaders:
    good vs., 31–33
    halo effect for, 105
    measurements of, 50–51
Growth mindset, 284

Halo effect, 62–67
    from fatal flaws, 128
    and strengths-based
        development, 105–106
Happiness, as contagious, 285
Harrington, H. James, 277
Harvard Business Review, 68, 265,
    285
Harvard Business School, 68
Hazlitt, William, 91
Herd immunity, 215
Higgins, Tory, 143

High performers, study of, 194
High potential employees, 213,
    219–222
High standards, 156
High-integrity organizations, 121
Hoffman, Reid, 285
Honesty, 163, 168–169
HP, 123
HR systems:
    competencies missing from, 61
    leadership development
        embedded in, 242–243
    and leadership development
        systems, 230–231
Humility, 181

IBM, 47
Impact, of leaders, 17, 31–52
    on bottom line, 41
    challenging good leaders to
        improve, 41–48
    on commitment of employees,
        40–41
    on company culture, 48–50
    on customer satisfaction, 38–39
    on employee engagement, 33
    good and bad leaders, 31
    great vs. good leaders, 31–33
    and ideas about leaders, 52
    on intention to leave
        organization, 38
    measurements of, 50–51
    on net profits, 34–35
    and organizational leader
        development, 51
    on sales, 35–36
    on turnover, 37
"Improving" view, 145–146

Individual achievement approach,
9–10
Individual competencies, 68–70
Initiative, taking (competency),
79, 220
gender differences in, 268
and problem-solving skills,
160–162
Innovation (competency), 77
lack of, 136–138
and learning from failures, 163
and rigid competencies, 60
The Inspiring Leader (Zenger and
Folkman), 111, 169
Inspiring others to high
performance (competency),
81, 169, 221
and changing strategic
perspectives, 170–171
improving, 173–174
lack of, 131–132
of leaders, 191
Institute for Corporate
Productivity, 202
Insurance company, 37
Integrity:
and Character, 159–160
and consideration of others,
158–159
Intention to leave organization,
38
Internal promotions, 205, 210
Interpersonal Skills, 80–82
and Character, 85–86
competency companions for,
166–169
and Focus on Results, 87–89
lack of, 135–136

and Leading Organizational
Change, 88
and Personal Capability, 87
and powerful communication,
166
and technical competence, 154–
156, 158
in tent model, 16
Interrelatedness, of model
elements, 72, 85–89
Intimacy, 133
Inuit language, 11

Jobs, Steve, 76
Johnson, T. R., 255

Kaiser, Robert, 102, 103
Kaplan, Robert, 102, 103
Katzenbach, Jon, 9–10
Kearns, David, 170
Kelley, Robert, 154, 160
Kelly, H. H., 63–64
Kelly, Kevin, 274–275
Kelly, Walt, 42
Ken Blanchard Company, 203
Knowledge:
and behavioral change, 253
business, 77
expanding, 243
general business, 77
product, 77
Kotter, John, 230
Kouzes, Jim, 74, 179

Language, about leadership, 11
Leaders:
behaviors of, as contagious,
286–287

born vs. made, 12, 23–24, 45–48, 177–179
change championed by, 83–84
effect of, on employee engagement, 287, 288*f*
good vs. bad, 31
good vs. great, 31–33
halo effect for great and bad, 105
impact of, 17
investing in younger, 217–219
leadership teams vs. individual, 8
subordinates' appraisals of, 10
uniqueness of, 110–111
women, 265–275
Leadership:
differing activities for, 7
differing styles of, 9–10, 20
in diverse environments, 6
evolving nature of, 8
lack of adequate, by many companies, 197–198
as mystery, 3–4
and performance outcomes, 18
personality traits vs., 45
research on, 11–13
teaching at a younger age, 218
Leadership Development Center (Ford Motor), 194
Leadership development solution:
executive support and purpose of, 226
ideal, 209–210
Leadership effectiveness:
and age, 271–273
and confidence, 185
as contagious, 26–27
effect of, on direct reports, 286–287
effects of poor, 215–216
and employee engagement, 290
factors correlated to, 10–11
improved with self-development, 24
increased with strengths, 98–101
philosophies of, 93–97
purpose of assessing, 277–278
success vs., 7–8
trickle-down effect of, 287–289
of women, 266–267
Leadership skills, emergence of, 178
Leadership sweet spot, 113, 115
Leadership teams, 285–293
development of, 290–293
emotions and behavior as contagious, 285–289
importance of, 289–290
individual leaders vs., 8
"Leadership-employee-customer-profit chain," 35
Leading Organizational Change, 82–83
and Character, 88
competency companions for, 170–171
and Focus on Results, 88
and Interpersonal Skills, 88
in tent model, 16
Learning:
from failures, and innovation, 163
from mistakes and negative experiences, 188

Learning, *continued*
  proposed phases of, 253–255
  retention of, 253
  by watching, 188
  from work experiences, 189–190
Learning agility (competency),
  77–78
Learning methods, 233–240
  common elements of effective,
    236–238
  effective, 234–236
  ineffective, 234
  selection of, 238–239
Learning organizations, 121
Lectures, in leadership
  development, 234
Lewin, Kurt, 193, 252
Lincoln, Abraham, 178
Linear development plan, 149–
  151, 171
Listening, 168
Lofty standards organizations,
  122
Lombardo, Michael, 134
Louis Vuitton, 75

MacArthur, Douglas, 20
Machiavelli, Niccolò, 193
Malhotra, Vik, 274
Management, trying new skills
  in, 245
Managers:
  assessments of, 281, 282*f*
  effect of, on direct reports,
    286–287
  involvement of, in leadership
    development, 209, 236,
    245–249

perspectives of, 12
  in sustainment process, 258–
    259, 261
  as targets of leadership
    development program, 213
McCall, Morgan, Jr., 134
McClelland, David, 86–87
McDermott, Rose, 285
McKinnon, Paul, 47
McKinsey & Co., 10, 68, 197
McLaughlin, S. D., 255
Medicine, science in practice of,
  210–211, 238–239
Mercer, 266
Michelangelo, 18
Millennials, 218
Mission, values, and pride
  approach, 9
Modern change theory, 252
Monitoring system:
  following leadership
    development, 259–261
  self-monitoring, 192–193
Morgan, Howard, 255
Mortgage bank, 34–35
Multiple fatal flaws, 131
Musical talent, 46–47

Natural abilities, development of,
  46–47
Needham, Richard, 127
Negative statements, 94
Nelson, C., 64
Net profits, 34–35
Neutral position, to learning
  initiative, 227
Nomenclature, consistent use of,
  242–243

Noncompetitiveness, 168
Nonlinear development paths, 23,
  151–153, 236
Nonlinear development plan,
  171–172
Nordstrom, 75
Nurturing competencies, 269

Openness, 168
Opposition, to learning initiative,
  226
Organization(s):
  analysis of, 203
  competencies as unique to,
    56–57
  competencies valued by, 119–
    120, 208
  current reality of, 190
  great leaders in, 17–18
  intention to leave, 38
  involvement of, in leadership
    development, 25, 283–284
  leadership behavior in, 26
  objectives of, in leadership
    development, 51
  types of, 120–125
  values of, 208
Organizational competency
  drivers, 118–119
Organizational culture:
  changing, 205
  competency models fit to,
    207–208
  development valued in, 210
  leadership development
    embedded in, 241
  and prized competencies,
    120–125

Organizational fit, 20, 109–126
  barriers to, 115–118
  CPO model for, 113–115,
    118–120
  organizational culture and
    prized competencies,
    120–125
  organization's and individual's
    competencies, 57
  and personal strengths, 111–113
  research on, 115
  and uniqueness of leaders,
    110–111
Organizational influence, of
  executives, 224–225
Organizational leadership
  development, 25, 201–212
  analysis of past efforts in,
    203–204
  business levers and activities as
    focus for, 208–209
  competency model for,
    206–208
  context for, 201–203
  developing program for,
    198–199
  embeddedness of, 241–250
  as evidence-based, 210–211
  executive support for, 223–232
  ideal leadership development
    solution, 209–210
  learning methods used,
    233–240
  organizational analysis for, 203
  scale and scope of, 213–222
  sustainment and follow-through
    of, 251–262
  targets of, 204–205

Organizational needs:
  in CPO model, 113–120
  in discovering strengths,
    112–113
Outcomes:
  and leadership, 18
  and sustainment of leadership
    development, 257–262

Passion:
  in CPO model, 113–120
  in discovering strengths, 112
Patton, George, 20
Peak Performance (Katzenbach), 9
Pearson, Andrall, 68
Peers:
  effect on others, 287–289
  perspectives of, 12
PepsiCo, 68
Performance:
  acceptance of mediocre, 132
  development of people with low,
    213
  inspiring others to high, 81
  and leadership, 18
  measurements of, and leadership
    development, 242
  methods for eliciting, 9–10
  past vs. current, 219, 221
  raising levels of, 59–60
  reviews of, 93–94
Personal attributes, 63–65
Personal Capability, 76–78
  competency companions for,
    160–163
  and Focus on Results, 87
  and Interpersonal Skills, 87
  in tent model, 15

Personal commendation
  organizations, 124
Personal development plans:
  based on weaknesses, 175
  in leadership development,
    234–235
  linear, 149–151
  managers' involvement in, 248
  as outcome of development
    training, 204–205
  and strengths-based
    development, 97–102
Personal Knowledge (Polanyi), 12
Personality traits:
  changes in, over lifetime,
    177–178
  feedback about, 146–147
  leadership vs., 45
  and organizational influence,
    225
Planning, 244
Pogo (character), 42
Polanyi, Michael, 12
Political organizations, 122
Positive energy, 191
Positive expectations, of others,
  169
Positive relationships, building, 81
Positive statements, 94
Posner, Barry, 74, 179
Post-assessments, 278–281
The Practice of Management
  (Drucker), 177
Pre-assessments, 278–281
Prevention orientation, 144–147
Problem-analysis and problem-
  solving skills (competency), 77
Problem-solving skills, 160–162

Process metrics approach, 9
Process organizations, 125
Product endorsements, 105–106
Product knowledge, 77
Productive feedback, 189
Productivity, 165–166
Professional skills, 77
Profits, net, 34–35
Promotion orientation, 143–144, 146
Promotions, internal, 205, 210
"Proving" view, 145–146

Quoits experiment, 87

Recognition and celebration approach, 9
Reflection, 244
Refreezing phase, of change, 252, 254
Relationships, building, 81, 243
Reliability, 133
Research, on leadership, 11–13
Resistance to change, 136–138
Responsibility, 164–165
  for learning initiative, 228–229
  of participants, in development programs, 237
Results driven (competency), 79, 104
Results-Based Leadership (Ulrich, et al.), 15, 79, 179
Risk taking (competency), 79–80, 164
Rohn, Jim, 31
Role models, 134, 187–188
Root Inc., 253
Rosenberg, S., 64, 65, 156

Saari, L. M., 255
Sales, 35–36
Sales organizations, 125
Sandberg, Sheryl, 265
Sandholtz, Kurt, 112, 113
Savage, Brett, 103
Self-development, 24, 177–196
  broader assignments in, 187
  change initiatives in, 193
  coaches for, 182–183
  communicating with stories, 190–191
  as continuous, 162–163
  decision for, 180
  and development of others, 85, 158, 167
  development of others in, 191–192
  developmental experiences for, 182
  as fatal flaw, 138
  fixing fatal flaws, 187
  focused on strengths, 101–102
  lack of, 134–135
  leaders as made vs. born, 177–179
  learning from mistakes and negative experiences, 188
  learning from work experiences, 189–190
  personal character, 180–181
  positive energy, 191
  preparation for future, 196
  productive feedback, 189
  repetition of vision, 195–196
  role models in, 187–188
  self-monitoring in, 192–193
  strategic thinking, 190

Self-development, *continued*
  strength identification in,
    183–186
  study of high performers for,
    194
  study of organization's current
    reality, 190
  teaching and training in,
    193–194
  team building in, 192
  volunteering in, 195
  weakness identification in,
    186–187
Self-interest, 133
Self-monitoring, 192–193
Seligman, Martin, 93
Senior management:
  competency lists created by, 60
  involvement of, in
    organizational leadership
    development, 209, 235
  as role models for younger
    leaders, 188
  support of, for leadership
    development, 223–224
  in sustainment process, 258,
    262
  as targets of leadership
    development program,
    213
  women leaders in, 266
Senn, Larry, 39
Shadow, of leaders, 47–50
Shaffer, Jim, 74
Shaw, George Bernard, 201
Sherlock Holmes, 5
The Sign of Four (Doyle), 5
Simon, Herb, 179

Simulations, in leadership
  development, 235
Sins of commission, in
  Interpersonal Skills, 135–136
Sins of omission:
  in Interpersonal Skills, 136
  most fatal flaws as, 139
Skills:
  building, through practice or
    rehearsal, 235
  and career stages, 6–7
  developing new, 182
  emergence of leadership, 178
  implementation of new, 252
  interpersonal (*see* Interpersonal
    Skills)
  problem-solving, 160–162
  professional, 77
  social, 136
  as transferable, 67
  trying new management, 245
Smallwood, Norm, 79–80
Snow, language about, 11
"Social contagion," 285–286
Social learning theory, 188
Social skills, 136
Southwest Airlines, 9
Special interest groups, 244
Spencer, Lyle, 57
Start-up organizations, 125
Statistics, 153
Stereotypes, 63
"Stop Overdoing Your Strengths"
  (Kaplan and Kaiser), 102
Strategic perspective, 82
  championing change in,
    170–171
  of high potential employees, 221

Strategic thinking, 190
Strengths:
  assessments of, pre- and post-
    development, 279f, 280
  combinations of, 21–22,
    103–105
  defining, 97–98
  as focus of feedback, 95–96
  identification and building of,
    21, 183–186, 237
  impact of, 98–101
  optimization of, 103
  and organizational fit, 111–113
  overlap between leaders and
    subordinates of, 49
  "tent poles" in model as, 73
  too much focus on, 21,
    102–103
Strengths-based development,
    91–108
  as approach to improvement,
    91–92
  combinations of strengths,
    103–105
  and halo effect, 105–106
  and personal development plan,
    97–102
  and philosophies of
    effectiveness, 93–97
  and self-development, 184
  too much focus on strengths,
    102–103
  and views of others, 107–108
Stretch goals (competency), 79,
    163–164
Subordinates:
  appraisals of leaders by, 10
  perspectives of, 12

Success:
  aspiration level increased by,
    68
  confidence increased by, 67
  effectiveness vs., 7–8
  in self-development of
    strengths, 186
Sullivan, John, 37
Supervisors:
  assessments of, 281, 282f
  as targets of leadership
    development program, 214
"A Survey of Management
    Training and Education
    Practices in U.S. Companies"
    (Saari, et al.), 255
Sustainment, 27, 251–262
  effective activities for, 257
  importance of, 251–252
  need for ongoing, 252–255,
    256f
  and outcomes, 257–262
Sweet spot, 115

Taffer, Jon, 223
Target population, 213–222
  age of, 216–219
  high potential employees as,
    219–222
  selection of, 213–214
  widening scope of, 214–216
Teaching, 193–194
Team building, 192
Team leaders, 214
Team leadership, development of,
    290–293
Team player, 133–134
Teamwork, 81, 167–169

Technical/professional acumen (competency), 77, 154–156, 158, 220
Technology, 8–9
Technology emphasis organizations, 123
Tent model, 14–16, 71–89
  change championed by leaders, 83–84
  Character in, 15, 74–76
  Focus on Results in, 15, 78–80
  Interpersonal Skills in, 16, 80–82
  interrelations among elements of, 85–89
  Leading Organizational Change in, 16, 82–83
  Personal Capability in, 15, 76–78
The Theory of Cognitive Dissonance (Festinger), 106
Thinking:
  binary, 52
  strategic, 190
Thompson, Paul, 112, 114
Total leadership, 195
Total quality movement, 137
Training:
  cross-, 67
  in self-development, 193–194
Training magazine, 202
Transferability, of skills, 67
"The Trickle-Down Effect of Good (and Bad) Leadership" (Zenger and Folkman), 285
Tricon Global Restaurants, Inc., 68
Truman, Harry, 178

Trump, Donald, 7, 76
Trust:
  and communication, 159
  loss of, 133
  and teamwork, 167–169
Turnover:
  impact of leaders on, 37
  and intention to leave organization, 38
  and sales, 36

Ulrich, Dave, 79–80
Unfreezing phase, of change, 252, 253
U.S. Marine Corps, 9

Valerio, Anna, 187
Valuing diversity (competency), 81–82, 274
Virtual organizations, 125
Virtual teams, 9
Vision:
  lack of, 132–133
  repetition of, 195–196
Vivekananthan, P., 64
Volunteer work, 195

Watson, Tom, Jr., 47
"We Wait Too Long to Train Our Leaders" (Zenger and Folkman), 217
Weaknesses:
  development plans based on, 175
  as fatal flaws, 128
  feeling need to eliminate, 22–23, 93
  as focus of feedback, 95–96

identification of, in self-
    development, 186–187
overlap between leaders and
    subordinates of, 49
Weick, Karl, 11
"When Women Thrive" report,
    266
Women leaders, 28, 265–275
    and age, 271–273
    assessments of, 267–268
    and confidence, 273
    at different levels, 268, 269*f*

effectiveness of, 266–267
as nurturing, 269–271
suggestions for organizations
    about, 274–275
Wooden, John, 188

Xerox, 170

Yum, 68

Zenger, Jack, 79–80
Zimmerle, D. M., 255

ABOUT THE AUTHORS

John H. (Jack) Zenger

John H. (Jack) Zenger is the cofounder of Zenger-Folkman and a best-selling author and consultant on the subject of leadership development. For the past six decades his career spanned academia, the corporate world, and being an entrepreneur.

In 1977, Jack cofounded Zenger-Miller and served as its president and CEO until 1991. The *Wall Street Journal* named it one of the 10 best suppliers of executive development.

For his contributions to the field of leadership development and training he was inducted into the Human Resources Development Hall of Fame, and in 2011 was awarded the Lifetime Achievement Award by the Association of Talent Development. The training industry twice awarded him their "Thought Leadership Award."

He received a doctorate in business administration from the University of Southern California, an MBA from UCLA, and a bachelor's degree in psychology from Brigham Young University.

He is the author or coauthor of 14 books on leadership, coaching, and self-managing work teams and 180 articles. He is a regular columnist for *Harvard Business Review* and *Forbes*.

Jack served for 10 years as a Regent in the Higher Education system of the State of Utah, and before that had been the Chair of the Board of Trustees of Utah Valley University. He was a former president of the Brigham Young University Alumni organization.

Jack and his wife, Holly, reside in Midway, Utah.

Joseph R. Folkman

Joe Folkman is the cofounder and president of Zenger-Folkman, a firm that uses evidence-driven, strengths-based methods to improve organizations and the people within them. He is a respected authority on assessment and change and an acclaimed keynote speaker at conferences and seminars the world over. His topics focus on a variety of subjects related to leadership, feedback, and individual and organizational change.

As one of the nation's renowned psychometricians, his extensive expertise focuses on survey research and change management. He has more than 30 years of experience consulting with some of the world's most prestigious and successful organizations. His unique measurement tools are designed using a database composed of more than a million assessments on more than 100,000 leaders. Because these tools specifically address critical business results, facilitating development and change is the main focus of measurement efforts.

Joe's research has been published in several publications, including the *Harvard Business Review, Talent Quarterly, Wall Street Journal's National Business Employment Weekly,* and *Training and Development Magazine.* For the latest research and insights Joe also posts blogs on HBR .ORG, Forbes, and LinkedIn.

A distinguished expert in the field of survey design and data analysis, Joe consults with organizations large and small, public and private. He has had engagements with clients such as AT&T, General Mills, General Motors, RELX, Yale University, GIAG, Celgene, LinkedIn, Wells Fargo, and TreeHouse Foods. The diversity of industries and business models has provided him with a powerful learning opportunity and an exceptional research base.

Joe holds a doctorate in social and organizational psychology and a master's in organizational behavior from Brigham Young University. He is the author or coauthor of nine books, including *Employee Surveys that Make a Difference* (Executive Excellence, 1998), the best-selling *The Extraordinary Leader: Turning Good Managers into Great Leaders* (McGraw-Hill, 2002), *The Handbook for Leaders* (McGraw-Hill, 2004),

The Power of Feedback (Wiley, 2006), *The Inspiring Leader* (McGraw-Hill, 2009), *How to Be Exceptional* (McGraw-Hill, 2012), and *Speed: How Leaders Accelerate Successful Execution* (McGraw-Hill, 2017).

Joe and his family reside at the base of the Wasatch Mountains in Orem, Utah.

ZENGER | FOLKMAN

You and your organization can benefit from a unique experience based on this bestselling book.

It begins with two premises. First, everyone deserves to work with a great leader. Second, great leaders make a great difference in every business outcome—from employee engagement to profitability.

But that doesn't happen if the company elects to only develop a few leaders. *The Extraordinary Leader* program can be economically and effectively provided to your entire leadership group. It gives them practical insights into their strengths and behaviors needing improvement. Better yet, it provides a practical pathway for development plus the motivation to make it happen. Then, to make sure it is not "one and done," it provides long-term sustainment methods.

Put what you just read into action.

Visit www.zengerfolkman.com

or email info@zengerfolkman.com